Jesus
and the Nonviolent Revolution

The Christian Peace Shelf

The Christian Peace Shelf is a series of books and pamphlets devoted to the promotion of Christian peace principles and their applications. The editor, appointed by the Mennonite Central Committee Peace Section, and an editorial board, from the Brethren in Christ Church, General Conference Mennonite Church, Mennonite Brethren Church, and Mennonite Church, represent the historic concern for peace within these brotherhoods.

1. *Nevertheless* by John H. Yoder. 1971.
2. *Coals of Fire* by Elizabeth Hershberger Bauman. 1954. (For young readers.)
3. *The Original Revolution* by John H. Yoder. 1972.
4. *The Christian and Warfare* by Jacob J. Enz. 1972.
5. *What Belongs to Caesar?* by Donald D. Kaufman. 1969.
6. *Jesus and the Nonviolent Revolution* by Andre Trocme. 1973.

JESUS
AND
THE NONVIOLENT REVOLUTION

by Andre Trocme

Translated by Michael H. Shank
and Marlin E. Miller
With Introduction
by Marlin E. Miller

Herald Press
Scottdale, Pennsylvania
1973

Library of Congress Cataloging in Publication Data

Trocme, Andre, 1901-1971.
  Jesus and the nonviolent revolution.

  (The Christian peace shelf)
  Includes bibliographical references.
  1. Nonviolence — Biblical teaching. 2. Jesus Christ
— Person and offices. I. Title.
BS2417 .P2T7613   2329,54   73-9934
ISBN   0-8361-1719-0

Introduction to English Edition

Andre Pascal Trocme was one of the rare Christian pacifists who in the past fifty years refused to choose between impassioned action and intellectual clarity. He repeatedly used humble circumstances for the practice and proclamation of virile Christian obedience in a troubled and turbulent time and actively confronted situations of human conflict. The present book on *Jesus and the Nonviolent Revolution* is a fitting part of his legacy to militant pacifists whose touchstone remains the person of Jesus, as well as to those who by design or default have divorced the historical Jesus from the social and historical dimensions of human existence.

Born into a French and German family living in the northern French industrial town of St. Quentin in 1901, Trocme early experienced the conflict which was to divide Europe and the world twice in the first half of the century. When the German army, including some of his German cousins, marched into St. Quentin in 1914, Trocme's youthful patriotism inspired him to hang a French flag from the top branches of a towering tree on the edge of town.

Years later, when Hitler's specter began to haunt Europe, Trocme toyed with the idea of using his German language facility to infiltrate the group gathered around Hitler in order to assassinate him before he plunged the world into catastrophe. But Trocme's fear of "separating himself from Jesus who rejected armed violence to counteract the crime being prepared against Him" held him back. In addition, his "perseverance" as a Reformed pastor in an obscure south central French village discouraged such an adventure. Nevertheless, the current of events coupled with the characteristic initiative of Trocme were to propel him into another style of confrontation with Nazism.

In 1934 Trocme and his Italian wife, Magda, transferred from a pastoral and evangelistic ministry among miners and steel workers in northern France to the sleepy Huguenot village of Le Chambon-sur-Lignon. To help rouse it from its lethargy, Trocme and Edouard Theis, a fellow pacifist teacher and pastor, founded a Protestant preparatory school with high school and junior curriculums. Classes opened in 1938 with 18 pupils in the parish annex. Already the following year refugees from central Europe began to arrive in southern France in fear of impending military actions. From 40 in 1939, the number of pupils and students increased to 150 the next year and reached 350 by 1943. (Today the College Cevenol has a student body of 500 with a staff of 50.) By the pressure of events, the school became international in composition. Students came not only from French Protestant but from Roman Catholic and Jewish families as well. Several Jewish professors, expelled from the public schools by the Petain regime, also became members of the teaching staff.

By the turn of the decade, rumors had reached Le Chambon about internment camps and deportations toward "forced labor" in Germany. At Trocme's initiative, the parish sent him to visit several of the camps to offer emergency assistance. Stopping first, however, in Marseille, Trocme was advised by the American Friends Service Committee representative, Burns Chalmers, not to visit the camps. Several organizations were already at work in the camps, cooperating with French doctors to have inmates dismissed as "unfit for work" in order to save them from deportation. Chalmers proposed instead that Le Chambon become a refuge for those who could be released from the camps. During the remaining war years Le Chambon thus became a mountain harbor for Jewish and anti-Nazi refugees and released prisoners. At least hundreds and perhaps several thousand were hidden, or smuggled into Switzerland. The International Fellowship of Reconciliation and the American Friends Service Committee continued to forward funds for the operation until the end of the war.

In 1943 Trocme and Theis were arrested for their resistance activities, interned in a prison camp, and released after two months, even though they refused to swear allegiance to Marshal Petain and to refrain from all further resistance. Not long afterward, two Gestapo informers, who also served the French resistance, reported to Trocme and Theis that the Gestapo had decided to assassinate them. On the advice of the informers and of the French Reformed Church. Theis and Trocme took to the woods and remained in hiding ten months.

After the war, Trocme was decorated with the "rosette of the resistance" (rather than with the more common "medal of the resistance"), even though his resistance had been consistently nonviolent. And shortly before he died in June 1971, he was awarded the "medal of the just ones" in commemoration of the part he and the populace of Le Chambon had played in saving hundreds of Jewish lives. In 1972 his wife planted his tree along the "path of the just ones" at Yad Vashem, the Jewish memorial for the six million Jews who were killed during the Second World War.

Trocme had already learned in the 1920s that a military armistice did not suffice for reconstructing peace and the moral fabric of the victors, as well as the victims. As the guns of the war were silenced in 1945 his energies turned toward reconciliation and the rebuilding the foundations of international good will. From 1947-60, he served as an international secretary of FOR. His travels and lectures took him to the United States and the Soviet Union, to Western and Eastern Europe, to North Africa and the Middle East, to Japan and Southeast Asia. He became one of the links in an international chain which united such leaders of nonviolence as Gandhi, Kagawa, and Martin Luther King. From 1950-60 the Trocmes founded and directed the House of Reconciliation, an international peace center in Versailles. Ironically enough, the house had been one of the two "Mills of Peace" built by Louis XVI to grind grain for the starving French populace prior to the Revolution. In the final decade of his life, Trocme returned to a pastoral team ministry with his pulpit at Saint Gervais, a fifteenth-century church in Geneva which converted to the Reformed faith in 1535.

Trocme's international travels and lecturing did not, however, blind him to the conflicts that held France on the verge of civil war in the 1950s. The French colonial empire was crumbling and the Algerian war was dividing the soul of the nation. The Trocmes again took the road of personal confrontation. In the spring of 1956 they set out for a situation of conflict in North Africa to gather information and seek constructive alternatives to the tension. They were prepared to be misunderstood and threatened by both sides. But through projects such as sewing and literacy training among Arab women, reconciliation training among Arab men, and the solicitation of French volunteer teachers who had previously remained on their side of the city, the Trocmes demonstrated that individuals and small groups could live by trust and peace in the midst of a seemingly hopeless historical impasse. Little wonder that Trocme was one of the founders of Eirene International Service for Peace in 1957 and that Eirene sent its first volunteers to North Africa. Little wonder that Eirene today has 50 persons at work in Morocco, the country where Trocme, during his military service in the early twenties, turned in his gun and ammunition under threat of being court-martialed for deserting colors under attack.

Besides numerous articles in French and foreign Protestant papers, Trocme has written two book-length treatments of peace and nonviolence. The *Politics of Repentance* was first delivered as the Robert Treat Paine Lectures for 1951 and published by Fellowship Publications (New York) in 1953. *Jesus and the Nonviolent Revolution* was in the making during the "Mill of Peace" years. The French original was published by Labor et Fides (Geneva) in 1961, has been published in Italian (1969) and is scheduled for publication in Portuguese (Brazil). The earlier book, which proposes to the church a strategy for peace and paradigmatic action in conflict situations, merits rereading, particularly together with the present volume.

Trocme's account of Jesus' nonviolent revolution begins with the thesis that Jesus' inauguration of the kingdom of God included the proclamation of a jubilee year in AD 26/27. This thesis is based on Jesus' first sermon according to Luke 4, as well as upon allusions throughout Jesus' teaching. The prescriptions of jubilee thus assumed a central place in Jesus' theology, ethics, and in His vision of the kingdom. This social and economic revolution based on the jubilary law of Moses took on a political dimension as well when Jesus asked the Jewish villages and their authorities to recognize Him as the Son of David and the King of Israel. The refusal of the authorities to accept Jesus' messianic claim led to the conflict which ended on the cross.

In the second part of the book, Trocme surveys the history of violence and nonviolence in Jewish history from Elijah to the time of Herod. Among the various social groups and Jewish parties contemporary to Jesus, Trocme uncovers within the broader nationalist and messianic stream a nonviolent resistance current in continuity with the vision of the major prophets. Within this movement Trocme recounts several demonstrations of nonviolent resistance to the Roman occupation to show that such an alternative was, historically speaking, a live option for Jesus as well.

In the final section of the book Trocme traces Jesus' extension of the Jewish religious horizon. Although Jesus' social and political program remained constant to the time just preceding His death, His reformulation of the notions of election and the Sabbath threatened to shatter the ethnic unity of the Jewish people, as well as their ethical vision. When the Jewish leaders refused Jesus' messianic claim, as well as His transformation of peoplehood and ethics, Jesus was faced with the alternative of withdrawal or continued confrontation. At crucial points in His ministry, Jesus chose the latter option. But, according to Trocme, He consistently chose nonviolent resistance rather than the way of sacral violence to institute the kingdom. He went so far as to sacrifice His "cause" for the sake of the human person. The book closes with a moral interpretation of the eschatological problem and a comparison between Gandhi and Jesus.

Without doubt, Trocme's vision of the historical Jesus reflects his own pacifist orientation. That could, however, hardly be considered a devastating critique. Albert Schweitzer has demonstrated both by historical survey and personal example that even exegetes employing the most sophisticated tools of linguistic and historic analysis invariably formed the historical Jesus after their own image. The reader will need to examine the degree to which Trocme's proposed interpretation nevertheless remains faithful to the New Testament presentation. It would also be naive to assume that Trocme simply projects his own prejudices upon the New Testament writings. He has also been committed to permitting the biblical record to shape his prejudices. The degree to which he has accurately interpreted Jesus' stance will thus need to be evaluated both by exegetical care and Christian obedience.

Without doubt, the reader may find Trocme's interpretation of several parables and incidents of Jesus' life somewhat imaginative. Nevertheless, Trocme has asked for nothing more than an exegetical and historical reevaluation by others whose exegetical and historical competence may be greater. His book is meant to raise a legitimate question and support a proposed answer, not to provide a definitive treatment. Within those limits, *Jesus and the Nonviolent Revolution* commends itself to both the scholar and the activist. It has so far been refuted by neither.

Marlin E. Miller
Paris, France
February 1973

Author's Preface

In the following pages, the author attempts to respond to the anguish of our generation.

On the one hand, the population explosion renders more difficult each day a peaceful solution to the problems of hunger, national independence, education of the masses, and social justice. Simultaneously, the threat of nuclear destruction hovers over the future of humanity. On the other hand, Gandhi has demonstrated that the Sermon on the Mount, long considered even by Christians as utopian, can at times resolve the problem of social relations. The Bible should be reread in this new perspective.

However, an ever-widening gap is developing between the mentality of our contemporaries, shaped by our industrial civilization where man controls nature, and our traditional theology, conceived during a rural epoch when man bowed under the weight of nature. While the machine is upsetting the conditions of human existence, Christian thought, frightened by the responsibilities it should assume, refuses to see anything in the gospel except a message of individual salvation.

Even more serious, some theological tendencies condemn all actions for the physical salvation of the human race and any effort of authentic Christian obedience as presumptuous and pharisaical — and that in an age devoted to the might of technology and armaments. Such a reversal of the teachings of Jesus Christ must be rectified. Without this correction, the Christian churches risk disqualifying themselves as leaders of the human race now bordering on suicide.

Neither a professor of history, nor of theology, the author will attempt little more than brushing lightly those areas reserved for specialists. However, it may be said that after having flirted with the theologies and philosophies of despair, as everyone else of his generation, the author now rejects this poison. He will no longer let himself be attracted by the dialectics of the relative and the absolute, of the horizontal and the vertical, of the devil and God. He is sated with lucid analyses, which define the problems without ever proposing a manly obedience capable of resolving them. He considers such forms of thought subtle excuses which are used by the intellectual in order to evade his responsibilities to those like him, a characteristic of periods of moral and religious decadence.[1]

In actual fact, the disciple of Jesus, as well as the non-Christian, is responsible for the hunger, the injustice, the egoism, the exploitation, and the wars which devastate our time. He is even more responsible so far as he is confident that men have not been abandoned by God. Knowing that God can change both men and things, the disciple of Jesus Christ brings the future of man and of things to God.

One day, God intervened in history. Since then, everything which happens on earth has become important. Because of one event without precedent and without duplication — the birth, the life, the death and the resurrection of Jesus Christ — every birth of "an ordinary man," every life and death of man becomes in turn an event without precedent and duplication.

If each "ordinary man" has thus been invested with such value, how great is the worth of human history! Regardless of whether one agrees or not, whether one believes in His divine sonship or not, Jesus is the central event of history, because *de facto* man is not the same after Jesus Christ as before. It is therefore essential to ascertain who the historical Jesus was if we wish to measure the value of contemporary man.

Recent works have reopened this old debate. Everyone is agreed today that the authors of the New Testament, when they attempted to explain Jesus to the people of their generation, used certain beliefs current in the Mediterranean basin. They employed doctrines colored by Judaism, by Neoplatonic philosophy, or Oriental dualism. Jesus and His disciples obviously spoke the language of their contemporaries.

We should not, however, be alarmed by this state of affairs. Behind this religious and philosophical vocabulary, today outmoded, we can discover the lasting Christ. The ancients, and Jesus along with them, believed that the universe had three levels: heaven, the earth, and the lower places. Today we know differently. Indeed, men of the 18th century thought that the atom was indivisible.[2] Even though we know today that the atom is divisible, we continue to use the word "atom" and invest it with new meaning. Similarly we continue to speak about "heaven," without locating it overhead as did Jesus. Are we going to dispute the value of what men of the first century have said because our knowledge of the universe continues to grow unceasingly? Would we enslave ourselves to certain words? That would hardly be an honor to our intelligence. And the gospel merits being read with as much intelligence as faith.

In the name of this intelligence and of this faith, we shall, however, not give way to the demythologizing zeal of some. Sooner or later, all those who have tried to weed out the gospel have transformed it into a desert.

It was indeed the case that angelology, demonology, and apocalyptic literature were widespread in Jesus' time.[3] Jesus borrowed certain concepts from them, among others, the notion of the Son of Man's return from heaven on clouds. Furthermore, it is true that the oldest apocalyptic work which first mentions the figure of the Son of Man is the Book of Daniel. But we should not forget that the canon of the Old Testament was closed two hundred years before Jesus Christ. Consequently, the Holy Scripture which was the teacher of John the Baptist, Jesus, and Saul of Tarsus, terminated with Daniel. The popular Jewish apocalypses were not read in the synagogue, but rather the law, the psalms, and the prophets, in other words, a Word singularly sober and spare. The authors of the Old Testament were hardly gifted in the invention of myths.

If the New Testament should be demythologized, it should not be done with the help of our modern myths but with the assistance of the Old Testament. The more the strict monotheistic faith in the God of Israel is exalted, the more visible becomes the thought of Jesus Christ. Let us never forget that the God of Jesus Christ was the God of Israel. The Christian faith dissolves into mythology as soon as it no longer leans upon Judaism. Nothing can be lost by rejudaizing Christianity. Judaism is the point of departure for all research destined to rediscover the Jesus of history. We need not hesitate to examine those ideas which the authors of the New Testament borrowed from sources other than the Old Testament in order to explain Jesus to their Jewish and Greek contemporaries. But let us not sacrifice the Old Testament.

Nevertheless, even the Old Testament is not without myth. In the first chapter of this book, we shall recall certain paradoxes of Jewish doctrine. This is where the Old Testament in turn stands in need of the New. That which was too crushing in the original story of man's Fall has been lifted by Jesus. The narrowness of the dogma of an elect people has been broadened by Jesus. That which was too ritual in the law of Moses has been humanized by Jesus. That which the prophets announced has been accomplished by Jesus. Thus one loses nothing by Christianizing Judaism, because Jesus Christ is the One who has done so.

However, the Jesus of history surpasses both the Old and the New Testament. He is the point of encounter between two theological edifices, the Jewish and the Christian. He has fulfilled the first and engendered the second. That which came before and after Him must be explained by Him. The light dawns when we ask Jesus Himself to interpret Judaism and Christianity for us. One uses a lamp to lighten the darkness. One doesn't put it under a bushel before even using it. Jesus has linked two historical epochs together by an arched bridge. This bridge is His life and His teaching, namely the few parables and aphorisms which He spoke. We should again today try to grasp their deeper meaning. This depth is more striking than any rigorously consistent doctrine. Its quality springs from the living presence in Jesus of the loving God, who reveals Himself as the Father of men. This presence of God manifests itself; it does not prove itself.

A further remark on the method of this book should be made. The author limited his ambitions to the modest goal of interrogating Jesus Christ by Jesus Christ. In the attempt to discover whether Jesus was nonviolent, the author saw (appearing in the Gospels), the portrait of a vigorous Revolutionary who is capable of saving the world without using violence. The author wishes to share the enthusiasm of his discovery with the reader.

Before writing the following pages, the author spent some time examining the literature on the subject. He, however, wishes to underline his limited exegetical and historical competence, because his other activities prohibit scholarly work. He would nonetheless indicate that on the subject of the biblical jubilee, he had recourse to an article by F. M. Lemoine, O.P., "Le Jubile dans la Bible," in the October 1949 issue of Vie Spirituelle, as well as to the exhaustive work by Robert North, S.J., Sociology of the Biblical Jubilee, published in the collection Analecta Biblica, by the Pontifical Biblical Institute of Rome, 1954.

The theses concerning the proclamation of a biblical jubilee by Jesus are the author's.[4] If their somewhat unusual character can stimulate the curiosity of the specialists and provoke a movement of research on the nonviolence of Jesus, the author will have reached his goal.

Contents

I. JESUS AND JUBILEE

1. Jesus — A Jewish Prophet

Much has been said in recent years about the syncretic character of the Gospels. In Jesus' time, Galilee was a place of transition. Three languages, Hebrew, Aramaic and Greek, were used. Dualistic doctrines from the East on the devil, angels, and demons took the place of strict Jewish monotheism.[1] Hellenistic civilization was invading the last strongholds of Judaism. Raised in this complex environment, Jesus could have laid the foundations of Christianity by borrowing from all the surrounding sources.

The only authority we have for challenging the validity of this thesis is common sense. We need merely to read the three Synoptic Gospels to discover that Jesus was a Jewish prophet, the last in a line which begins with Amos and ends with John the Baptist.

The writers of the Synoptics (Matthew in particular) had one obvious intention. To demonstrate that Jesus was really the Messiah whom the prophets had announced, they embellished their stories with quotations from the Old Testament. Because this demonstration took place after the event, it may have distorted some of the Master's authentic words and influenced the account of His Passion. We should note three things.

First of all, the authors of the Gospels had no trouble whatsoever in showing the Jewish character of Jesus' thought. The contrary would have been more difficult to prove because Jesus, as a Jew, had only one library at His disposal, namely the law, the prophets, and the psalms, which inspired His teaching and several of His parables. As a matter of fact, the Jews made no mistake on this score. The ones who refused to recognize Him as the Messiah saw Him until the end as an authentic Jewish prophet (Matthew 14:5; 21:23-26; 21:46; Luke, chapters 9 and 8; etc.). Moreover, the theology and moral teaching of Jesus were none other than Jewish theology and Jewish moral teaching less the ritual elements which clouded their simplicity. Jesus could not even conceive of a moral teaching other than the Mosaic law. "I have not come to abolish the law and the prophets but to fulfil them," he affirmed. "What did Moses command you?" He asked His questioners. When He gave the Golden Rule ("Whatever you wish that men would do to you, do so to them," still considered today as the supremely lay expression of morality), He justified it with a peculiarly Jewish expression, "for this is the law and the prophets."

Second, the law of Moses, enlarged and commented upon by the prophets, was the law of the Jewish people. It mixed together prescriptions of the religious, moral, social, and political order. When the prophets Amos, Hosea, Isaiah, and Jeremiah sounded their calls to repentance, they addressed themselves to Israel, Judah, and Jerusalem as to a corporate personality. They called the entire people to repentance. Jewish justice had to be restored, Jewish religion purified, Jewish customs transformed, and the law of Moses put into practice at all levels. In the pure prophetic tradition, Jesus addressed His reproaches and His appeals to the entire Jewish people. When He proclaimed the *metanoia,* that is, the radical change of heart, He was not addressing Himself to the pagan "nations," but rather to the Israelite community (Matthew 9:35; Luke 3:8). Jesus traveled up and down Galilee preaching the good news from God: "The time is fulfilled, and the kingdom of God is at hand; repent, and believe in the gospel" (Mark 1:15). When he commissioned the Twelve, he instructed them: "Go nowhere among the Gentiles, and enter no town of the Samaritans, but go rather to the lost sheep of the house of Israel" (Matthew 10:5, 6).

Keeping in mind that the Jewish religion was a national religion, we may thirdly mention some of the typically Jewish notions that Jesus accepted and taught without hesitation. The nonmodern and nonrational character of these notions should not surprise us. Jesus' universalism did not spring from Greek rationalism, nor from Roman legalism, nor from Enlightenment philosophy. Nor is it the offspring of a happy marriage between Judaism and Neoplatonism. It grows out of orthodox Judaism, a Judaism that "exploded" under the pressure of the messianism borne within it. The universalisms of Greece or Rome, whether rational or scientific, all suffer from the same infirmity: they lack dynamism. They are too well balanced, too symmetrical to inspire action. The universalism which grows out of Judaism is, on the contrary, asymmetrical. It contains a creative impulse that enables it to last for centuries while continuously renewing itself.

When confronted with the great revolutionary passions, Western democracies, inspired by eighteenth-century philosophy, share the same sickness as the Greco-Roman civilization. Their rationalism cannot resolve their internal contradictions. Their philosophy is too static, too optimistic, too conservative. It took Christianity's asymmetry, rooted in Judaism, to rescue Greco-Roman civilization from the collapse threatening it. Is modern Christianity still close enough to Judaism, still asymmetrical enough to get our rationalism-infested Western civilization out of trouble? That is the question.

But in what sense is Judaism asymmetrical?

1. The Idea of the Chosen People

The Old Testament recounts as a historical event how God chose Abraham of Ur. "Go from your country and your kindred and your father's house to the land that I will show you. And I will make of you a great nation and I will bless you. . . . I will bless those who bless you, and him who curses you I will curse; and by you all the families of the earth will bless themselves."

The call of the people of Israel, descendants of Abraham, in which pious Jews still believe today, has not ceased to cause suffering for the Jews themselves and to be a scandal for non-Jews. Islam was originally and continues as a protest of Ishmael's descendants deprived of their heritage by Israel's descendants who claimed to be God's preferred people. But despite its irrational character, the notion of election reappears constantly throughout history. The disequilibrium it inspires is a generator of movement and energy. The Jewish people, the object of divine choice, has gone through centuries of vicissitudes, but still stands today, the lone witness to vanished antiquity.

Following in Israel's footsteps, the Christian church understands itself as divinely chosen. It affirms that there is no salvation outside of its Lord, Jesus Christ, and it undertakes in His name the conquest of the world through its reforming and charitable missions. The conviction of the church that it has been chosen by God often creates tragic tensions between itself and other religions. But every time it doubts its election, its capacity to convert others also diminishes.

Whereas the church today has lost much of its conquering dynamism, the proletariat, that is the common class, considers itself the heir of Christianity's chosenness. Because it is "free from the sin of exploitation," that is, because it possesses no capital, the proletariat feels called to guide humanity in the "movement of history." Its messianic faith has proven its ability to undertake and bring off the greatest social revolution of all times. The proletariat thus compels the Christian West to arouse itself from the rational torpor which it so much enjoys.

But let us return to Israel's election. It is the result of a divine choice as inexplicable as love, because Israel is "the least among the nations." Strangely enough, even though God's choice is arbitrary, it binds the responsibility of the elect. For if God makes a covenant with Israel to which He will be faithful, Israel is in return required to uphold its part of the contract. Israel must be "holy" to its God because it is a witness among the nations, of which God is the Light. As a result of this witness, all nations will finally recognize that Israel's God is the only God and will come to Jerusalem to worship. But if Israel breaks the stipulations of the contract, becomes unfaithful to Yahweh and disobeys the law, terrible punishments will come. Israel will be devastated, carried off in bondage, destroyed. Only a small remnant will escape. With this remnant, God will, however, rebuild a faithful people. Jesus obviously shared this belief in Israel's election. Because of His orthodox faith, He could address His prophetic call to the people. After having drawn the consequences from the Jews' disobedience, He dared to announce the rejection of this stiff-necked people, but also, according to Scripture, the birth of a "remnant," of a "small flock," to which the Father would give the kingdom.

Thus the concept of election repeatedly activated certain minority groups who were filled with the certainty of a redemptive mission to be accomplished. Thanks to these minorities, the recurring failures of humanity (seen by Greek antiquity as the hand of destiny and by Oriental wisdom as proof that action is illusory by definition) have become the very material God uses to resolve history's dilemmas.

2. The Individual's Moral Responsibility in the Midst of History

Perhaps even more important than the belief in election is what we shall call the "moral bias of the Old Testament." Like the Greek philosophies, Oriental cosmogonies tried to explain the creation of the world and the origin of evil and death. Man always came out as the irresponsible victim of a fate he did not choose. Some talked about the Fall as a cosmic catastrophe; others explained evil as the necessary shadow cast by the good. For some, creation was subjected to the perpetual cycle of new beginnings. For others, the problem of evil was resolved by successive reincarnations of the human soul until its final absorption into God. The majority found consolation for this world's injustices in the hope for a celestial paradise where sin and death would be abolished.[2]

Only the Old Testament dares attribute evil and death to a strictly moral cause. According to the Old Testament, man dies because of his own fault (Genesis 3:17-19). Moreover, man is the one who dragged the other creatures with him into death (Genesis 6:5-7).[3] At first glance, such an assertion is revolting. It cannot be reconciled with modern paleontology. Science nowadays tells us that disease and death affected plants and animals long before man ever appeared on earth! Moreover, if the Old Testament were right, a good man should receive the reward of his virtues. Even if it is true that the descendants of a good man are often blessed by God and the descendants of an alcoholic or a rake often suffer, such examples can hardly be made a general rule. How many depraved families enjoy impudent happiness and how many virtuous ones are struck by inexplicable catastrophies! How many inoffensive nations are annihilated while the brute force of unscrupulous conquerors prevails! No. Man's sin is not the only cause of suffering and death. Job and the psalmists of the Old Testament already protested against such an unjust doctrine.

However, there is another way of looking at the doctrine of the Fall and its consequences. If one abandons the search for an explanation of evil and death, one can find another of the asymmetric, revealed teachings of the Bible. Here I am, thrown into the world, a man alone before the God of Israel. If I use my reason and declare, "I was born by chance; I am not responsible for my temperament and I am conditioned by my environment; I am the toy of heredity and of events that drag me along; I received my breath from a blind creator who no longer cares about me," I will lack the energy I need in order to act. But if I am spurred on by the paradoxical and extreme doctrine of the Bible, I perk up, "offended."[4] "What? God says I am the only one to blame for my sins? Yes. The only master of my temperament? Yes! Of my environment? Certainly. Of my nation and the way it behaves? Indeed. Of my death and the fall of a world headed straight for suicide? Exactly. But you are not going to go so far as to say that I am responsible for the innumerable sins of my forefathers and even for Adam's sin? No, *we* claim nothing since *we* are not the Bible, but men just like you. We have nothing to force upon you, but the Bible tells us, the speakers, as well as you, the listeners, that we are responsible for our death and the death of the people around us. And because the Bible is not a philosophical dissertation, it adds one paradox to another by stating: "You know very well you are guilty, because you are forgiven! You would not be guilty if your heredity had no cure, but you are guilty insofar as you neglect the cure that God freely gives you!"

Jesus gave no other explanation to those who questioned Him about the death of eighteen people crushed by a falling tower. "Do you think that they were worse offenders than all the others who dwelt in Jerusalem? I tell you, No; but unless you repent you will all likewise perish" (Luke 13:4). In other words, repentance comes first. Fall on your knees before God and confess your sin. Then get up and change the course of history!

Thus, the Bible gives no explanation of evil. But it does give us a way to get out of it: repentance and faith. By requiring of men that they repent, God acts in history not as a Creator, but as a Redeemer. Through the repentance of a few, He says to the whole of a sick history, "Rise and walk!" Such an injunction awakens in everyone who hears it the response of faith at a level deeper than that of reason. Such faith gives man his true measure and moves history forward.[5]

3. The Requirements of an Inexorable Justice

Here again the peculiar genius of the Bible reveals itself to us. The law of Moses certainly contains nothing unique. Like other ancient codes, it confuses the ritual purity of a people dedicated to its God with the legal principles that are necessary for life in society. But whereas the flow of centuries has brought about a softening of the harsh primitive laws among other nations, the legal frame of reference of the Bible was transformed without fundamental alterations.

Take, for example, the law of retaliation expressed for the first time in the Book of Genesis after Cain had killed his brother. Abel's blood demanded revenge. Justice had to be established. Cain was to die because he had killed. But God decreed that whoever would kill Cain must also pay the price of blood: "If anyone slays Cain, vengeance shall be taken on him sevenfold." Genesis 9:6 adds, "Whoever sheds the blood of man, by man shall his blood be shed; for God made man in his own image." This principle of justice was codified by Moses in the following terms: "You shall give life for life, eye for eye, tooth for tooth, hand for hand, foot for foot, burn for burn, stripe for stripe." From then on, strict accounting regulated the relationship of man to man and man to God.

Today, our customs are less rigid. Of the law of retaliation, our legislators have retained only provisions concerning liability.[6] Israel, however, could not rid itself of its peculiar election. God had said, "You shall be to me a holy nation." He therefore required much more of the Jews than of the other nations. They had to pay for every sin before it could be erased.

In its relations with other nations, Israel was also marked by the dreadful and holy law. No compromises were allowed. Yahweh had ordered the destruction of the conquered pagans so "that they may not teach you to do according to all their abominable practices which they have done in the service of their gods, and to sin against the Lord your God" (Deuteronomy 20:16-18). This was the law of *herem* or of the *ban*. The Pharisees of Jesus' time continued to observe this law, for example, when they ordered the Jews to avoid all contact with pagans or Samaritans (John 4; 9). They acted this way to save their people from all idolatrous contamination. The historians of this period describe the Jewish people, who had temporarily given up violence as a means to reconquer their independence, as ready at all times to use holy violence as soon as the purity of worship was desecrated. One inscription has even been discovered that threatened death for any pagan who dared venture into the court of the temple.

The Christian faith, rooted in the Jewish faith, does not deny the necessity of sacred violence — far from it. But this violence has assumed a different form, thanks to the person of the *goel*.

Who is the *goel?* He is precisely the "avenger of blood." According to the law of Moses, if someone had been assassinated, the *goel* had the responsibility of carrying out the vendetta against the guilty person. "The avenger of blood shall himself put the murderer to death; when he meets him, he shall put him to death" (Numbers 35:19). The *goel* was the victim's next of kin. He was also the appointed protector of his relatives. If an indebted kinsman were forced to sell his land, the Book of Leviticus decreed, "If your brother becomes poor, and sells part of his property, then his next of kin [*goel*] shall come and redeem what his brother has sold" (Leviticus 25:25). Thus, in the Old Testament, the idea of vengeance and redemption are closely intertwined.

The *goel* also had to marry the wife of his deceased kinsman as well as redeem the kinsman that had become enslaved. "If your brother . . . becomes poor and sells himself . . . one of his brothers may redeem him, or his uncle, or his cousin may redeem him, or a near kinsman belonging to his family may redeem him . . ." (Leviticus 25:47 ff.).

In Isaiah and the Psalms, the word *goel* often refers to God Himself, with the double meaning of Avenger and Redeemer of the people of whom He is the kinsman. "Go forth from Babylon, flee from Chaldea, declare this with a shout of joy, and proclaim it. . . . The Lord has redeemed [*ga'al*] his servant Jacob" (Isaiah 48:20). "Fear not, for I have redeemed you; I have called you by name, you are mine. When you pass through the waters, I will be with you; and through the rivers, and they will not overwhelm you. . . . For I am the Lord your God, the Holy One of Israel, your Savior. I give Egypt as your ransom, Ethiopia and Seba in exchange for you. Because you are precious in my eyes . . ." (Isaiah 43:1 ff.). As one can see here, the payment of a ransom is never omitted from the duties of the *goel*.

However in Deutero-Isaiah, chapters 52 and 53, another idea of *goel* appears: he is the one who redeems Israel by taking upon himself the chastisement of God. The figure of the "Servant of Yahweh," who gives his life in ransom for the guilty ones fallen into slavery, thrusts itself upon Jesus. In this way the law of retaliation was transmuted. Its demand for justice could never be abolished. But God's vengeance would now be borne by God Himself, by the God who is the *goel* of His people in the person of His Son.

2. Jesus Proclaims Jubilee

At the beginning of His public ministry, Jesus gave an extremely important speech in the synagogue of His hometown, Nazareth. Matthew and Mark give us merely a brief summary of this event, but Luke's account (4:16-32) is quite detailed. Here it is in its entirety:

And he came to Nazareth, where he had been brought up; and he went to the synagogue, as his custom was, on the sabbath day. And he stood up to read; and there was given to him the book of the prophet Isaiah. He opened the book and found the place where it was written,
"The Spirit of the Lord is upon me,
because he has anointed me to preach good news to the poor.
He has sent me to proclaim release to the captives
(and recovering of sight to the blind),[1]
to set at liberty those who are oppressed,
to proclaim the acceptable year of the Lord."
And he closed the book, and gave it back to the attendant, and sat down; and the eyes of all in the synagogue were fixed on him. And he began to say to them, "Today this scripture has been fulfilled in your hearing." And all spoke well of him, and wondered at the gracious words which proceeded out of his mouth; and they said, "Is not this Joseph's son?" And he said to them, "Doubtless you will quote to me this proverb, 'Physician, heal yourself; what we have heard you did at Capernaum, do here also in your country.'" And he said, "Truly, I say to you, no prophet is acceptable in his own country. But in truth, I tell you, there were many widows in Israel in the days of Elijah, when the heaven was shut up three years and six months, when there came a great famine over all the land; and Elijah was sent to none of them but only to Zarephath, in the land of Sidon, to a woman who was a widow. And there were many lepers in Israel in the time of the prophet Elisha; and none of them was cleansed, but only Naaman the Syrian." When they heard this, all in the synagogue were filled with wrath. And they rose up and put him out of the city, and led him to the brow of the hill on which their city was built, that they might throw him down headlong. But passing through the midst of them he went away.
And he went down to Capernaum, a city of Galilee. And he was teaching them on the sabbath; and they were astonished at his teaching, for his word was with authority.

This narrative deserves some rather lengthy comments. First, let us note that Matthew and Mark place this incident after a long ministry of Jesus in Galilee. Luke, who spent some time on more precise chronological research, places it at the beginning of His public activity, immediately after a first preaching tour in the synagogues and following the temptation. We will follow Luke's chronology. It was indeed logical for the Spirit-filled Jesus to begin His ministry in His hometown and to try to secure the adherence of His own people to the kingdom of God. Moreover, Matthew (4:12 and 13) follows the account of the temptation with these words: "Now when he heard that John had been arrested, he withdrew into Galilee; and leaving Nazareth, he went and dwelt in Capernaum by the sea." John 2:12 also places the trip to Capernaum at the beginning of Jesus' ministry, though he does not mention the dramatic events of Nazareth. All this agrees quite well with Luke's account (4:30, 31): "But [Jesus] passing through the midst of them, went away, and he went down to Capernaum, a city of Galilee."

Second: The next part of Jesus' speech, the part beginning with the words, "Doubtless you will quote to me this proverb, 'Physician, heal yourself,' " set off a wave of anger which chased Jesus from the synagogue and provoked an attempted assassination. But one cannot see at all why Jesus would have wanted to offend His fellow citizens if they had not already disbelieved the beginning of His speech. Furthermore, Matthew and Mark also present the succession of events in this light.

Third, Even under these circumstances, it is hard to understand at first glance why some of Jesus' audience react with explosive violence while others display astonishment and even enthusiasm. It would have taken more than a few comments about the widow of Zarephath or about Naaman the Syrian to initiate the attempt to kill Jesus. According to Jewish law only crimes, blasphemies against God, or violations of the Sabbath deserved the death penalty. But Jesus had committed neither of these offenses.

Had He threatened the life or interests of a part of Nazareth's population? This is what we must now investigate.

The passage Jesus read from Isaiah 61 will give us the answer. This is the only Old Testament text where the Messiah, the Anointed One of the Lord, speaks in the first person: "The Lord has anointed me." Jesus chose to read precisely this passage in the synagogue of His youth, before His parents and friends, "The Lord has anointed me." And He added: "Today this scripture has been fulfilled in your hearing." In other words, to our knowledge, Jesus officially stated for the first time in the synagogue at Nazareth that He was the Messiah whom the prophets had announced. It is now easy to understand the amazement of some and the skepticism of others.

But this messianic proclamation alone could not have aroused such murderous anger. The rest of the passage from Isaiah will help explain it.

The Messiah announced by the prophets was the liberator. People thought He would reestablish the legitimate Davidic dynasty and free the people from foreign domination. Isaiah 61 does indeed refer to a liberation, but it is a social liberation: "To bring good tidings to the afflicted, to proclaim liberty to the captives, and the opening of the prison to those who are bound, to proclaim the year of the Lord's favor." To imagine that such a text meant nothing more to Jesus than a succession of vain words would be an insult. In effect, He attached the greatest importance to each of these terms. Being the Messiah, He meant to accomplish word for word what the prophet announced as the task of the Messiah. Thus He was setting out to liberate all the oppressed of Israel. He was proclaiming (Luke 4:19) a "year of freedom" ("the year of the Lord's favor" or the "acceptable year of the Lord").

We now hold the key to the problem. By proclaiming a "year of freedom" in Nazareth, Jesus was threatening the interests of property owners and thus excited their murderous anger. His adversaries never admitted the real motives behind their fear and hate. As good conservatives do, they hid behind noble pretexts to discredit the prophet from Nazareth. They wanted to defend the sabbatical institutions, the temple in Jerusalem, and the tradition of their fathers.

Exactly what was this "year of the Lord's favor" which Jesus proclaimed? Exegetes agree that it was nothing less than the sabbatical year or Jubilee instituted by Moses.[2]

Moses had instituted a genuine social revolution aimed at preventing the accumulation of capital in the hands of a minority. This social revolution was to recur every seven and every forty-nine years. We use the term "revolution" intentionally because the social readjustments ordered by Moses were second to none of the claims of the modern revolutionary. However, according to their own doctrinaires, contemporary revolutions grow only out of economic transformations forced upon modern societies by technological discoveries. Jesus' revolution, on the contrary, drew its strength from the source of all revolutions, God's justice. God has revealed His justice to Moses, and Moses, with his legislative genius, had planned its periodic re-establishment in the dynamic form of the Jubilee. By proclaiming the Jubilee, Jesus wanted to transform the present from the perspective of the future according to the code of justice God had promulgated in the past.

Now these rules of Jubilee were known to the poor, as well as to the rich people of Nazareth. Was not the law of Moses read every Sabbath in the synagogue, without, however, being put into practice? In His speech, Jesus suddenly demanded that the law be put into effect immediately. This implied among other things expropriating the lands of the wealthy and liquidating the usurious system from which the ruling classes lived. It is easy enough to understand the enthusiasm of the poor, as well as the fear of the rich, and the reasons that prompted them to try to stop a social revolution by means of a crime.

Before specifying the details of the jubilean provisions and regulations, we must point out the meaning of certain terms used in the Bible to describe the Jubilee. They are: year of favor, year of liberty, and year of release.

1. Year of Favor (Luke 4:19; Isaiah 61:2)

The adjective "favorable," in Hebrew *ratson*, comes from the verb *ratsah*, which means either "to pay a debt" when it refers to the man paying it or "to be favorable" when it refers to God accepting the payment. The RSV uses "acceptable year" which points to the double meaning of *ratson*.

For example, in Leviticus 26:41, God says, "If then[when they are in exile] their uncircumcised heart is humbled and they make amends for their iniquity," and further on (v. 43), "But the land shall be left by them and enjoy its sabbaths [it will lie fallow to compensate for all the unobserved sabbatical years] . . . and they shall 'make amends' for their iniquity."[3]

In Isaiah 58:5, God asks: "Will you call this a fast and a day acceptable [*ratson*] to the Lord?"

In Psalm 119:108 the psalmist says to God: "Accept [that is, be favorable to *ratson*] my offerings of praise."

In Isaiah 49:8, the roles have changed. God takes the initiative and announces: "In a time of favor [in a time of acceptance, *ratson*], I have answered you; in a day of salvation, I have helped you."

Finally, in the passage quoted by Jesus (Isaiah 61:2), the Messiah proclaims: ". . . the Lord has anointed me to . . . proclaim the year of the Lord's favor [a year of acceptance: *ratson*] and the day of vengeance of our God." For the prophet, the God "of vengeance" and the God "of mercy" are one and the same divine person, in whom there is no contradiction.[4] In this context the "year of favor" proclaimed by Jesus involved a judgment as well as a pardon or forgiveness of God. This was the content of the good news, the gospel.

2. Year of Liberty (Luke 4:18; Isaiah 61:1)

"The Lord has anointed me . . . to proclaim liberty to the captives." The Hebrew word *deror*, which means "liberty" in Isaiah 61, is also found in Leviticus 25:10: "And you shall . . . proclaim liberty throughout the land, to all its inhabitants; it shall be a jubilee for you." Ezekiel (16:17) calls the Jubilee the "year of liberty" *deror*. It seems that *deror* was used as a technical term referring to the periodic liberation of slaves as prescribed by Moses.

3. Year of Release

This word (in Hebrew, *shemitta*) is found neither in Isaiah nor in Leviticus, but only in Deuteronomy (chapters 15 and 31) where it corresponds exactly with the "liberty" *(deror)* of Leviticus. The verb *shamat*, from which *shemitta* stems, means "to let alone, to let rest, to release, to remit (the payment of a debt)." *Shemitta* occurs six times in Deuteronomy 15:1-11, where it means "release, periodic remittance of debts."

4. The "Aphesis"

With this one word, *aphesis*, the Greek version of the Old Testament (Septuagint) translates both *shemitta* and *deror*, which we have analyzed in the preceding paragraphs. Thus, the Septuagint translated Isaiah 61: "The Lord has anointed me to proclaim the *aphesis* to the captives." The substantive *aphesis* comes from the verb *aphiemi* (to send away, to liberate, to leave aside, to remit a debt).

Sometimes it means "liberty," — or better, the "liberation" — of a slave, sometimes, "the remittance of a debt."

This word occurs quite frequently in the Gospels both as a substantive and as a verb. Following are a few characteristic references. When John the Baptist preached the baptism of repentance (Mark 1:4) it was for the *aphesis* (release) of sins (considered as debts). When Jesus presented Himself to John the Baptist to be baptized (Matthew 3:15), He overcame John's hesitation by saying, "Release at this time [*aphes arti*, translated by let go now], for thus it is fitting for us to fulfil all righteousness." "Then," says Matthew, "he [John the Baptist] released him [*aphiesin auton*]." These mysterious words seem to indicate that Jesus wanted His baptism to have some jubilean significance. Before proclaiming liberty to the captives, was it not necessary for Him to inaugurate the Jubilee of justice and liberation for Himself? Baptism would then be the first act of this liberation.

Later, referring to the healing of the paralytic, Jesus stated (Matthew 9:6) "The Son of Man has authority on earth to forgive [release, verb *aphiemi*] sins!" For the Messiah, the jubilean remission of debts extended to all areas of life: physical, moral, and social. In the parable of the unforgiving servant, Jesus portrays God as a King who remits (*aphiemi*) debts acquired by his servant (Matthew 18:27-32). In the Sermon on the Mount, Jesus advises us to also "let go" or "remit" our cloak to him who wants our coat (Matthew 5:40).

The jubilean significance of *aphesis* in the first three Gospels is beyond doubt. Peter, Andrew, James and John, called by Jesus, "left everything [*aphientes panta*] and followed him" (Luke 5:11). Shortly before the triumphal entry of Jesus into Jerusalem, the apostles happily reminded their Master that they had put the jubilean ordinance into practice as soon as they had heard his call: "Lo, we have left everything [*aphekamen panta*] and followed you" (Matthew 19:27). And Jesus told them that their obedience meets God's generous jubilean initiative: "Truly, I say to you, in the new world, when the Son of Man shall sit on his glorious throne . . ." (Matthew 19:28). "There is no one who has left [*apheken*] house or brothers or sisters or mother or father or children or lands for my sake and for the gospel, who will not receive a hundredfold now in this time, houses and brothers and sisters and mothers and children and lands, with persecutions and in the age to come, eternal life" (Mark 10:29-30). Finally, Jesus uses the same word during the institution of the Lord's Supper where the Jubilee is announced in eschatological terms (Matthew 26:28, 29): "This is my blood of the covenant which is poured out for many, for the forgiveness [remission, *aphesis*] of sins. I tell you, I shall not drink again this fruit of the vine until that day when I drink it new with you in my Father's kingdom." The supreme Sabbath celebrated in the kingdom of God is thus announced by a terrestrial Jubilee that foreshadows it.

5. The "Apokatastasis"

This Greek word means to reestablish something or somebody to his previous state, a restoration or restitution of prisoners or hostages. This is the word used by the Neoplatonic Jewish philosopher Philo of Alexandria, a contemporary of Jesus, to designate the Jubilee, a subject to which he devotes several chapters throughout his works (cf. his *Decalogue*).

In fact, the purpose of Jubilee was to "reestablish" the tribes of Israel in the condition they were in at the time they entered Canaan. The word *apokatastasis* expresses this idea very well. The New Testament uses it several times with this meaning. In Matthew 17:11, it refers to the messianic "restoration" of the kingdom of Israel. Jesus said, "Elijah does come and he is to restore [*apokatastasei*] all things." In Acts 1:6 the disciples who had come together ask Jesus, "Lord, will you at this time restore [*apokathistaneis*] the kingdom to Israel?" This passage seems to indicate that the idea of an impending restoration of Israel was expressed by the term *apokatastasis*. In Acts 3:19-22, Peter, quoting Deuteronomy 18:15-19, declares: "Heaven must receive Jesus until the time for the [*apokatastasis*] of all things that God spoke by the mouth of his holy prophets from of old. Moses said, 'The Lord God will raise up a prophet from your brethren as he raised me up.' "

In the last passage, which exegetes consider to be very ancient because it presents a Christology that is both elementary and close to Judaism, Peter describes Jesus as a second Moses, who will once again enforce the ancient ordinances. Moses' return and consequently the reestablishment of the Jubilee through repentance and remission of sins are described in this text as the condition for the great restoration marked by Jesus Christ's return.

Let us notice that the Gospels also use *apokatastasis* to mean the "reestablishment" or "recovery" of a sick person (Mark 3:5; 8:25;

etc.). This term should be translated with a strong emphasis on its jubilean connotation. The "reestablishment" of the sick — as well as the "reestablishment" of Israel and the "reestablishment" of property — was a part of the Messiah's duties.

6. Jubilee

The word "Jubilee" itself (*Yobel*, in Hebrew) does not seem to have had any particular meaning. The *Yobel* was probably the ram's horn used in the land every 50 years on the Day of Atonement, the tenth day of the seventh month, to proclaim the beginning of the year of Jubilee. Later, it became associated with the Latin word *jubilum* (from *jubilare*, to rejoice, to exult), but this was merely a verbal coincidence. As a matter of fact, the year of Jubilee was celebrated every 49 (or 50) years, that is every seventh sabbath of years (7 times 7). Just as the week ended with a "day of release" called Sabbath, and as the "week of years" ended with the sabbatical year (every 7 years), each period of 49 years ended with a year of Jubilee.

Let us now recall the religious principles upon which the year of Jubilee was based.

First Principle: God Is the Owner of the Land of Israel

In Leviticus 25:23, God says, "The land shall not be sold in perpetuity, for the land is mine; for you are strangers and sojourners with me." In the ancient Orient, such a declaration was not unique. The land, along with the flocks, constituted the only source of capital, and its possession guaranteed wealth and power. As a general rule, the land belonged to the god of the area or country. In practice, this meant that it belonged either to the priests of the god or to the king who incarnated the god (as in Egypt). The situation was then somewhat similar to state collectivism: the king granted the use of his lands to whomever he pleased.

But the remarkable thing about the Jewish institution of Jubilee was that it did not lead to this type of collectivism. On the contrary, the arbitrariness of the sovereign was limited by the jubilean provisions.[5] Furthermore, the interval between Jubilees did not paralyze individual initiative. It gave everyone the opportunity to invest his capital, to buy and sell goods.[6]

The redistribution of the land every 49 years prevented the accumulation of capital in the hands of a minority. At the time of the Jubilee every tribe repossessed the land it had received when the people of Israel settled in Canaan. Similarly, each family regained the lands it might have lost in the interval. In this way, even though God was the only Owner of the land, He did not operate as an Oriental potentate oppressing His people in slavery. Rather, He acted as a good Father, entrusting to His servants the administration of His goods, which He let them enjoy, but whom He would call to account at regular intervals, and once again distribute the capital He alone possessed.

Second Principle Complementary to the First: God Is the Liberator of His People

"I am the Lord your God who brought you forth out of the land of Egypt to give you the land of Canaan" (Leviticus 25:38). Because God set you free from Egyptian bondage by a liberating act, liberation (from debts, from slavery, from land) will have the force of law among you. This is how Deuteronomy justifies the institution of the Sabbath: "The seventh day is a sabbath to the Lord, your God. . . . You shall remember that you were a servant in the land of Egypt, and the Lord your God brought you out thence with a mighty hand and an outstretched arm; therefore the Lord your God commanded you to keep the Sabbath day" (Deuteronomy 5:14, 15).

Consequently, the mercy that manifests itself during the year of favor is not arbitrary. It is not the result of the king's despotic benevolence, similar to the *bon plaisir* used by the prince in the Middle Ages. It does not contradict the requirements of justice which characterize Yahweh's will for His people. It is a moment of justice, a sabbatical moment which occurs at regular intervals to regularize the relations between God and His people. The people's debts to God will not stack up indefinitely; accordingly, debts between Jews will also be cancelled periodically.

If we now try to summarize how the sabbatical year and the Jubilee should have been celebrated in Israel, we come up with the following description:

First Measure: Every seven years, the land should lie fallow.

By a special blessing of Yahweh, the land was supposed to produce a double harvest during the sixth year.

Second Measure: During the seventh year, all debts between Hebrews were to be cancelled.

Third Measure: After six years of slavery, every Hebrew slave was to be set free by his master.

Fourth Measure (reserved for the Jubilee, every 49 years): Each family should regain possession of the land and houses it had lost in the meantime. Between two Jubilees, a buyer owned the land only temporarily. As the year of Jubilee got closer, the value of the land dropped in proportion to the remaining years of tenure.

It seems that the inapplicable character of the sabbatical year, which recurred too often, was the prime motive in creating the year of Jubilee. The economic life of the land would have been paralyzed by the recurrence every seven years of a measure as radical as the abolition of debts or the freeing of slaves. Nevertheless, the year of Jubilee which in addition required the redistribution of land, does not seem to have been followed any more closely than the sabbatical year.

After the return from exile, both the *Mishnah* and the *Talmud* justified the neglect of the more rigid sabbatical and jubilean measures with various unconvincing arguments. Indeed, the sabbatical year and the Jubilee had faced opposition from the ownership classes both before and after the exile. In vain the prophets of Israel had demanded the restoration of these institutions, in which they saw one of the precursory signs of the coming of David's reign. Unfortunately, unfaithfulness did always get the upper hand. The two most remarkable attempts at restoring the Jubilee, namely those of Jeremiah and Nehemiah, will be of interest to the reader.

Under the reign of Zedekiah, the last king of Judah (598-587 BC), the rich had agreed to free their Hebrew slaves according to the Jubilee ordinance but soon regretted their decision and took them back. Their disobedience aroused Jeremiah's indignation and he prophesied that it would cause the destruction of Jerusalem.

"Thus says the Lord, the God of Israel: I made a covenant with your fathers when I brought them out of the land of Egypt, out of the house of bondage, saying, 'At the end of six years, each of you must set free the fellow Hebrew who has been sold to you and has served you six years; you must set him free from your service.' But your fathers did not listen to me or incline their ears to me. You recently repented and did what was right in my eyes by proclaiming liberty, each to his neighbor, and you made a covenant before me in the house which is called by my name; but then you turned around and profaned my name when each of you took back his male and female slaves, whom you had set free according to their desire, and you brought them into subjection to be your slaves. Therefore, thus says the Lord: You have not obeyed me by proclaiming liberty, every one to his brother and to his neighbor; behold, I proclaim to you liberty to the sword, to pestilence and to famine, says the Lord. I will make you a horror to all the kingdoms of the earth" (Jeremiah 34:13-17).[7]

The second attempted reform the Bible mentions was undertaken by Nehemiah after the return from exile, around 423 BC (Nehemiah 5).[8] Having called the leading citizens of Jerusalem together, Nehemiah rebuked them for requiring the poor to pawn their sons and daughters "that they may eat and keep alive." And he tells them,

"Return to them this very day, their fields, their vineyards, their olive orchards and their houses and the hundredth of money, grain, wine and oil which you have been exacting of them." And they said, "We will restore these and require nothing from them."

Because this attempt was not followed up any better than the previous ones, the last chapters of Isaiah as well as Ezekiel still count the Jubilee among the institutions to be reestablished. (Cf. Isaiah 56 to 66; Ezekiel 45:7-9; 46:16-18.)

A few additional remarks will be helpful in understanding the scope of the jubilean ordinances:

1. According to Leviticus 25, slaves were set free after seven years of service. This liberation did not necessarily coincide with the sabbatical year.

2. The freed slaves were Hebrew. The jubilean ordinances did not apply to foreigners. The Jews had no obligation to free the foreign slaves they might have owned. Loans with interest were also forbidden among Jews but could be made to foreigners. A Jew could also require the reimbursement of a debt from a foreigner, in spite of the Jubilee.

These distinctions which the law of Moses made between Jews and foreigners belong to the background of the Gospels. In a later chapter, we will examine Jesus' struggle to abolish them.

3. The Roman or Oriental type of slavery was nonexistent among the Jews. Slavery for the Jews was a consequence of mortgages taken by a creditor on the lands of an insolvent debtor. The creditor could use the lands until their revenue had paid off the amount of the

debt. If this did not suffice he could require the debtor (with his wife and children) to work for him until the entire debt had been paid off. This resulted in a form of effective slavery which was still practiced in Jesus' time. If a Jubilee occurred, the "slave" would be *ipso facto* freed, since all debts were cancelled, and he could regain his ownership rights.

In Jesus' time, a period which we will study in more depth in chapter 3, the situation could be summed up as follows: The anonymous author of the *Book of Jubilees*, as well as Philo of Alexandria, attached merely ritual significance to the Jubilee years. It was limited to celebrating the days, months, and years, according to an orthodox calendar. On the other hand, the Pharisaic rabbis, as we shall see later, recommended the observance of sabbatical years, while simultaneously trying to attenuate their strictness. Letting the land lie fallow every seventh year was the sole surviving sabbatical practice obeyed by the people.

Certain historical events prove that this practice was still observed. According to the First Book of the Maccabees (6:48-53), the Jews who in 162 BC had given up defending Beth Zur against Lysias' Syrian troops were also forced to abandon the defense of Mount Zion. "There was no food in storage because it was the seventh year; those who found safety in Judea from the Gentiles had consumed the last of the stores." The historian Josephus also reports the same event, although he dates the sabbatical year as 164-163 BC. This does not contradict the Book of the Maccabees. In effect, during the sabbatical year (164-163), people relied upon the harvest of the preceding year. Consequently, 162-163 would have been the year the population felt the pinch of hunger.

Josephus refers to two other famines that were aggravated by sabbatical years: one in 135-134 BC, which occurred during the siege of the Dagon Fortress by John Hyrcanus, and the other in 38-37 BC, while Herod the Great was besieging Antigonus in Jerusalem. This last date raises a rather embarrassing problem. Indeed, if one uses the first dates given by Josephus as points of reference, the sabbatical year should have occurred in 40-39 BC, rather than 38-37. However, such uncertainties in a historian's chronology should not create doubts about the correctness of his information. We must not forget that Josephus was writing 100 to 250 years after the events he reported. (The relative accuracy of his information is rather admirable for a time when there were no newspapers!)

After Christ, the chronology becomes more precise. We know that AD 47-48 marked the beginning of a great famine which affected the whole empire. This was the famine announced by Agabus in Acts 11:28. In Palestine it was aggravated by the return of the sabbatical year.

According to the *Sotah* tractate of the *Mishnah* (VII, 8), the preceding sabbatical year (AD 40-41) had been celebrated with particular solemnity by Herod Agrippa I, grandson of Herod the Great. He is the Herod mentioned in Acts 12, to whom Emperor Claudius, out of gratitude, had given back the entire kingdom of his grandfather in AD 41.

To please the Jews, Herod Agrippa persecuted the Christians (he beheaded James, the brother of John) and practiced the Jewish religion with ostentation. In AD 41 he publicly read the law of Moses to mark the end of the sabbatical year, as prescribed in Deuteronomy 31:10. Having gathered the people in Jerusalem, he began to read but broke out in tears when he came to Deuteronomy 17:15: "One from among brethren you shall set as king over you; you may not put a foreigner over you, who is not your brother." In fact, the Herodians were Idumaeans, and therefore foreign to Israel. But the people reassured the king by shouting, "You are our brother, you are our brother!" because they were quite fond of Agrippa.

This story is of great interest for our chronology because it enables us to set AD 26-27 (two septennials earlier) as the date of the sabbatical year Jesus inaugurated in the synagogue of Nazareth with the words, "I have come to proclaim the acceptable year of the Lord." It would then have been in AD 26, on the tenth day of the month of Tishri (September-October) which is the Day of Atonement (*Yom hakippourim*) that Jesus announced the complete restoration of the jubilean practices in Israel. We say "jubilean practices" because as we have seen that the ordinances of the sabbatical year and of the Jubilee coincided. The calendar of jubilean years — recurring every 49 years according to some authors and every 50 years according to others — was subject to controversy even among the Jews. It is all the harder for us to recreate it with accuracy.

Setting the beginning of Jesus' ministry at such an early date creates difficulties, especially with Luke's chronology. Luke, with his great concern for accuracy, sets the beginning of John the Baptist's ministry in the fifteenth year of Emperor Tiberius' reign (Luke 3:1, 2). Because Tiberius came into power on August 19, 14 AD,

John the Baptist's ministry would have started 15 years later, that is during the summer of AD 28. But many of the more authoritative exegetes estimate that Jesus died before the Passover Feast of AD 28 and Jesus could hardly have been crucified before the beginning of John the Baptist's ministry! However, historians have managed to resolve the difficulty. As early as AD 11, Tiberius was associated with the power of the weakening Emperor Augustus. It is possible that Luke counted fifteen years from that date, which would add up to AD 26.

Such a chronology coincides with a detail found in the Gospel of John. He places the expulsion of the merchants from the temple at the beginning of Jesus' ministry, shortly after the celebration of the Passover. On this occasion, the Jews tell Jesus, "It has taken 46 years to build this temple and will you raise it up in three days?" or in other words, "For 46 years, they have been building the temple," which was still under construction in Jesus' day. The date of the beginning of the construction of the temple by Herod the Great is perfectly well known as 20 BC. Thus the words recorded by John 2:20 which date the beginning of Jesus' ministry in Jerusalem would have been uttered in the spring of AD 27.

In conclusion, this study of dates seems to confirm our thesis rather than weaken it. When John the Baptist began his "cry in the desert" in AD 26, Jesus was among the first to be baptized. Soon after the temptation, He would have returned to Galilee where He began preaching. In September, AD 26 He proclaimed the Jubilee in Nazareth. During the Passover of AD 27, He went to Jerusalem. In AD 28 — a year and a half after the beginning of His ministry — He died, crucified in Jerusalem on the eve of the Passover.

Two centuries after Jesus Christ, the orthodox Jews who remained in Palestine still observed the sabbatical year since Rabbi Abrabu recalls the way some Gentiles made fun of Jews. They would bring an emaciated camel to the theater and rail: "Why is this camel so afflicted? Because the Jews are observing their sabbatical year, and since they have run out of vegetables, they are eating the thorns this camel used for food."

3. Implications of Jubilee

The speech at Nazareth alone would not be enough to prove that Jesus really did proclaim a Jubilee. A more complete reading of the Gospels will be the only way to either confirm or invalidate our thesis.

As we have just seen, the Jubilee or sabbatical year prescribed four provisions: (1) letting the land lie fallow; (2) the remittance of debts; (3) the liberation of slaves; (4) the return to one's patrimony.

The purpose of this chapter is to discover whether the Gospels make other references to these four steps.

First Provision: Letting the Land Lie Fallow

Jesus does not mention this provision directly. His silence on the subject is not surprising since this sabbatical prescription was the only one to have been accepted by the people. It was therefore useless to encourage the Jews to put it into practice. But somewhat like the Ramadan fast which all Muslims practice — often with moaning and groaning and sometimes with cheating — the Jews needed much courage to let their land lie fallow every seven years while counting on God to give them what they needed!

Many worried about it. In Leviticus (25:20, 21) the Lord foresaw this uneasiness and declared: "And if you say, 'What shall we eat in the seventh year, if we may not sow or gather in our crop?' I will command my blessing upon you in the sixth year so that it will bring forth fruit for three years."

Jesus talked to the disciples in precisely these same terms. The proclamation of the Jubilee in AD 26 may have troubled them because they had abandoned their land and their boats by the lake to follow Jesus. "Do not be anxious, saying: 'What shall we eat?' or 'What shall we drink?' or 'What shall we wear?' For the Gentiles seek all these things; and your heavenly Father knows that you need them all. But seek first his kingdom and his righteousness and all these things will be yours as well."

Such an exhortation is often misunderstood as apparently encouraging laziness, but it can easily be explained in the framework of the expectation of God's kingdom (of which the Jubilee was one of the premonitory signs). This is how we should interpret it: "If you work six days (or six years) with all your heart, says Jesus, you can count on God to take care of you and your loved ones. Let your land lie fallow without fear. Just as He does for the birds of the sky who neither sow nor reap, nor gather away in barns, God will also provide for your needs. The Gentiles who ignore the Sabbath are no richer than you are."

Second and Third Provisions: Remittance of Debts and Liberation of Slaves

Contrary to the preceding one, the second and third jubilean provisions are not marginal, but central to Jesus' teaching. They are central even to His theology.

The Lord's Prayer, which sums up Jesus' thinking about prayer, contains the following request: "And forgive [remit, *aphes*] us our debts as we forgive our debtors." Numerous versions translate this passage incorrectly by: "Forgive us our trespasses as we forgive those who trespass against us." In reality, the Greek *opheilema* means a money debt, a sum owed, *in the material sense of the word*. In the Lord's Prayer Jesus is not vaguely recommending us to forgive those who have created problems for us, but He is telling us to completely cancel the debts of those who owe us money, that is, to practice the Jubilee.

It is remarkable that the verb used by Jesus was *aphiemi* (to send away, to free, to remit a debt), a word with an unquestionable jubilean connotation. The material connotation of the word "debts" in the Lord's Prayer was so obvious that Matthew (or Jesus Himself?) thought it fitting to add a commentary to the prayer, to explain that the words concerning the debts *also* applied to "trespasses" in general (Matthew 6:14, 15). "If you forgive men their trespasses [the term He uses here is *paraptoma* or transgression] your heavenly Father also will forgive you, but if you do not forgive men their trespasses, neither will your Father forgive your trespasses [*paraptoma*]."

Thus, the Lord's Prayer is truly a jubilean prayer which means: "The time has come for the faithful people to cancel all the debts which bind the poor of Israel because your debts to God have also been cancelled." (This is the good news, the gospel.) Moreover, this is the way Jesus' listeners understood His prayer: He was setting up a rigorous equation between the observance of the Jubilee and the grace of God. Although He was not otherwise a legalist and unhesitatingly forgave even prostitutes and ill-famed people, Jesus was very strict on one point: only he who grants forgiveness can become an object of forgiveness. God's *aphesis* toward you is vain if you do not practice *aphesis* toward your brothers.

Two parables will help us further clarify Jesus' thought. Certainly the more impressive of the two is known as the parable of the unforgiving servant, which expresses the strictness of the "equation" of the Lord's Prayer: No mercy for him who has none.

Why has this parable been detached from its sociological background? Why has it all too often been understood as a rather pale portrayal of the forgiveness of sins granted by God to those who forgive their brothers? In fact, its sorry hero was a real person, a Galilean peasant whose name was probably known to Jesus' disciples. As all those to whom Jesus spoke, he had been a beneficiary of the proclamation of the Jubilee. He had been granted forgiveness by God. All his debts had been cancelled though they were enormous: 10,000 talents (approximately ten million dollars!). This astronomical figure should not surprise us. It expresses the debtor's insolvency toward the prince.

S. W. Baron[1] describes how Galilean peasants who had been free proprietors before Jesus' time had been forced into slavery by their progressive indebtedness. To a large extent, Herod the Great was to blame for this situation. He had overburdened the people with taxes and expropriated the recalcitrant proprietors. To avoid expropriation, the peasant borrowed money from a usurer who usually worked hand in hand with the king's steward or the tax collector. His pawned property would soon become the usurer's and the peasant his sharecropper (or "servant"). But this did not solve the peasant's problems. His unpaid debts accumulated until they reached horrendous proportions. The creditor sought repayment and ordered that the sharecropper be sold (along with his wife, children, and all he owned) in order to reimburse the debt. This is exactly the "unforgiving servant's" situation. Jesus describes the relation between the peasant's indebtedness, the loss of his property, and the alienation of his freedom (a direct consequence of his indebtedness).

But because of the Jubilee, the servant appears before the king who cancels his debt. The king "released him and forgave [*aphiemi*] him his debt." This story would be quite encouraging if it stopped there. But it was told at a time when Jesus was facing opposition to the Jubilee from the majority of His fellow citizens, sometimes even from very humble ones. The rest of the story reflects the bitter disappointment in the face of this rejection.

Upon meeting one of his fellow servants who owed him about 25 dollars, the newly freed slave refuses to grant his debtor the same jubilean privilege which set him free. He seizes him by the throat and says, "Pay what you owe." Denounced by his fellow servants, the unforgiving servant is arrested and taken before the king. The Jubilee is no longer applicable for such an unmerciful and thankless man. He will be sold along with his wife and children to pay for his debts. There is no divine Jubilee for those who refuse to practice it on earth.

However, a too frequent occurrence of the remittance of debts had one very serious drawback, which is pointed out in Deuteronomy 15:7-11: it froze credit. Because of this, some of the most orthodox rabbis, even champions of the integral restoration of the Mosaic law such as Hillel and Shammai, hesitated to require a strict application of the Jubilee. In fact, as the sabbatical year approached the rich were more and more hesitant to loan money to the poor for fear of losing their capital. This practice paralyzed the land's economy.

The rabbis had tried to find a solution to this problem. As skilled commentators of the law, they could make it say the opposite of what it decreed. Strangely enough, one of the most likable of them was the famous Pharisee Hillel, the grandfather of Gamaliel, who later became Paul's teacher and from whom Jesus probably drew some of His inspiration. Hillel took it upon himself to find an elegant solution to the problem.

This solution was called the *Prosboul*.[2] *Prosboul* probably comes from the Greek *pros boule* (a deed carried out before a law court). According to the *Gittin* tractate of the *Mishnah*,[3] Hillel by this deed gave the creditor permission to use a court as his attorney in recovering a debt which the sabbatical year had abolished. By means of this subterfuge, loans with interest, which had been abolished by the Mosaic law (Exodus 22:25) and limited in time by the provisions of the sabbatical year, once again became possible. The rich, and particularly the Pharisees, whom Jesus accused of "devouring widows' houses," did not restrain themselves from using this measure to its fullest.

The *Mishnah* has preserved a text which refers to the *Prosboul*: "I (so and so) transfer to you (so and so), the judges (in such and such a place), my right to a debt, so that you may recover any amount which (so and so) owes me, at whatever time I will so desire."[4] The *Prosboul* was then signed by the judges and the witnesses. Jesus was an avowed adversary of the *Prosboul*.

A clarification seems necessary at this point. Usually, Jesus is pictured as an opponent of the sabbatical laws. But in this case, the opposite is true. When it was a question of bringing out the humanitarian prescriptions of the Mosaic law, Jesus was even more radical than the Pharisees.

His continuous controversies with them would lose all meaning if they merely centered on religious practices. In reality, the conflict went much deeper than that. It revolved around the nature of moral law. "What is goodness?" the Pharisees would ask themselves, and they would answer with a multitude of detailed ordinances in the midst of which they lost the essential idea.

"What is goodness?" Jesus would ask. He would neglect the details in order to go back to the essential idea which he recognized in the Mosaic law, without detouring through the scribes' tradition. This radicalism was exactly the opposite of surrendering the law. When Jesus said that God made the Sabbath for man, He meant, "God set the Jews free by taking them out of Egypt. The sabbatical year, like the Sabbath, must be put into practice. They are made to set men free, not to enslave them." That is why the *Prosboul*, as well as all other human traditions added to the law to alter its liberating and revolutionary character, provoked Jesus' indignation.

But how can one avoid freezing the credit if the lure of profit is taken away? In the Sermon on the Mount (Luke 6), Jesus gives His answer: the rich man must prove himself generous by eradicating his fear of not being reimbursed because God will take the matter into His own hands. "If you lend to those from whom you hope to receive, what credit is that to you? Even sinners lend to sinners, to receive as much again. . . . But . . . lend expecting nothing in return; and your reward will be great, and you will be sons of the Most High, for he is kind to the ungrateful and selfish. . . . Forgive and you will be forgiven; give and it will be given unto you; good measure, pressed down, shaken together, running over, will be put into your lap" (Luke 6:34-38).

The honesty of the debtor must nevertheless coincide with the generosity of the lender. The debtor should not hide behind the protection of the sabbatical year in order to escape his own obligation. The Sermon on the Mount contains two striking paragraphs where Jesus points out possible solutions to the problem upon which Hillel and the Pharisees had stumbled.

Hillel would tell the worried creditor: "Take your claims to the court. Your money will be restored to you there." Jesus tells the careless debtor: "Do not wait for a court summons to repay your debt, 'If anyone [your creditor] would sue you [using the *Prosboul*] and take your coat[5] [which he holds as a pledge for the debt you have not repaid] let him have [Jesus uses the verb *aphiemi*] your cloak as well' " (Matthew 5:40). Before that, Jesus said, "Make friends quickly with your accuser while you are going with him to the court lest your accuser [using the *Prosboul*] hand you over to the judge and the judge to the guard and you be put in prison; truly, I say to you, you will never get out till you have paid the last penny" (Matthew 5:25). According to the parallel passage in Luke (12:52-59), Jesus asks, "And why do you not judge for yourselves what is right?" His disciples were to avoid court proceedings. They should not rely on the courts to decide whether or not it is right to pay their debts.

Let us now turn to the other parable with a jubilean teaching, the parable of the "dishonest steward" (Luke 16:1-9). It too revolves around the peasants' status in Jesus' time.

Let us recall our prior discussion. Due to the extortions of King Herod — as well as those of his son and the Roman occupant — most of the older proprietors had lost their independence. Forced to mortgage their property in order to pay their taxes, they had been driven into semi-slavery. The taxes in kind (oil, wheat) which they paid to their masters often amounted to one half or more of their harvest.[6]

The peasants' conditions in Israel were aggravated by yet another evil: the owners' absenteeism. A hierarchy of middlemen (toll-gatherers, publicans, customs officials, stewards, and managers) had the task of collecting debts. They extorted from the sharecropper arbitrary sums of money that exceeded the rent, debts, and taxes they actually owed. The poor were always in the wrong. They could rely on no one because the stewards presented falsified accounts to their masters. With the help of these accounts, they were able to gather up in a few years what Jesus called "unrighteous mammon." It was by constantly seeking these unjust riches that the stewards lost their genuine riches, namely, the friendship of their fellow citizens.

This parable tells how a landowner one day discovered the dishonesty of his steward. Not only did the steward plunder the sharecroppers, he also stole from his master to whom he showed falsified records. Once his cheating had been discovered, the steward began to feel the pangs of conscience. He understood that he would never be able to reimburse the entire amount of his swindling. But he decided at least not to require of the sharecroppers exaggerated amounts they had not yet paid. He then erased the amount by which he had unjustly increased their debts. Jesus describes him calling the debtors together and reducing their debts to their correct amount: 50 measures of oil instead of 100, 80 measures of wheat instead of 100, etc.

Such a decision certainly increased the steward's insolvency. It forced him into poverty. But by acting as he did, he would acquire genuine riches, that is the thankfulness and friendship of his previous victims. Poor among the poor, man among men, he would be received as a brother in their homes and this hospitality would be practiced unto eternity. That, says Jesus, is the joy of God's kingdom.

"Make friends for yourselves by means of unrighteous mammon" (Luke 16:9) he concludes. That is, put the Jubilee I'm announcing into practice. By liberating others from their debts, you set yourselves free from the bonds which keep you from being ready for the coming of God's kingdom.

The most remarkable part of the parable is the praise Jesus puts into the mouth of the proprietor, who symbolizes God. "Here is an intelligent man," says God, "more intelligent than the average man who wants to become my disciple!" In the parable of the unforgiving servant, God was the One who took the initiative. God was the first to cancel man's debt, and He expected man to do the same. In the parable of the dishonest steward, man takes the initiative. *He* is the first to put the Jubilee into practice by obeying the messianic call and remitting the debts of those who are debtors to God, as well as debtors to himself. Consequently, God praises this intelligent man for practicing the redistribution of wealth even before being touched by divine grace. This man was able to read the signs of God's kingdom and understand that the rule of unjust riches is over.

These two parables confirm the inferences of the speech at Nazareth, the Lord's Prayer, and the Sermon on the Mount. Jesus was indeed proclaiming a Jubilee, consistent with Moses' sabbatical instructions in AD 26, a Jubilee capable of solving the social problems of Israel at that time. It would abolish debts and set free the debtors whose insolvency had turned them into slaves. But putting such a Jubilee into practice was not optional. It was one of the premonitory signs of the kingdom. Those who refused to take that road could not enter into the kingdom of God.

Fourth and Last Jubilean Provision: The Redistribution of Capital

During the time of Jesus, before the invention of the machine, land and flocks were the only wealth of a people, or in today's terminology, their "capital."

All the evidence indicates that Jesus accepted voluntary poverty in view of the kingdom and ordered His disciples to practice the jubilean redistribution of their capital. "All the nations of the earth seek these things, and your Father knows that you need them. Instead seek his kingdom and these things shall be yours as well. Fear not, little flock, for it is your Father's good pleasure to give you the kingdom. Sell your possessions and give alms" (Luke 12:30-33). No one doubts these words. However, people have wondered whether the redistribution of wealth was commanded by Jesus for all Christians of all times everywhere or whether it was only a "counsel of perfection" addressed to saints.

Traditionally, the church has chosen the second solution, the easy one. Only the person with a particular vocation, such as the monk, is called to abandon all his possessions. The ordinary believer can be content to "give alms," that is to distribute part of his income to the poor.

Such a position would be quite justifiable had Jesus not been so harsh toward those very people who in His own day were complacently satisfied with their almsgiving: the Pharisees. They gave one tenth of all their income, no mean accomplishment. But Jesus thought this was not enough: "Woe to you, scribes and Pharisees . . . you tithe mint and dill and cummin, and have neglected the weightier matters of the law, justice, mercy, and faith. These you ought to have done, without neglecting the others" (Matthew 23:23). Once again, this confirms our previous statement about Jesus' radicalism. He did not want to abolish the tithe. He merely wanted people to go beyond the level of the easy moral satisfaction they reached when they tithed and to attain the level of justice, mercy, and faith.

But what did Jesus mean by these three words? Everything leads us to believe that He meant the gratuitous act by which the disciple ceased planning for his own future and distributed what he needed for himself, namely his capital. "Unless your righteousness exceeds that of the scribes and Pharisees, you will never enter the kingdom of heaven" (Matthew 5:20).

One day, as He was comparing the generosity of the rich, who ostensibly put large gifts into the offering box, and that of a poor widow, Jesus cried out, "This poor widow has put in more than all of them; for they all contributed out of their abundance, but she out of her poverty put in all the living that she had" (Luke 21:1-4). In today's language, this means: "It matters little how much one gives. What matters is *what* one gives. If it is a part of the income, it isn't justice, mercy, and faith. If it is the capital one is sharing, then all is right."

We do not believe, however, that Jesus prescribed Christian communism. If He had done so, He would have left with His disciples either monastic rules similar to those of the Essenes, or some constitutional project in view of a collectivistic Jewish state. But He did neither of these things. Collectivism was contrary to the spirit of the Mosaic law.

When Jesus in Luke 12:33 gave the famous commandment, "Sell what you possess and give to the poor" (a better translation would be: "Sell what you possess and practice kind deeds"), it was neither a counsel of perfection as in Matthew 19:21, nor a constitutional law in view of founding a utopian Israel. It was rather a jubilean ordinance to be put into practice *hic et nunc* in AD 26 as a "refreshment" foreshadowing the restitution of all things. "Give what is within yourself," as in Luke 11:41.

Such a redistribution of capital every fifty years, out of faithfulness to God's justice and in the hope of the kingdom, would not be utopian even today. Many bloody revolutions would have been avoided had the Christian church shown itself more respectful than Israel of the jubilean prescriptions in the Mosaic law.[7]

When interpreted as jubilean commandments, other teachings of Jesus fall into place with little trouble: "Sell what you possess and give to the poor; make friends for yourselves by means of unrighteous mammon; give to everyone who begs from you; and of him who takes away your goods, do not ask them again."

We have seen that Jesus was also thinking about the salvation of His people when He prescribed practicing the Jubilee, because He made a rigorous equation between the Jubilee practiced on earth and the grace of God. In this context, the following words are somewhat surprising: "Sell all that you have and distribute to the poor and you will have treasure in heaven" (Luke 18:22). "Sell your possessions, and give alms; provide yourselves with purses that do not grow old, with a treasure in the heavens that does not fail" (Luke 12:33). The redistribution of capital in these verses appears to be a selfish act in view of securing a place in heaven. Such texts have opened the door to monastic ethics in which the believer rids himself of all his possessions in order to purchase his salvation!

By inverting the order of Jesus' words, a superficial reader of the gospel could make Jesus say what He is not really saying. In reality, according to Jesus, compassion for the poor precedes the acquisition of a treasure in heaven. Compassion comes first and imposes itself as the blunt condition for entry into the kingdom of God. Salvation comes later. God's compassion toward man is nevertheless conditioned by my compassion toward my neighbors.

What matters primarily to God is the lot of the poor. It is for them that the "rich young ruler" must sell his possessions. To practice compassion is to reestablish the poor in the primordial condition God willed for all. The well-known parable of Lazarus and the rich man can leave no doubts in our minds (Luke 16:19-31). God will, in any case, entirely reestablish the poor, with or without the help of the rich man. "Blessed are you poor, for yours is the kingdom of God." If it does not happen on earth, it will be realized in "Abraham's bosom." In the end then, the one in a precarious situation is not the poor man but the rich man who refuses to put the Jubilee into practice. If he does not distribute his capital now, it will be too late tomorrow. "Woe to you that are rich, for you have received your consolation" (money is your *paraklesis*, your consolation). A large gap separates the kingdom of God from the place of pleasure where the rich man likes to enjoy himself.

At this point, we can refer to the living examples of two people to whom Jesus proposed a jubilean redistribution: Zacchaeus who accepted the practice of the Jubilee and the rich young ruler who did not.

The former belonged to the scorned class of publicans and usurers whose disastrous activities were described above. Zacchaeus had become rich by lending money at usurious rates to the insolvent poor with one hand so that they could pay the government taxes he collected with the other hand. But even before meeting Jesus, Zacchaeus had heard rumors about His proclamation of the Jubilee. Zacchaeus' conscience was seriously troubled by the unjust riches he owned. The story tells us that instead of fleeing from the prophet, he climbed a tree to be certain to see Him. We also recall that Jesus went to Zacchaeus' house and that His very presence made Zacchaeus see that his wealth resulted from robbery. Applying to himself the commandment of Exodus 22:1-4, [8] which tells the robber to return four for the one he stole, Zacchaeus cried out, "The half of my goods I give to the poor; and if I have defrauded anyone of anything, I restore it fourfold" (Luke 19:1-10).

By this action, Zacchaeus was joining the great movement of jubilean reform undertaken by Jesus. He was practicing what Jesus preached by abolishing his part in the system of exploitation under which the people of Israel were suffering. Jesus exclaimed, "Today salvation has come to this house, since this man is also a son of Abraham. For the Son of Man came to seek and save the lost." Shall we conclude that those men who did not practice the Jubilee were, according to Jesus, excluding themselves from among the sons of Abraham?

It is interesting and sobering to notice that Jesus considered the rich who did not redistribute their capital as lost. Referring to the rich young ruler, Jesus had said, "How hard it is for those who have riches to enter the kingdom of God!" and the disciples had cried out, "Who then can be saved?" Indeed, the rich young ruler had refused to sell his possessions and return them to the poor. He had received the command as the disciple candidates had — to put the fourth jubilean ordinance into practice, but he had not obeyed. Despite Jesus' sympathy for him, he could not be one of His disciples who were waiting and preparing for the great reestablishment of Israel.

The contrast between the bitter sorrow of the rich young ruler and the joy of the apostles, who had responded to Jesus' jubilean call by getting rid of their possessions, is very striking.

It was, in fact, after the rich man's departure that Peter said to Jesus, "Lo, we have left [all] . . . and followed you." Jesus answered, "Truly, I say to you, there is no man who has left house or wife or brothers or parents or children, for the sake of the kingdom of God, who will not receive manifold more in this time, and in the age to come eternal life" (Luke 18:28-30).

No other text can give a better summary of the revolution Jesus effected. He was not concerned with the reform of certain details, but with overturning the entire economic hierarchy of society. The rich, who are too attached to their possessions, are relegated to the last rank; the "poor in spirit," who have voluntarily thrown off their possessions in order to obey the Jubilee, are now in the first rank. "Blessed are you that hunger now, for you shall be satisfied. . . . Woe to you that are full now, for you shall hunger" (Luke 6:21, 25). These words from the Sermon on the Mount reveal the entire scope of their meaning only in the light of Jubilee.

An honest reading of the Gospels thus confirms that Jesus was truly proclaiming a Jubilee in Nazareth. The implementation of the four jubilean prescriptions had a central place not only in Jesus' ethics but also in His proclamation of the kingdom of God and His theological teaching. In fact, the Jubilee was the sign of God's justice on earth, which fulfills itself through years of conscientious labor followed by the year of favor that crowns the completed work with the good news of divine forgiveness.

4. The "Politics" of Jesus

Christian ethicists almost unanimously agree that Jesus left us no political teaching.

In one sense they are right but only up to a certain point. Any hope of finding in the Gospels some type of criticism of first-century political regimes, such as the kingdom of the Herod dynasty or the Roman Empire, are futile. Nor is anything concerning the nature of church-state relations to be found.

But these ethicists are wrong on two counts. After having affirmed that there is no political ethic in the Gospels, they take some of Jesus' sayings out of context. For example: "Render . . . to Caesar the things that are Caesar's and to God the things that are God's"; or "You would have no power over me unless it had been given you from above." From these they conclude that, in the absence of any Christian sociology, the wise thing for the disciple to do is to submit humbly to the legitimate authorities. Such assumptions have almost totally stifled any attempt to apply Jesus' teachings on the social level. Besides that, traditional Christian ethics looks down with suspicion of heresy upon any courageous Gospel-inspired attempts to transform social institutions. Thus, a majority of church members blindly obeys the established order and supports conservative regimes, or even the most tyrannical dictatorships, on the other side of the iron curtain, in Latin America, or in Africa.

But contrary to this traditional view, we have just seen that Jesus attempted a social revolution based on Moses' jubilean law. We would now like to show that this revolution also had a political character.

In Jesus' time, the verb *politeuo* meant "to live as a citizen," that is, to live according to the laws of a city (Acts 23:1; Philippians 1:27). The adjective *politikos* applied to everything which concerned the *polites*, or citizen of a *polis* (city).

Joseph submitted himself to the census ordered by Emperor Augustus and had to go to Bethlehem, *polis* of David, of which he was a *polites*. Paul in Acts 21:39 declares: "I am a Jew, from Tarsus, in Cilicia, a citizen [*polites*] of no mean city [*polis*]." The Roman tribune who, years later, arrested Paul in Jerusalem discovered that Paul was a Roman citizen and said to him, "I bought this [*politeia,* citizenship from Rome] for a large sum of money," to which Paul proudly answered, "But I was born a citizen." Thus Paul was simultaneously a *polites* of Tarsus and a *polites* of Rome. The concept of a Roman nationality (with the same connotation as French nationality) developed much later.

In Jesus' time, the Roman Empire was still only a constellation of cities, submitting willy-nilly to Rome of course, but each forming a separate "state," a *polis* with its *politeuma* (civil government), its laws, its institutions, its authorities (*archontes* or *exousiai*), its cults and gods (Diana of Ephesus, Cybele of Pergamum, Artemis of Ancyra, Astarte of Damascus, Mithra of Cappadocia, and Yahweh of Jerusalem).

Each of the cities which Paul visited during his trips (Antioch of Syria, Perga, Antioch of Pisidia, Colossae, Iconium, Lystra, Derbe, Ephesus, Troas and Priletus in Asia, Philippi, Thessalonica and Beroea in Macedonia, and Athens and Corinth in Achaia) enjoyed a particular status and kept its gods, its laws, and its magistrates. Some were Roman colonies, such as Lystra, Philippi, and Troas. Others had the status of free cities, such as Tarsus, Perga, Thessalonica, Athens, and, for a time, Joppa, which Caesar later returned to the Jews. The free cities were tied to Rome by a *foedus* or covenant. Most of them had kept their freedom, had autonomous finances, and were sometimes exempt from paying the tribute to Caesar.

In the completely pacified regions, Rome only maintained a small number of soldiers. On the other hand, the troubled provinces, called imperial provinces, were directly under the emperor's control through the intermediary of a legate. The legate of Syria resided at Antioch. He had the procurator of Palestine, who resided in Caesarea, under his orders.

In principle, the Roman governor of the province merely served as the protector of the cities. His work was limited to regulating relations between cities, guaranteeing the judicial privileges of the local magistrates, listening to complaints against them, and forbidding religious practices that disturbed the peace.

As one can see, the framework of the Roman "nation" barely existed. In the midst of all this, the Jewish nation was an exception. Those of its members who had settled throughout the empire recognized only one God, the God of Jerusalem. They made a pilgrimage to the temple once a year. Among the inhabitants of the pagan cities, only the Jews had managed to be exempted from sacrifices to the local gods. They were also exempted from military service because its requirements violated the observance of the Sabbath.

But Israel's religious unity had not led to its political unity. After the death of Herod the Great, the province of Palestine was subdivided into six different territories placed under the authority of three sovereigns. Judea and Samaria, with their well-known quarrels, were directly under the authority of the Roman procurator in Caesarea; Galilee and Perea were governed by Herod Antipas, Decapolis and Trachonitis formed the tetrarchy of Philip, the brother of Herod Antipas.

The particularism of the Jewish cities and provinces resisted all attempts of fusion: one was either Galilean or Judean, Samarian or Syro-Phoenician. The Gospels mention Simon "of Cyrene," Joseph "of Arimathea," Mary Magdalene (of Magdala). Jesus, a citizen of Nazareth, could not be recognized as the Messiah by Nathaniel, a citizen of Jerusalem.

The historian Josephus says that there were in Galilee alone fifteen fortified cities (*polis*) and behind their walls life had a distinct and well-characterized "political" flavor. There was a similar number of such cities in the tetrarchy of Philip, in Perea, in Samaria, in Judea. The Gospels mention the names of Nazareth, Capernaum, Cana, Nain, Magdala, Chorazin in Galilee, Bethsaida and Gadara in the tetrarchy of Philip, Sychar and Shechem in Samaria, Jericho, Ephraim, Bethlehem, Emmaus, and, of course, Jerusalem in Judea. To this list one should add the cities mentioned by Josephus: Gisehala, Gadara, Gabara, Jezreel, Pella, Bethel, Tekoa, Hebron, and so forth.

The "political" thought of Jesus did not apply to the problems of a Roman Empire, but rather to the "cities of Israel" to which His calling was directed. Like the prophets of old, He spoke to these cities as if they were persons. When He recruited His first disciples, it was with the intent of sending them as "apostles" (messengers) to the cities of Israel to implore all of them together to change their behavior. Everything in them had to be transformed, the institutions as well as the hearts.

The fact that the proclamation of the kingdom was directed only to the cities of Israel underlines the "politically Jewish" character of Jesus' program. Sepphoris, north of Nazareth, Caesarea of Philippi, and even Tiberias, which was at the center of Jesus' sphere of action, are not mentioned in the Gospels. Why not? They were foreign cities, founded by the Herod dynasty or by the Romans. They did not belong to the "twelve tribes of Israel." The kingdom of God was no concern of theirs. However, the kingdom of God was announced very concretely to the cities of Israel and to their leaders.

It is not very difficult for us to imagine the intense life of these small communities, their streets buzzing with the vitality of a crowd of people of humble condition: artisans, carpenters, weavers, fullers, potters. The wealthier people owned a piece of land on the outskirts of the town, planted with vines and fig and olive trees. The sons of the poor would hire themselves out as shepherds and lead the flocks to the pastures on the hilltops. By the side of the lake, at Tiberias, Magdala, Capernaum, and Bethsaida, the artisan became a fisherman and probably owned a boat.

The city had both its rich and its poor — alas, more poor than rich! The poor included the sick, the blind, the lepers, the crippled for whom no hospital cared. There were also the widows who lost all their rights if a *goel* did not redeem them.[1] They would then become the victims of the usurers who forced them into mortgaging their houses and sometimes even their clothes.

The rich included the public officials. The Roman presence, with its garrisons at the city gate (Capernaum was "blessed" with a centurion, the commander of a company), guaranteed the stability of the Herodian usurpers, represented by the governor *(hegemon)*, the steward *(epitropos)*, the publican *(telones)*.

But the legitimate Jewish authorities were at Jerusalem. The four Gospels constantly underscore the preeminence of these authorities. They were the ones who should have recognized the Messiah, because they incarnated the people. The Sanhedrin was the supreme authority, chaired by the high priest *(archiereus)* who held the power *(exousia)*. This power affected life on three levels: the political, the judicial, and the religious. Every city had its magistrates *(archontes)*, endowed with power *(exousia)*. It also had its judge *(krites)*, its chief tax collector *(architelones)*, and its head of the synagogue *(archisynagogos)*. The latter was influential because he was the interpreter of Israel's theocratic traditions.

Indeed, the synagogue was the place where the lawyers taught and commented upon the Mosaic law and where they defined the practical rules of its implementation. But it was precisely on the level of the law that Jesus made His political claims. When He said: "You have heard that it was said to men of old, but I say to you. . . . Something greater than the temple, than Jonah, than Solomon is

here . . ." He was claiming *exousia*, the power which belonged only
to the legitimate authorities of Israel. When He spoke for the first
time in the synagogue of Capernaum, the crowd was stupefied because He taught as One who had "the power" (*exousia*), not like
their scribes.

It is easier to understand the conflict between Jesus and the
archontes of the cities of Israel if *exousia* is translated by "power."
The entire discussion with the scribes centered on the question of
power: there could not be two legitimate powers in Israel. If Jesus
was the Son of David, the legitimate king of Israel (Matthew 12:23),
He had the *exousia*, the power from God, and in this case the leaders (*archontes*) of the people should place themselves under His
authority. In Jerusalem the crowd even thought for a moment that
the Jewish leaders had surrendered to Him: "Can it be that the
authorities really know that this is the Christ [the messianic King]?"
(John 7:26). Alas, very early in the struggle the opposition prevailed.
Already in Galilee the Pharisees (from whose ranks came most of the
lawyers and who had come to Jerusalem to stop the messianic movement) had loudly declared that the power Jesus claimed was illegiti-
mate. It came, they said, not from Yahweh, but from Baal, the ancient
Canaanite god denounced by the prophets. Luke 11:14-19.

No slanderous remark could have hurt Jesus more than this
one, which explains His quick reaction and His fulminating response.
The sons (i.e., the disciples) of the Pharisees were also casting out
demons. Jesus was quite happy to find this out. Hence He was not
the only one to be announcing the coming of the kingdom of God
through miracles. He thought of Himself as the ally of the Pharisees'
disciples. "Do not forbid him to cast out demons," He had told His
disciples. "He that is not against us is for us" (Mark 9:38-40). God's
Spirit ("God's finger," according to Luke) uses various means for the
advancement of the kingdom.

But at this point, Jesus' answer to the lawyers was incisive and
comprehensive. There is but one kingdom, He says, one finger of
God, one Spirit which manifests itself in "power" (Luke 11:20). The
kingdom cannot be divided against itself: "He who is not with me is
against me (Luke 11:23). "By accusing me of being an instrument of
Baal you are giving way to pure jealousy; you are knowingly sinning
against the Spirit of God. And, of all sins, the sin against the Holy
Spirit cannot be forgiven" (Matthew 12:31, 32).

Thus Jesus was claiming for Himself all power on the religious, social, and political levels. He was rejecting any compromise; He wanted to be recognized by the *archontes* of the cities of Israel as the Son of David and King of Israel.[2]

These considerations enable us to gain a better understanding of the nature of the *Kerygma*[3] He entrusted to His apostles. Matthew 10:27, Luke 9:2-6, etc. It had a "political" character, since it was directed to cities *(polis)*, to their citizens *(polites)* and to their magistrates *(archontes)*.

Jesus certainly believed in the possibility of a collective and sudden repentance of each city in Israel, since He ordered His disciples to remain in each city long enough to tell the inhabitants about the *kerygma*, that is, the good news of the imminent kingdom: "You will not have gone through all the towns of Israel, before the Son of man comes" (Matthew 10:23).

His proclamation took the form of an ultimatum. The cities of Israel had to decide on the spot for or against the kingdom of God.

"Whenever you enter a town and they receive you . . . heal the sick in it and say to them, 'The kingdom of God has come near to you.' But whenever you enter a town and they do not receive you, go into its streets and say, 'Even the dust of your town that clings to our feet, we wipe off against you; nevertheless know this, that the kingdom of God has come near' " (Luke 10:8-11).

The poor, the sick, and the outcast gave an extraordinary reception to the proclamation of the kingdom by Jesus and His apostles. Whether in Galilee or in Judea, crowds began to move as soon as the word spread that Jesus was coming. But the *archontes* were not converted. Their resistance jeopardized the success of the messianic plan because Jesus wanted to convert the entire town to the kingdom with its authorities and its crowd: "Woe to you, Chorazin! woe to you, Bethsaida! for if the mighty works done in you had been done in Tyre and Sidon, they would have repented long ago, sitting in sackcloth and ashes. But it shall be more tolerable in the judgment for Tyre and Sidon than for you" (Luke 10:13, 14). Even Capernaum — the center of the Messiah's activities — had slipped out of His grasp. "And you, Capernaum, will you be exalted to heaven? You shall be brought down to Hades. . . . I tell you, it shall be more tolerable on that day for Sodom than for that town" (Luke 10:15, 12).

These well-known curses prompt several indispensable remarks. First of all, Jesus continued to see each city of Israel as a "political" community called to repentance as a whole, even after the failure of

His *kerygma*. Similarly, after concluding that the *archontes* of Jerusalem would reject Him, Jesus did not individualize His call to conversion, but continued to speak to the city as a whole, "O Jerusalem, Jerusalem, killing the prophets and stoning those who are sent to you! How often would I have gathered your children together as a hen gathers her brood under her wings, and you would not! Behold, your house is forsaken. And I tell you, you will not see me until you say, 'Blessed is he who comes in the name of the Lord' " (Luke 13: 34, 35).

The second remark pertains to the nature of the judgment that will strike Chorazin, Bethsaida, Capernaum, and Jerusalem. These cities are subject to a divine vocation and are called to "heaven," that is, to the kingdom of God. Sodom's disobedience caused its destruction by fire from heaven. The other cities of Israel and Jerusalem will similarly be destroyed and deserted.

But God's judgment does not stop there. On "the day of judgment" Tyre, Sidon, Sodom, and with them Chorazin, Bethsaida, Capernaum, and Jerusalem, will appear before God. The pagan cities will be treated with less rigor than the Jewish ones who had witnessed the miracles of the Messiah more frequently and had more opportunities to acclaim Him as King.

One can wonder what Jesus meant when He talked about a city's judgment before God. To understand His prophecies as mere rhetoric would be an insult to His seriousness. It is, however, hard to visualize cities being taken up into heaven to be judged, destroyed, or restored. Jesus' thinking, as we see it, is on the historical level; the judgment does take place "in heaven," that is, before God, but the cities stay on earth. After the judgment, God's will shall "be done on earth as it is in heaven." Some cities, those definitively condemned, will have ceased to exist, whereas others, the forgiven, regenerated, and restored ones, will have opened their doors to the Messiah. "I tell you," says Jesus to Jerusalem, "you will not see me until you say, 'Blessed is he who comes in the name of the Lord.' "[4]

Our discussion about "power" in Israel and about the hope for a collective conversion of its cities seemingly puts the traditional discussion of Jesus' messianic titles — King of the Jews, Son of David, Son of Man, Son of God, Christ (in Hebrew, Messiah) — in the background. But the Jews, in particular the Pharisees who listened to Jesus, seem to have used these titles indiscriminately without doubting Jesus' royal claims. Moreover, it is remarkable that in the first three

Gospels the titles which are directly associated with the historical throne of Israel (i.e., King of the Jews, Son of David, and Son of Man) have disappeared from the Apostle Paul's vocabulary. This fact points to their ancient origin. Paul retains only the two terms "Son" and "Christ." He uses the former with the possessive "his" (His Son, referring to God) and the latter, the Greek translation of Messiah, as a proper noun, unrelated to any historical context.

This point underscores the primitive character — closer to historical Judaism — of the messianic titles used by the Synoptics. The Greek or the Roman to whom Paul was talking would not have understood these titles. It is obvious that the writers of the Synoptic Gospels did not doubt that Jesus was the King of the Jews, the historical Messiah announced by the prophets. But for the pagans to whom Paul was speaking, this historical aspect was meaningless.

On one point, however, Jesus disappointed the messianic expectations of His day. Whereas they were awaiting a triumphant messianic King who would overcome His enemies by armed might, Jesus — while also preparing Himself for a brilliant victory — thought that for the time being He was called to humiliation and voluntary sacrifice, like the suffering servant announced by Isaiah. The Son of Man, the very One who was to come on the clouds of heaven, in His day did not even have a stone on which to lay His head. Abandoned by His own people, He would later be handed over to the *archontes* and put to death.

Without a doubt, Jesus considered both the humiliated Messiah and the triumphant Messiah to be one and the same person with whom He identified. Were this not true, several of His well-known parables would lose all meaning.

How should we understand, for example, the parable of the marriage feast (Matthew 22)? Jesus describes Himself as a king's son, for whom his father is giving a banquet. The Jewish people respond to the invitation with indifference, insults, and violence toward the messengers. The affront to the king and his son is humiliating, but the invitation still stands. When the wedding is ready, the son's triumph takes place, but the guests come from the crossroads and along the hedges (from among the pagans). This parable reveals an elementary Christology, so elementary, in fact, that it could not have been invented by the theologians of the early church. Jesus describes Himself as the Son of God (or the Son of the King) whose wedding God wants to celebrate. The feast honoring the King's Son will take place, no matter what happens, with or without the Jews.

The parable of the great judgment (Matthew 25:31 ff.) probably defines with even more clarity Jesus' royal character. Who is the Son of Man, coming in His glory with all His angels and sitting on His glorious throne, if not Jesus Himself who at present is hungry, thirsty, naked, ill, a stranger in prison? It is impossible to give this parable any meaning if one claims, as some exegetes do, that Jesus did not see Himself as the Son of Man who was to come in His glory. The humble Messiah and the victorious Messiah are one person, firmly based on the Old Testament teaching.

The christological teaching of these parables is confirmed by the account of Jesus' double trial, before Pilate and before the Sanhedrin.

Unquestionably, both trials had a political character. The elders of the people, the chief priests, and the scribes knew that Pilate would have refused to become involved in the theological quarrels between various Jewish sects. Thus they formulated a politically oriented accusation against Jesus, "We found this man perverting our nation, and forbidding us to give tribute to Caesar, and saying that he himself is Christ a king" (Luke 23:1-3).

When Pilate heard this accusation, he asked Jesus a political question, "Are you the King of the Jews?" Jesus, according to Luke 23:2, 3, answered him unambiguously by assuming the political title of King of the Jews, "You have said so." (*Su legeis*.) Some contemporary exegetes claim that this was an evasive answer.[5] But if Jesus had reassured Pilate with an evasive answer, why then did Pilate order the inscription "Jesus, King of the Jews" to be put on the cross as the reason for his condemnation[6] since he really would have preferred to spare His life? Matthew 27:37; John 19:19, 22.

Pilate may have doubted that the Christian revolution could present any danger to the order of his province, but he had no doubts about the political demands of a Man who so clearly claimed to be the King of the Jews. So he classified Him with the Zealot leaders who from time to time laid claim to the throne of Israel. Jesus' royal claims were obvious to the Romans. The cohort mocked Him for precisely those reasons. They covered Him with a royal robe, set a grotesque crown on His head, placed a ridiculous scepter in His hand, and kneeled before Him, simulating an audience at a king's court saying, "Hail, King of the Jews!" (Matthew 27:27-31). Indeed, if one wanted to remove any of Jesus' claims to the throne of Israel, it would be necessary to rewrite the four Gospels!

The Sanhedrin itself was politically motivated in arresting Jesus. During the well-known meeting that finalized Jesus' death, the chief priests and the Pharisees said, "If we let him go on thus, every one will believe in him, and the Romans will come and destroy both our holy place and our nation" (John 11:47, 48). Thus political rationale was the reason that impelled them to condemn Jesus. In their view His popularity was endangering both the political system they represented and even the existence of the nation. He had entered Jerusalem as a pretender to the royal throne. His imposture had to be unmasked.

Consequently, the high priest questioned Jesus in no ambiguous terms, "I adjure you by the living God, tell us if you are the Christ, the Son of God" (Matthew 26:63). (Cf. Mark: "Are you the Christ, the Son of the Blessed [God]"; and Luke: "If you are the Christ, tell us.") And Jesus answered, as He did to Pilate, "You have said so"; and added, "But I tell you, hereafter you will see the Son of man seated at the right hand of Power, and coming on the clouds of heaven" (Matthew 26:64).

People often discuss what Jesus meant by "Son of man." For the reader who is not acquainted with the prophecies of Daniel, the Son of Man coming on the clouds of heaven is a mythical character quite unrelated to the King of Israel. Nothing could, however, be farther from the truth. Without a doubt, the Son of Man mentioned by Daniel is a king of Israel who will succeed a dynasty of tyrants.

Following are the words of Daniel's prophecy which inspired Jesus when He answered the high priest, "You will see the Son of man seated at the right hand of Power, and coming on the clouds of heaven": "Thrones were placed and one that was ancient of days[7] took his seat. . . . The court sat in judgment, and the books were opened. I looked then because of the sound of the great words which the horn[8] was speaking. And as I looked, the beast was slain, and its body destroyed and given over to be burned with fire. As for the rest of the beasts, their dominion was taken away[9] but their lives were prolonged for a season and a time. I saw in the night visions, and behold, with the clouds of heaven there came one like a son of man,[10] and he came to the Ancient of Days and was presented before him. And to him was given dominion and glory and kingdom, that all peoples, nations, and languages should serve him; his dominion is an everlasting dominion, which shall not pass away, and his kingdom one that shall not be destroyed.

"These four great beasts are four kings who shall arise out of the earth. But the saints of the Most High shall receive the kingdom, and possess the kingdom for ever, for ever and ever."

By presenting Himself as the Son of Man coming on the clouds of heaven, Jesus was laying unequivocal claim to the throne of Israel, a claim as unequivocal as the question put to Jesus by the high priest. In effect, the judiciary problem facing the Sanhedrin was a two-sided one. The first aspect was religious. Was this Jesus really the Son of God as He claimed? The other was political. When Jesus said He was the King of Israel announced by Daniel and the prophets, was He telling the truth?

When Jesus answered: "You say that I am" (Luke), "You have said so" (Matthew), and "I am" (Mark), the judges of the Sanhedrin thought He was lying. The high priest tore his garments and cried out, "Why do we still need witnesses? You have heard his blasphemy. What is your judgment?" They answered, "He deserves death." For the law of Moses stated, "He who blasphemes the name of the Lord shall be put to death; all the congregation shall stone him" (Leviticus 24:16). Thus Jesus was condemned to death for having claimed the title of Messiah, King of Israel.

Having outlined the political role Jesus had assigned to Himself, we must show that He also associated His disciples with His reign.

Christian theology tends to isolate Jesus from any social context because of His universal redemptive role. As Son of God and Son of Man, Jesus would have entered his invisible kingdom after all His disciples either denied or betrayed Him. Thus there would be a complete break between the old Israel, ending at the cross, and the new Israel (the church) that grew out of the resurrection and Pentecost.

Up to the end of His earthly life, however, Jesus insisted upon the continuity of Israel. Of course, there was only a remnant, a handful of disciples who remained faithful. But insofar as the suffering Messiah and the triumphant Messiah are one and the same person, Jesus' apostles, despite their betrayal, will also take part in the construction of the kingdom, even after His crucifixion. Let us consider Peter, for example. In the same passage where Jesus predicts the denial, He tells Peter, "I have prayed for you that your faith may not fail, and when you have turned again, strengthen your brethren."

But Jesus is not talking to Peter alone. He is addressing all the apostles. According to Luke 22:28, Jesus tells the Twelve, "You are those who have continued with me in my trials; and I assign to you, as my Father assigned to me, a kingdom." A better translation would read, "Therefore I bequeath to you the kingdom as the Father bequeathed it to me."

It is hard to see the meaning of such a bequest made by Jesus at the time of His departure from the earth if the kingdom to which He referred was purely celestial. In Jesus' mind the kingdom was both earthly and heavenly. He leaves the apostles on earth to continue His work. The rest of this passage from Luke underlines the double character of the kingdom, "I assign to you . . . that you may eat and drink at my table in my kingdom, and sit on thrones judging the twelve tribes of Israel." Eating and drinking at the King's table clearly evokes a messianic banquet that will take place when the kingdom of God will have come,[11] and it is difficult to say whether it will be on earth or in heaven.

Let us now try to understand what Jesus meant when He told the disciples they would be called to "[judge] the twelve tribes of Israel."

First of all, the evocation of the twelve tribes brings out the continuity between the ancient Israel with its laws and institutions and the new Israel. (Cf. our prior reference to the importance Jesus conferred upon the Jewish people.)

One must also recall the role of the "judges" in Israel. He was not only a magistrate in charge of administering justice, but also a governor, administering the people under God's direct authority. When Jesus told His disciples, "You will judge the twelve tribes of Israel," He was not referring to the last judgment. Rather, He was announcing that His apostles would be installed as judges, that is, as governors of the twelve tribes of Israel. These were responsibilities He Himself had inherited from His Father.

The parable of the pounds (Luke 19:11-27) confirms this. One could wonder whether it is really a parable. In this case, the symbolic element usually found in parables is reduced to a minimum. Jesus gave this speech at the end of His life as He was going up to Jerusalem when the people had heard His messianic call and were convinced that "the kingdom of God was to appear immediately."

At this point Jesus spoke to His disciples and to the crowd with the intention of making His position clear. He plainly told His disciples that they would soon be called upon to govern the cities of Israel. Herein lies the entire emphasis of the parable, "You shall have authority over ten cities. . . . And you . . . are to be over five cities." Without a doubt, He was referring to the enthronement we mentioned above and to the cities of Israel.

Thus, despite the grim predictions Jesus was making about Himself and the outcome of His trip to Jerusalem, He had no doubts about the final success of the campaign He had inaugurated a year and a half earlier in Nazareth's synagogue. He had chosen and drawn the apostles around Him so that they might fill the leadership positions of Israel.

However, the disciples and the crowd needed to realize that a period of trials would precede the final triumph. Jesus explained this by recalling one of the memories of His youth. When Jesus was a child, Archelaus, one of Herod's sons, who was to succeed his father as one of the kings of the Herodian dynasty, had become very unpopular among the inhabitants of Jerusalem. He therefore traveled to Rome in order to receive the confirmation of his kingship from Emperor Augustus. But a Jewish delegation of his opponents caught up with him in Rome and Augustus granted them Archelaus' deposition instead.

In similar words, Jesus was saying to the crowd: "The authorities in Jerusalem do not want me for their king. I must appear before God, the supreme sovereign to receive my investiture from him and then I will come back. Do not think that what happened to Archelaus will also happen to me. The objections which Jewish authorities present before God's throne against my rule will not stand. I will surely return soon, invested with power. Then a twofold judgment will take place: first, a judgment against my enemies, who do not want me to rule over them: they will be destroyed; second, a judgment over my disciples, who will have administered my kingdom during my absence: the careless and doubting ones will be excluded from my kingdom, while the active and faithful ones will receive the government of the cities of Israel."

Several more remarks should be made at this point, if one wants to grasp the full meaning of this parable.

First, the parable mentions only ten of the twelve apostles. One can wonder whether Jesus had already foreseen the denial of some of them.

Second, the extremely violent conclusion is quite striking. It does not coincide with our usual ideas about Jesus' meekness: "But as for these enemies of mine who did not want me to reign over them, bring them here and slay them before me." This ruins any philosophy that would attempt to turn the Messiah into a weak being, eternally destined not to resist the wicked. There will be a judgment, says Jesus. Those who will have deliberately rejected the kingdom of God will receive a terrible punishment.

However, this punishment is put off until later because God is granting a delay for the investiture of the Messiah with royal authority. During this time, the Messiah will surrender His prerogative as judge. He will become a sacrifice and die at the hands of the wicked. This is God's will.

Thus Christian nonviolence is not a part of the fabric of the universe, as is Hindu nonviolence. Rather, it has a temporary character. It is tied to the delay God grants men because of the voluntary sacrifice of the messianic King. By deriving nonviolence not from a philosophy of the universe (which may be utopian) but from His sacrifice on the cross, Jesus gives it historical precision and a much greater impact. Through redemption, nonviolence thrusts itself upon all Jesus' disciples. It becomes an article of faith, a mark of obedience, a sign of the kingdom to come as it was for Jesus Himself.

A third remark is that the delay God granted grows out of His unbelievable patience. In the parable of the vineyard God's patience comes to an end and punishment follows. In the parable of the pounds, however, God still has pity on Israel and the punishment is put off until the day the king will return, invested with supreme authority.

Now we can understand Jesus' frame of mind as He went to Jerusalem mounted on His donkey in order to be acclaimed King. He was accomplishing a historical act. He was passing a new milestone on the way to the reestablishment of the kingdom of Israel and the founding of God's reign. He knew, however, that the kingdom would yet have to wait, and He exhorted His disciples not to be deceived but to persevere throughout their trials.

As the crowd was acclaiming Him King,[12] and as He approved the cries of the children in the temple, "Hosanna to the Son of David," Jesus was not lamenting the tragic events awaiting Him. Instead, He was crying over Jerusalem, over the cities of Israel, over the women and children He had tried to bring together under the leadership of the *archontes*, all of whom had rejected Him.

5. The Jubilean Revolution and the Ethics of the Early Church

How shall we bridge the gap between the old Israel and the new Israel (the church), between the law of Moses and the ethics of today's Christian community?

The year of Jubilee was a Sabbath, a "sabbath of sabbatical years," which was to return every 49 years. If we are to understand the high importance of the Jubilee, we must go deeper into the meaning of the Sabbath itself.

We recall that the Sabbath was instituted in the fourth commandment of the Decalogue. In Exodus 20, weekly rest is justified in the following terms: "In six days the Lord made heaven and earth, the sea, and all that is in them, and rested on the seventh day; therefore the Lord blessed the sabbath day and hallowed it." Thus, the Sabbath had an eschatological significance. It announced God's rest, the completion of His work in final perfection. In Deuteronomy 5:15 the Sabbath is a reminder of the Exodus from Egypt, "You shall remember that you were a servant in the land of Egypt, and the Lord your God brought you out thence with a mighty hand and an outstretched arm; therefore the Lord your God commanded you to keep the sabbath day." This historical liberation was announcing the supreme liberation which is the end of history. You shall commemorate it and proclaim it by resting yourself and by granting rest to the stranger, to the slaves, and to the cattle. Thus the humanitarian concerns that inspired Jesus already fill the pages of Deuteronomy, "In it you shall not do any work, you, or your son, or your daughter, or your manservant, or your maidservant, or your ox, or your ass, or any of your cattle, or the sojourner who is within your gates, *that your manservant and your maidservant may rest as well as you.* You shall remember that you were a servant in the land of Egypt" (italics author's).

In Deuteronomy 15, as we have already seen, the freeing of slaves during the sabbatical year was inspired by a similar consideration, "You shall remember that you were a slave in the land of Egypt and the Lord your God redeemed you." Deuteronomy 24 justifies the ban on taking the garments of a sojourner, an orphan, or a widow as a pledge with the same statement, "You shall remember that you were a slave in Egypt and the Lord your God redeemed you from there."

According to Isaiah, the redemption of God's people is the essential work which God Himself accomplishes by means of his *goel*, the Messiah.

Jesus believed He was the *goel*, that is, the instrument chosen by God to carry out redemption. When Jesus healed a woman with a deformed back in the synagogue, the ruler of the synagogue became indignant because Jesus had healed someone on the Sabbath, and he told the people, "There are six days on which work ought to be done; come on those days and be healed and not on the sabbath day." And Jesus answered, "You hypocrites! Does not each of you on the sabbath untie his ox or his ass from the manger, and lead it away to water it? And ought not this woman, a daughter of Abraham whom Satan bound for eighteen years, be loosed from this bond on the sabbath day?" (Luke 13:14-16).

This response clarifies the meaning Jesus was giving to His own mission as well as His attitude toward the Sabbath, the eschatological day above all others. It is erroneous to believe that He wanted to abolish the Sabbath. On the contrary, He wanted to give it its full significance. The Sabbath was not to be a day of servitude, but rather the premonitory sign of the supreme liberation God is accomplishing for His people and for the whole of creation.

The eschatological expectation of the supreme Sabbath is admirably defined in the latter part of the Book of Isaiah, chapters 56 to 66, probably written after the return from exile. Once back in their own land, the Jews had tried to establish a theocracy. They had restored the Sabbath to its place. Messianic hopes grew in intensity, "Arise, shine, for your light has come . . . the Lord will arise upon you . . . nations shall come to your light and kings to the brightness of your rising. . . . The sun shall be no more your light by day nor for brightness shall the moon give light to you by night, but the Lord will be your everlasting light and your God will be your glory."

And to prepare the reign of light, the entire people were to put the Sabbath into practice: "If you turn back your foot from the sabbath . . . and call the sabbath a delight . . . then you shall take delight in the Lord and I will make you ride upon the heights of the earth; I will feed you with the heritage of Jacob your father. . . . Behold, in the day of your fast you seek your own pleasure, and oppress all your workers. Behold, you fast only to quarrel and to fight and to hit with wicked fist. . . . Is not this the fast I choose: to loose the bonds of wickedness, to undo the thongs of the yoke, to let the oppressed go free and to break every yoke? Is it not to share your bread with the hungry, and bring the homeless poor to your house; when you see the naked to cover him, and not to hide yourself from your own flesh? Then shall your light break forth like the dawn, and your healing shall spring up speedily" (Isaiah 58).

"And the foreigners who join themselves to the Lord . . . every one who keeps the sabbath, and does not profane it, and holds fast my covenant — these I will bring to my holy mountain and make them joyful in my house of prayer; their burnt offerings and their sacrifices will be accepted on my altar; for my house shall be called a house of prayer for all peoples" (Isaiah 56).

"For as the new heaven and the new earth which I will make shall remain before me, says the Lord; so shall your descendants and your name remain. From new moon to new moon, and from sabbath to sabbath, all flesh shall come to worship before me, says the Lord" (Isaiah 66).[1]

We know that Jesus had nourished His faith by reading Isaiah and that He had found the expression of His vocation in one of the sabbatical texts from Isaiah 61, the very text He read in the synagogue at Nazareth to affirm His messiahship and proclaim the Jubilee.

The Book of Daniel contains another striking sabbatical prophecy: "Seventy weeks of years are decreed concerning your people and your holy city, to finish the transgression, to put an end to sin, and to atone for iniquity, to bring in everlasting righteousness, to seal both vision and prophet, and to anoint a most holy place. Know therefore and understand" (Daniel 9:24, 25).

The author of the letter to the Hebrews reechoes this prophecy in his fourth chapter: "So then, there remains a sabbath rest for the people of God. . . . Let us therefore strive to enter that rest."

The disciples on the road to Emmaus described the messianic expectation of the Jews and their disappointment concerning Jesus of Nazareth by telling the stranger accompanying them, "We had hoped that he was the one to redeem Israel. And beginning with Moses and all the prophets, [the stranger] interpreted to them in all the scriptures the things concerning himself." Once back in Jerusalem, the Emmaus pilgrims and the apostles saw a vision of the resurrected One in the upper room and He said to them, "These are my words which I spoke to you, while I was still with you, that everything written about me in the law of Moses and the prophets and the psalms must be fulfilled . . . that repentance and forgiveness of sins should be preached in his name to all nations, beginning from Jerusalem. You are witnesses of these things."

Thus it was in an atmosphere of eschatological expectation that the church in Jerusalem was formed. "Lord," the disciples asked Jesus before Pentecost, "will you at this time restore [derived from *apokatastasis*] the kingdom to Israel?" And Jesus did not dissuade them from expecting the restoration of the kingdom. He merely warned them as He did in Jericho on the eve of His trip to Jerusalem, "It is not for you to know times or seasons which the Father has fixed by his own authority."

In his speech to the people, after healing a lame man, Peter links the rejuvenation of the Jubilee with the final restoration and spells out a perfectly clear eschatological program: "Repent therefore, and turn again, that your sins may be blotted out, that times of refreshing may come from the presence of the Lord, and that he may send the Christ appointed for you, Jesus, whom heaven must receive until the time for establishing [*apokatastasis*] all that God spoke by the mouth of his holy prophets of old. Moses said, 'The Lord God will raise up for you a prophet from your brethren as he raised me up. You shall listen to him in whatever he tells you' " (Acts 3:19-22).

For the first Christians, in the period immediately following the crucifixion, the resurrection, and Pentecost, the expectation of the restoration of all things required an immediate application of Moses' sabbatical teachings, interpreted by Jesus. And the Jubilee was a part of these teachings; so they put them into practice: "There was not a needy person among them, for as many as were possessors of lands or houses sold them, and brought the proceeds of what was sold and laid it at the apostles' feet; and distribution was made to each as any had need" (Acts 4:34, 35).

Many debates have centered around the "impossible communism" of the church in Jerusalem. Some exegetes think the idyllic description of the Book of Acts is exaggerated. They underscore the fact that the text mentions only one concrete example of land sharing, that of Joseph, called Barnabas, who sold a field. If all those who owned land sold it, why did the author think it necessary to emphasize Barnabas' example? Others think that the communism of the early church did indeed exist, but that it was short-lived. It belonged to the "interim ethics" Jesus preached, and became impossible to practice as soon as the church recognized the length of the interval still separating it from the "restoration of all things."

In both cases, the exegetes see the "communism of the early church" as a rule inapplicable to modern society and they mourn the utopian character of an experiment reserved for a limited number of "latter day saints."

A third school of thought seems to come closer to the truth. In their view, Jesus gave the Sermon on the Mount in a spirit of eschatological expectation. The Beatitudes in particular announce the coming deliverance which will reward the poor, the mourners, the meek, the hungry, the merciful, the pure, the peacemakers, and the persecuted.

However, these "kingdom ethics" are in tension with today's world. They were given to us, we are told, to help us measure the depth of our failure, to inspire us to repent, and to open the door of grace. Situational ethics would align itself with this interpretation. The believer, faced with the requirements of the kingdom of God, his own incapacity to do good and the power of divine grace, receives in every situation and in due course the inspiration of the Holy Spirit and "invents" each time an answer that corresponds to God's direction.

But this interpretation of Jesus' ethics has several weaknesses:

1. It neglects the gospel's entire social message, which Jesus expressed clearly.

2. It places each individual person in a series of "situations" where he alone must always resolve the tension between the absolute and the possible. This pushes him into clashes of conscience he cannot always overcome because man is rarely capable of bearing the weight of his own existence alone.

3. It destroys the permanence of God's commandment and thereby of ethics itself.

4. Simultaneously, it shakes the message of the church, which shrinks to nothingness if the church ceases to be the channel of God's commandment and forgiveness.

5. Once the commandment has been undermined, man can no longer really see himself as a sinner. God's message of grace is perfectly meaningless for someone who fails to see himself as a sinner before God.

o   o   o

There should be, then, another interpretation of Jesus' ethics, that of the early church. Would it not be jubilean ethics?

Jesus did not want to crush His people under the weight of an impossible absolute. He did not try to establish a monastic order. The Essenes had done this before Him. Nor was he the victim of an eschatological illusion. He simply proclaimed a Jubilee, that is, to use Peter's words, "times of refreshing" announcing "the time for establishing all that God spoke. . . ."

With this, we are finally treading upon the solid ground of Jewish ethics. The Jubilee was a revolutionary year for an entire people and not only for some individuals.

Jesus' ethic is therefore a revolutionary doctrine applicable to a society, as well as to an individual, an ethic of possibility, adaptable to each age, every time the expectation of the kingdom becomes more intense under the influence of God's Spirit.

It is adapted for four reasons: (1) Its foundation remains God's commandment, revealed to Moses, indestructible throughout the centuries and reinterpreted by Jesus Christ. (2) Its goal is the imminent kingdom of God and the justice of God, that is, His impending judgment. (3) It is adapted because the delay God granted is not an empty one with vain tensions and endless conflicts, but a history, with Jubilees for landmarks, the first of which was inaugurated by Jesus. (4) It is adapted because in every historical situation between Mount Sinai and the kingdom, the Spirit tells the church what form of injustice, violence, or false witness must be eliminated and in what terms the Jubilee must be proclaimed as a premonitory sign of the reestablishment of all things.

It is actually a form of "situational ethics," *but historical situational ethics and not individual situational ethics*; an ethic of the church of the elect, no longer of leaderless snipers; a social ethic, no longer a sectarian one; a revolutionary ethic, no longer a static one; a concrete, practical ethic, no longer the hopeless struggle of a limping Israel with the angel of the absolute. [2]

What then happened in the early church?

The "time of refreshment," which followed Pentecost and to which Peter refers, soon went by. Then this Jubilee which had been characterized by the restitution of land and houses to the poor, by sharing of possessions and by the recovery of health for the sick, made way for a period of stabilization. People returned to their work, got married, raised families without, it seems, being conscious of backsliding, since the Jubilee had elapsed.

Every time the gospel reached new groups, however, the proclamation of the Jubilee would ring out again. We will not attempt to follow here a preestablished calendar of septennial recurrences. But rather, let us say that as soon as Jews or Gentiles were touched by the apostles' message, they inaugurated their conversion with a Jubilee. It is in this spirit that one should read Paul's letters. In particular at the beginning of each letter we are reminded of the extraordinary favors manifested in each city on the day when Jesus was recognized there as the Messiah. Chapters 8 and 9 of 2 Corinthians (written around AD 57, 29 years after Pentecost) witness the jubilean joy that filled the Macedonians whose "extreme poverty [has] overflowed in a wealth of liberality on their part" (2 Corinthians 8:1-5) in aiding the members of the church in Jerusalem.

This picture may be too optimistic, but a second explanation will modify it.

In AD 66 the Jews who had refused to accept the Messiah revolted against Rome. In AD 70 Jerusalem was destroyed by Titus and the Jewish state ceased to exist. From then on the law of Moses lost its social and political thrust for the dispersed Jews. Indeed, in rabbinic literature the hopes for a reestablishment of Israel became vaguer and vaguer. The Christians were subjected to the same evolution as the Jews. Dispersed as they were throughout the Mediterranean countries, they adopted out of necessity a minority ethic. It was out of the question for them to reestablish the sabbatical laws. Their problem was that of remaining faithful under persecution, renouncing the impurities of the world, and keeping good relationships between the members of the church. The messianic vision of a kingdom of God which should begin in Israel and spread to the entire globe slowly died off. It would probably be more exact to say that it transformed itself into the expectation of heaven, meant for those who persevered in the present tribulations. Who could hope to reform the Roman Empire with the laws of Moses? The church even thought of the authority of Caesar and the *Pax Romana* as gracious heavenly gifts.

Also, insofar as Israel did not become converted and despite the hopes Paul formulated in Romans 11, the first Christians abandoned the ancient plan that set the conversion of Israel as the primary condition for the conversion of the nations. The church then specialized in the transformation of individuals. It recruited one by one and exhorted them to remain faithful. The example of the martyrs brought about new conversions, but the church's hopes for the world shrunk.

The unconverted, both Jews and Gentiles, came to be considered as definitively lost.

However, three centuries later, the impossible happened. Rome was converted to Christianity and Emperor Constantine turned it into a state religion. This could have been a unique occasion for the church. It could have attempted to make the Roman state adopt the laws of Moses as Jesus had taught them to the Jews so they could be put into practice by society, as well as by individuals. But nothing happened. The Roman state relied upon Roman law and ignored Moses. Once in power, the church adopted Rome's social ethics as its own and kept on teaching the admirable minority ethic which had constituted its strength during persecution. It forgot the Jubilee. Nevertheless, the Jubilee did linger on in the church's liturgy in the form of a vague nostalgia for forgotten messianic expectations.

But the spirit of the prophets never perished. Like the prophets of the old covenant, holy reformers shook up the church from century to century and attempted to bring it back to the original purity. These noble efforts sometimes resulted in the foundation of a new religious order, sometimes in the creation of a new reforming movement, often oriented toward the jubilean practice of shared possessions.

Be that as it may, we must retain from the Jubilee five useful teachings for our day:

1. Social and political revolutions are not contrary to the Old Testament or to the gospel. Their periodic recurrence is necessary to restore a justice of God that is always deteriorating. Their role is also to reform the structures of society and to adapt laws and customs to the new conditions created by economic transformations and evolution of morals.

2. The refusal of the privileged social classes or races to do justice and the often violent repression of revolutionary movements can be condemned in the name of Christ. For having refused the Jubilee, the Jewish leaders crucified the Christ and hastened Jerusalem's catastrophic end. The murderous violence of some revolutions is certainly contrary to the Gospel, but the revolutions themselves *cannot be condemned* when they are prompted by a spirit of justice.

3. It is wrong to believe that Christians should not worry about social justice. The divorce between individual ethics and social practices is found neither in the gospel nor even in Judaism. It is the result partly of the persecutions suffered by the early church for

nearly three hundred years and partly of the compromises the church made with a pagan society whose laws did not come from biblical revelation.

4. Whenever the Spirit of God speaks to the church, it is to call individuals to repentance, and also to transform laws and habits. Individual repentance and social repentance cannot be dissociated. The gospel ethic is an ethic of awakening, for in the Old Testament tradition, Jubilees were nothing less than religious awakenings. Any effort to limit an awakening by preventing it from bearing fruit on the social and political levels will make it abort. Man must not artificially limit the full scope of God's power, for it embraces every domain.

The "Jubilee awakenings" must involve a repentance and revolution on four levels:

a. On the individual level.

b. On the level of the church, the new Israel, in whose midst justice must reign, for God's judgment will start with the church.

c. On the ecumenical level. The world is in need of hearing the voice of the universal church.

d. On the level of the state. By demanding that the state practice God's justice, the church will be conforming to the election it inherited from the people of Israel and from the Messiah, its Leader.

5. In its proclamation of the Jubilee, the church must not take the place of the state. The Jubilee does not enslave man to laws; it frees the church from servitude. It can only be conceived in a spirit of repentance and prayer. Modern states have not inherited Israel's vocation. They can neither pray nor repent. So let the church be the New Israel for the greater good of the states throughout which it is scattered.

In conclusion of this first part, there is no tension between "the kingdom of God to come" and its so-called "absolute ethic" and "the world as it is" with its "relative necessities." The Christian citizen is not, as some would like to have him believe, inwardly torn apart by conflicting duties to his Christian conscience and his membership in the state.

The tension that remains in the world is that which separates the faithful church from the modern state, which is not a Christian state, but a state that fears the church, and cannot do without it.

If it is put into practice by the church whenever the Spirit blows, the Jubilee that announces the kingdom of God will propose practical solutions to the problems of ownership, exploitation of man by man, freedom of the oppressed, and capital sharing. The Jubilee will once again give the church its place in the modern world. The conscience of its members will then grasp the full scope and implications of the gospel applied in the concrete reality of today's world.

II. VIOLENCE
AND NONVIOLENCE
FROM ELIJAH TO JESUS

6. From Elijah to Herod

Elijah, who prophesied in Israel under Ahab (around 870 BC), was certainly the most ardent defender of sacred violence. To rid the Israelites of Canaanite idolatry, he did not hesitate to personally massacre 450 prophets of Baal, the rival of Yahweh. But this feat troubled him deeply. After having taken refuge in the desert, he did not find God's revelation in the earthquake or the fire, but in a "still small voice."

His disciple Elisha **was** also a man of indescribable violence. He had two bears tear some children to pieces because they laughed at his baldness. Nevertheless, he did advise the king of Israel with moderation. When the king asked Elisha whether he should execute Syrian prisoners he had captured, Elisha said, "You shall not slay them. Would you slay those whom you have taken captive. . . ? Set bread and water before them that they may go to their master." The king obeyed and sent the prisoners home. This act of mercy had providential consequences: According to 2 Kings 6:21-23: "The Syrians came no more on raids into the land of Israel."

Elisha died about 785 BC. Thirty-five years later, Amos, the first prophet-writer, ushered in the evolution of the ancient Hebrews' religious nationalism toward nonviolence. Amos was certainly not a sentimental man. He was not thinking of weakening Israel's virility. His prophecies against the enemies of the Jews are extremely violent, but the ones he pronounced against his own people are still more harsh. He blamed the Jews for their own sufferings, which he saw as chastisements sent by God for their crimes. The sacred violence necessary to reestablish God's justice had not been abolished, but it applied equally to the friends as well as to the enemies of Yahweh. At the same time, Yahweh ceased to be seen as a national God and became the universal Judge.[1]

With the prophet Hosea this trend was accentuated. He compared Israel to a woman who deceived her husband by "committing adultery" with foreign gods. Her infidelity was chastised by means of the Assyrians, but God continued to love her in spite of all.

Isaiah, who is usually considered to be the greatest among the prophets, acted as political counselor for Hezekiah, king of Judah. In

721 BC, Samaria, the capital of the Northern Kingdom, had been taken by the Assyrians and its inhabitants carried away. Jerusalem, the capital of the small Southern Kingdom, seemed doomed to the same fate. The Jews wavered between profound discouragement, reliance upon Egypt, and the most superficial optimism.

But Isaiah dissuaded the king from making an alliance with Egypt. The Jews were to trust God alone. He fought the optimism of some by announcing that the end of Jerusalem was near and uplifted the courage of others by prophesying an unexpected deliverance. As the tremendous armies of Sennacherib, king of the Assyrians, were moving in on the capital, deliverance came. The plague struck the Assyrians' camp, and they withdrew.

The same Isaiah left us the well-known series of portraits of "the servant of the Lord."

The "servant of the Lord" was the Jewish people, a people called to be the light to the nations and to establish justice on earth. The servant of the Lord could find his security nowhere but in God, for God alone was in charge of his protection. Thus, 2,650 years ago, Isaiah was already sketching "a new method of national defense" tied, of course, to Israel's acceptance of its particular vocation as "servant of the Lord."

After many centuries, the problem of the church's defense against the enemies of truth boils down to this: Did or did not the church inherit through Jesus Christ Israel's vocation of the "servant of the Lord"? Can or cannot the church count on God alone for its defense?

Jeremiah, the sorrowing prophet who witnessed Jerusalem's destruction, followed in Isaiah's footsteps. The generals of Nebuchadnezzar, king of Chaldea, laid siege to Jerusalem, but it refused to capitulate. Jeremiah disapproved military resistance and advised the people to have faith in God alone. He was thrown into jail for having attempted to escape the besieged city. From his dungeon cell, he continued to cry out even at the risk of his life, "Thus says the Lord, He who stays in this city shall die by the sword . . . but he who goes out to the Chaldeans shall live. . . . This city shall surely be given into the hand of the army of the king of Babylon and be taken" (Jeremiah 38:2, 3). The people did not listen to him and the divine warning was realized. Jerusalem was taken and destroyed in 587 BC and its people carried off to Babylon.

During the exile, which lasted from 587 to 538 BC, the Jews no longer had a problem of national defense. They were, in any case, captives and powerless. This is when the "Prophet of the exile," usually called the second Isaiah, who witnessed the unjust sufferings endured by the exiled, completed the portrait of the "Servant of the Lord." "The servant is not conquered," he said, "he will not fail or be discouraged till he has established justice in the earth." But he will establish this justice without breaking a bruised reed or quenching a dimly burning wick (Isaiah 42:1-4).

Certainly the people were to be punished for their disobedience and crimes, but a remnant was to survive. Jerusalem was to be restored. The sufferings of the Lord's servant would redeem the sins of many.

Thus the idea was gradually formed that Yahweh, the *goel* of Israel,[2] would participate with His people in a much wider redemptive act, intended for the entire human race. When God redeems the guilty, He is neither refusing to see the power of evil nor is He refusing to look at the world as it is, nor is He evading His responsibility. Redemption does not eliminate divine violence, but rather redirects it from the head of God's enemy to the Lord's servant, who is called to suffer instead of the guilty.[3]

From the exile until Jesus' time, Israel's history was nothing but a long spiritual struggle for the acceptance or the rejection of this grand and terrible vocation of the "servant of the Lord." In 538 BC, one of Cyrus' edicts had brought the Jews back to Palestine. The temple had been rebuilt and the people were filled with great hopes. Was the ideal theocracy imagined by Ezekiel about to become a reality? Alas, no! Subjected to the Persians from 538 to 333 BC, to the Greeks under Alexander the Great, then to the Ptolemys of Egypt, and finally to the Seleucids of Syria from 197 BC on, Israel became entrenched in religious legalism. Correct ritual celebration replaced living faith. Courage was not lacking, but the powerful nonviolent visions of the two Isaiahs and Jeremiah had vanished.

Moreover, a new ideology tended to supersede the old one. The tolerant Greek civilization was slowly invading Asia. Even the high priests in Jerusalem were becoming hellenized. Under the rule of the Seleucids of Syria, the Jews had gradually adopted their customs. In 175 BC, Jason, the father of the high priest Onias, became the advocate of the new ideas in Jerusalem. Hellenization was increasing at a steady pace when the accident happened. Antiochus Epiphanes, king of Syria, who thought the battle had already been won, abolished Jewish worship and erected a statue of Zeus in the temple of Jerusalem.

On the 24th of Chislev 167 BC, a pagan sacrifice defiled the holy place. (This was later called the "abomination of the desolation." Jesus thought that the recurrence of such a sacrilege after His death would be a sign of the end times.)

For fear of persecution, the majority of the Jews accepted the new cult. Only one priest, called Mattathias, filled with righteous anger, left Jerusalem and went to Modin in order to remain faithful to the law of Moses. His five sons followed him. The "Hasidaeans," a group of puritans that later gave rise to the pharisaic movement, also joined them. Quite a number of people concerned with justice and the law followed Mattathias' example and fled to the desert. Royal troops pursued and reached them.

Mattathias was not nonviolent since he had personally cut the throat of a Jew who had sacrificed to idols! However, his resistance was passive in its first stage. A group of the faithful refused to retaliate rather than fight their aggressors on the Sabbath. "Let us all die in our innocence," they said, "heaven and earth testify for us that you are killing us unjustly." The enemy attacked them on the Sabbath. They allowed themselves to be massacred without resisting, faithful to the law that forbade them to fight on the Sabbath.

After hearing about this massacre, Mattathias, however, chose violence, "If we all do as our brethren have done and refuse to fight with the Gentiles for our lives and our customs, they will quickly destroy us from the earth." He called the Jews to arms and began the war of liberation that his sons were to end victoriously.[4]

At Mattathias' death, his son Judas, nicknamed "the Hammer" (Maccabee), struck mercilessly the enemies of truth. In 164 BC, the temple was purified. In 160 BC, Jonathan succeeded his brother Judas, who had been killed at war. In 143, the third brother, Simon, became the high priest and ethnarch of Palestine. When the Maccabees had regained Jewish national independence, they took the titles of high priest and king. But, alas, the Maccabees or Hasmonaeans were unable to free themselves from the violence they had used to obtain their power. In order to reestablish the ancient boundaries of David's kingdom, they warred their neighbors and took Perea, Samaria, Idumea, and Philistia. After approximately one century, their quarrel- and violence-ridden dynasty yielded before foreign usurpers, the Herods.

The Hasidaeans (the pure), who had supported Mattathias, turned into a political party, the Pharisees, champions of strict ritual observances. They entered the struggle for power. Persecuted under Alexander Janneus, they triumphed under his daughter Alexandra.

Several pretenders to the throne hastened the decadence of the Hasmonaeans by their rivalries. In 65 BC Hyrcan, supported by a "mayor of the palace," Antipater the Idumean, contended with his younger brother, Aristobulus, who entrenched himself in Jerusalem.

Finally the Romans came onto the scene. Only too happy to serve as arbitrator between the two adversaries, Pompey took the side of Hyrcan in 63 BC and laid siege to Jerusalem. After three months, his soldiers made a breach in the wall, stormed and took the city. The victorious Roman general then entered the "holy of holies" with his forces, scandalizing the Jews. But he was wiser than Antiochus Epiphanes a century earlier. He ordered the temple to be purified and the traditional sacrifices to be offered. Hyrcan retained the pontificate but his role was reduced to that of ethnarch while his minister Antipater was given the Greek title of *epitropos* (equivalent to the Latin "procurator") by Pompey.

That day was the beginning of success for Antipater's family. Antipater was not a Jew. He was an Idumean, or Edomite. Neither he nor his son Herod had any right to the throne of Israel. However, by associating themselves with the changing fortunes of the Roman political figures who rivaled for the dictatorship (Pompey, Caesar, Anthony, and finally Octavius, the future Augustus), the Herods managed to obtain royal power from them. The trickery Antipater and Herod the Great employed to attain their ends (for example, by deserting the camp of the conquered general in order to make the most offers of service to the conqueror help us understand the Jews' repulsion for this dynasty of usurpers.

But Herod the Great was not lacking in genius; in fact, he was a man with a powerful intellect. As the last of the Hasmonaeans, Antigonus was besieging Herod in Jerusalem (he was convinced that his minister had betrayed him), Herod managed to escape to Rome and be declared king of Judea by Anthony. He was solemnly crowned in Rome (39 BC) but had to reconquer his kingdom by force. In 37 BC, he took Jerusalem, stopped the looting and reinstated the cult. Eighteen years later he began the construction of a magnificent temple (winter of 20 to 19 BC). This was the temple that became famous throughout the Orient and caused the admiration of Jesus' disciples. The date its construction was begun makes it possible for us to establish the date of Jesus' first "official" visit to Jerusalem. He appeared in public for the first time in the capital during the Passover celebration. And in the midst of a discussion the Jews told Him, "It has taken 46 years to build this temple and will you raise it up in three days?" These words were uttered in the spring of AD 27. Thus we can place the beginning of Jesus' ministry in Galilee in AD 26.

Herod the Great reigned for 33 years, until 4 BC. During his reign Jesus was born. It is, of course, well known that the traditional chronology which places Jesus' birth in the year AD 1 is incorrect. Jesus was two or three years old when Herod the Great died, after having attempted to kill Him with the children of Bethlehem. This fact is very important, because the period following Herod's death was troubled by a series of attempts by pseudo-messiahs to seize political power, as we shall see in a following chapter. Jesus often referred to these tragic events of His childhood.

Returning to Herod, one must say that history leaves us a rather unjust picture of him. The first part of his reign had been very prosperous. A great admirer of Greek customs, he had an amphitheater built outside Jerusalem's gates, as well as a theater and a magnificent palace for himself within the city. During a famine, he had ordered food distributions for the poor. But his family was busy plotting against him. Herod became morbidly jealous and had his father-in-law, his mother-in-law, one of his ten wives, and three of his daughters executed one after the other. The monstrous cruelties that marked the end of his reign erased in the people's minds any recollection of the positive aspects of his character. His death was acclaimed as a deliverance.

7. The Crises in Palestinian Politics

Herod the Great's death in 4 BC caused an extremely serious succession of crises. The kings's will divided the kingdom between his three sons. Philip received the land beyond the Jordan (Batanea, Auranitis, and Trachonitis). Archelaus inherited Judea, Idumea, and Samaria, with the title of king; and Herod, called Antipas, received Galilee and Perea.

In Trachonitis, Philip, like Antipas, had received only the inferior title of tetrarch, but he was satisfied with it. His reign lasted until AD 34 without problems. When Jesus crossed the Sea of Galilee, He would go into this peaceful territory, whose population was a mixture of Jews and Gentiles.

In Judea, Archelaus' reign lasted only ten years and was filled with disturbances. After having tried to please the people, he executed three thousand Jews to suppress an insurrection. His brothers contested the validity of their father's will, which had made Archelaus king while they were only tetrarchs. Archelaus went to Rome as early as AD 4 to petition Augustus for royal investiture which the emperor granted him. But Jewish delegations hostile to the king repeatedly went to Rome and finally obtained his deposition. He was exiled to Vienna in Gaul in AD 6. [1]

By getting rid of Archelaus, the Jews had hoped to regain their independence. But as it turned out, the exact opposite happened. Augustus turned Judea and Samaria into Roman provinces and incorporated them with Syria, which at that time were under the authority of an imperial legate. He governed Judea by means of a procurator residing at Caesarea on the coast. We know the names of the procurators of Judea: Coponius, Valerius Gratus, Pontius Pilate (from AD 26 to 36) and Marcellus, who succeeded each other until AD 37. After Marcellus, from AD 37 to 44, the Jewish kingdom was temporarily reunited under a grandson of Herod the Great, Agrippa I. Having spent his childhood in Rome, Agrippa had become a good friend of Caligula, who was to become emperor in AD 37.

At Agrippa's death, Judea again became a procuratorial province. Fadus, Cumanus, Felix, Festus, Albinus, and finally Gessius Florus succeeded each other quite rapidly. Under this last procurator the great revolt of AD 66 broke out, which was to cause the destruction of Jerusalem.

In Galilee, Herod Antipas, also a tetrarch and contemporary of Jesus, is closely tied to the gospel story. In honor of Tiberius, he had built a city on the Lake of Gennesaret, which he named Tiberias. He forced settlers to come and live there and turned it into his capital. Its being built on a cemetery was considered a sacrilege by pious Jews. They would not set foot in it.

During a trip to Rome, Herod Antipas met his niece Herodias, who was the wife of one of his numerous brothers, Philip Boetos (not Philip the Tetrarch). Antipas repudiated his first wife, daughter of the king Aretas of Arabia, and married Herodias. This insult to his father-in-law set off a war, which Antipas eventually lost.

John the Baptist, who was then preaching near the Jordan, had enough courage to reproach the king for a marriage that was considered incestuous. The gospel narrative of Herodias' vengeance and of John the Baptist's death is well known. The historian Josephus recorded another version of it. According to him, Antipas had John the Baptist executed because his preaching endangered the throne. It was a threat to the social and political order as was also later the case with Jesus' preaching.

In AD 37 at the time of the accession of Agrippa I to the throne of Judea, the ambitious Herodias became infuriated after seeing Agrippa receive a higher title than her husband and incited her husband also to go to Rome in order to obtain the title of king. Unhappily for Antipas, Caligula decided to send him into exile in Lugdunum in Spain. Historians are debating whether this Lugdunum was a town in the Pyrenees, near today's Spanish border, or whether it was the Lugdunum of Gaul (Lyon). In view of this latter possibility, Josephus may have made a geographical error.

In order to understand the rest of our study we must briefly recall how the Roman administration functioned in Palestine. The Roman procurator was a minor official. He depended upon the legates who succeeded each other in Syria: Quirinius, Saturninus, Varus, Vitellius, Petronius, Marsus, Longinus, Quadratus. When disturbances occurred in Judea, the procurator who headed only a small number of troops had to call upon the legate. Pilate, the sixth procurator, succeeded Valerius Gratus in AD 26 and held office for six years. We will describe the troubles that faced his term of office in a following chapter. After having been denounced before the legate of Syria,

Pilate was finally removed from office in AD 36 and sent back to Rome to justify himself. Some authors say he was executed. Eusebius in his *Church History* claims he was exiled to Vienna in Gaul. Apparently Gaul was destined to become a harbor for all the unsympathetic characters of the Gospels: Archelaus, Antipas, Pilate!

The political regime which the Romans imposed upon their Galilean protectorate and Judean province was actually not as harsh as it seemed at first. In theory, they respected the religion of a conquered people. Thus, religious services took place as usual at the temple in Jerusalem. A sacrifice to Yahweh was offered daily in the name of the emperor. The Roman cohort which resided in the Antonia tower, to the north of the temple, was even responsible for guarding the sacerdotal garb, because the Jews often quarreled over the succession of the high priest. Since the end of the Hasmonaean dynasty, the high priest was no longer king, but with the members of the Sanhedrin, he continued to judge the people according to the law of Moses. Though civil and religious laws were one and the same for the Jews, the Sanhedrin's power had been limited by the Romans. In particular they had taken away its right to pronounce and carry out capital punishment.

Roman garrisons occupied the land, but except for periods of mutiny, they seem to have had rare but correct contacts with the Jews.

However, Palestine remained one of the most restless provinces in the empire. At the time of Herod's accession to the throne in AD 37, Palestine was still, along with Egypt, the richest country along the eastern Mediterranean. Herod covered not only Jerusalem but Palestine as well with his generosities! He was a construction maniac, comparable to Louis XIV centuries later in France. He erected the Herodium, his fabulous fortress and retreat near Bethlehem in Palestine. The cities of Antipatris, Phasaelis Sebaste (Samaria), and especially Caesarea, the old Tower of Strato, were completely rebuilt. Such building projects were expensive and Herod had overburdened the people with taxes. Galilee was hit the hardest because it was much richer agriculturally than the rocky hills of Judea. Both Palestine's impoverishment and the reawakening of messianic hopes were important factors in the numerous revolts that shook the country during Jesus' youth.

The Jews were already heavily taxed. First, they paid the temple tax, expected of everyone; then the firstfruits and the tithe established by Moses to feed the sons of Levi. The Levites (approximately 20,000) took turns going to Jerusalem to serve in the temple, but the tithe rarely found its way to their homes. The high clergy appropriated it by force and thus grew richer. The low clergy often sided with the poor, as did the low clergy in France centuries later at the beginning of the Revolution. This explains the priest Zechariah's style of piety and the family setting into which Jesus was born (Luke 1 and 2).

Besides the tithe for the clergy, the Jews also paid another tithe for the poor which was again often embezzled by the high clergy.

All these taxes were prescribed by Jewish law. To these the Roman occupants added the tribute or tax to Caesar. This unpopular tax included a land tax, a poll tax paid directly to the employees of the imperial treasury, and indirect taxes collected by the toll-gatherers. Palestine was subdivided into fiscal provinces whose revenue went to rich intendants, who practiced absenteeism quite regularly. By means of their agents, these individuals pressured the population into paying much more than the toll required by Rome. They had under their orders a large number of Jews whose offices kept an eye on the roads, bridges, borders, and ports of the Lake of Galilee. These customs officers also grew rich at the expense of the people who hated and rejected them.

It has been calculated that approximately 60 or 70 percent of the peasant's income eventually fell into the hands of various collectors and creditors. Though loans with interest were theoretically forbidden by the Jewish law, the taxpayers who were unable to pay became victims of the userers who would impose on them annual interest rates as high as 24 percent.[2]

Within a few decades, small and middle-sized plots of land had disappeared, whereas the properties owned by the temple and the imperial crown grew beyond proportion. The administration of these lands was in the hands of dishonest intendants for whom the ex-owners had to work as slaves.

The religious custom that ordered all fields to lie fallow during the seventh year also contributed to the impoverishment of the land. Rarely, however, did a Jew ever remain a slave. His closest kinsman, his *goel*, usually sacrificed in order to pay his debts and set him free.[3] Thus, in Jesus' time, everybody was familiar with the concept of ransom or "redemption." But the system of redemption did not affect the Jews who had been sentenced to the mines or the galleys following revolts which had been harshly suppressed.

Driven to misery, many peasants abandoned their land and joined bands of robbers that survived by pillage and lived in caves in the mountains. The Herods and Roman procurators constantly had to suppress new revolts.

It is very difficult to determine to what extent these highway robbers who attacked peasants were common law criminals or patriots with the dream of freeing Palestine from the Roman yoke. In any case, they were forced to find, more or less legally, means of survival in the desert. Barabbas and the two robbers between whom Jesus was crucified were probably patriots of this type. This explains the bitter irony of one of the men hanging beside Jesus, "Are you not the Christ? Save yourself and us." He could not forgive Jesus for not having taken the leadership of the Palestinian underground!

Whatever the case may be, the rapid impoverishment of Palestine and Galilee in particular helps us to understand the extraordinary response Jesus' jubilean proclamations found among the poor and the outcast.

John the Baptist, who was baptizing near the Jordan River, had opened the way for the messianic revolution by proclaiming, "Prepare the way of the Lord; make his paths straight. Every valley shall be filled, every mountain and hill shall be made low. . . . He who has two coats, let him share with him who has one and he who has food, let him do likewise."

John the Baptist told the tax collectors, "Collect no more than is appointed you" by the royal or Roman administration. He said to the soldiers of Herod or of the occupation who probably accompanied the tax collectors on their rounds, "Rob no one by violence or by false accusation and be content with your wages." With these exhortations he was already announcing the imminence of a Jubilee.

8. Jewish Social Groups and Political Parties

There are eight groups to which the Gospels continually refer.

1. The High Priests. Jerusalem and the temple were at the heart of the Jewish nation. The great Sanhedrin of Jerusalem met on the hill of the temple and was controlled by a truly aristocratic dynasty. Annas remained high priest for approximately eight years, from AD 8 to 16, but after him five of his sons and his son-in-law held the office and apparently filled it under his supervision. Annas was proud of this situation. (Caiaphas, his son-in-law, was high priest from AD 18 to 36.) Throughout the Gospels the name of Annas is always associated with that of Caiaphas.

2. The Sadducees. Both Annas and Caiaphas belonged to the Sadducean party, which was said to have been started by a certain Zadok, high priest of the temple at the time of Solomon. The Sadducees had a political mind. They did not share the Pharisees' aversion for everything foreign. Under the Hasmonaean kings they had favored moderation. At the time of Jesus they were conservatives. They were suspicious of anything that changed the religious customs. They did not believe in the resurrection of the dead, which was not taught in the Old Testament. They favored a compromise with Rome and were alarmed by the unrest caused by Jesus' revolutionary speeches. The Sanhedrin that condemned Jesus was controlled by the Sadducees, whose members came exclusively from the upper classes of society.

3. The Galilean Crowd. The Sadducean spirit prevailed in Jerusalem and in all of Judea. Authentic Judeans were disdainful of the populations around Israel's borders: the peoples who lived beyond the Jordan who were strongly influenced by pagan customs, the Samaritans, and also the Galileans.

It is generally not known that the Galilean population did not belong to the "pure race." During the Babylonian exile, Phoenicians, Arabs, and Greeks had taken over the land. Once back from exile, some Jews mingled with them. The Judeans referred to Galilee as "a district of Gentiles." They scorned the Galileans, which they classified among the *Am-haerez*, "people of the earth," and forbade their daughters to marry them.[1] Furthermore, the Galilean language was coarse. For such reasons Nathanael, the Judean, asked after having heard that Philip had found the Messiah and that the Messiah was Galilean, "Can anything good come out of Nazareth?" When speaking of the *Am-haerez* the Pharisees would say, "This crowd, who do not know the law, are accursed" (John 7:49).

But even though the Galileans were naive, they were certainly more enthusiastic and thus more inclined to receive the gospel than the Judean aristocrats. Contrary to their reputation, they were far from being illiterate. Each of their cities had its synagogue where the law and the prophets were read and commented upon. As a whole the Jews, to whom rabbis taught the law in numerous schools, were the least ignorant of the peoples of antiquity.

4. The Scribes or "Lawyers." They had considerable influence in the synagogues where they explained the law. At the time of Jesus, the rabbis merely commented upon the law in the light of "the tradition of the fathers." As traditionalists everywhere, they felt called to justify their opinions by quoting the most famous rabbis of preceding generations: men like Hillel, a liberal mind, whose decisions sometimes foreshadowed the Sermon on the Mount; or his rival, Shammai, whose strictness and aggressiveness met the requirements of the most narrow-minded.

5. The Pharisees. The lawyers, who should not be confused with the Pharisees, did, however, generally belong to the Pharisaic party. Some of them, the disciples of Hillel, were sympathetic toward Jesus. A certain Simon, called "the Pharisee," invited Jesus to dinner. Nicodemus came to him by night. Joseph of Arimathea, a member of the Sanhedrin and probably also a Pharisee, offered him his tomb. The Pharisee Gamaliel, one of Hillel's grandsons, a member of the Sanhedrin and a lawyer, tried to stop the persecutions against the first Christians. He was the teacher of the future Apostle Saul of Tarsus, also of Pharisaic background.

This clarification is necessary because today the term "Pharisee" has taken on a pejorative connotation. In reality, no Jewish party was closer to Jesus' thinking. Having inherited the austerity of the first Maccabees, the Pharisees fought the dissolving influence of Hellenism under the Hasmonaeans. When the Hasmonaeans' regime ended they focused their activities on religious and moral reform rather than on politics. They were awaiting Israel's deliverance and some of them were even extremists with Zealot tendencies, who favored armed revolt. But the majority of them concentrated their energies on the scrupulous observance of the Mosaic law. Their influence dominated the synagogues, where they taught the people the strict observance of the Sabbath, the fasts, the purifications, the prayers, the tithes, the alimentary and sabbatical ordinances.

In their attempt to preserve for God the purity of the chosen people, the Pharisees had unfortunately imprisoned the Jews in a series of negative prescriptions which suffocated living faith and charity. But above all, their critical spirit was destructive. The moral censorship they practiced toward everybody drove not only the prostitutes, the drunkards, and the gluttons away from God, but also the non-Jews, whose contact they fled to keep from defiling their own ritual purity. These Gentiles included the Samaritans, Greeks, Syrians, Phoenicians, and all the Jews who collaborated with the Gentiles to earn their livelihood, such as the publicans, toll-gatherers, and Herodians.

The narrowness of their puritanism, their way of confusing faith in God and external observances, and their neglect of the true riches of the heart caused Jesus to dissociate Himself from the Pharisees. However, there was something tragic about their misunderstandings, because Jesus' faith generally corresponded with the Pharisees' piety. Both had a fervent confidence in God, an expectation of messianic times and hope in the resurrection of the dead. This was the culmination of the Jews' search during the preceding centuries. From it stemmed the authority of the Pharisees over the Jews. Had their pride been moved by Jesus' appeal, the history of the world would have been different. Unfortunately, they were the group which bore the primary responsibility for His failure and condemnation!

6. The Essenes. This group which stood to the right of the Pharisees has received considerable attention since the discovery of their famous manuscripts and the remains of their convent at Qumran by the Dead Sea.

The Essenes' theology resembled that of the Pharisees. They too believed in the resurrection of the dead and individual salvation, but they formed a closed community of which one became a member by abandoning one's possessions.

The Essenes remained celibate, were charitable toward the poor, and adopted the children of others. They did not take oaths except for the one they swore at the end of their probationary period.

They did agricultural work exclusively and rejected all professions which would have meant compromising with the world. Their monastic discipline included silence and obedience to the superiors they elected. Both before and after meals they frequently practiced ablutions that

had a sacred character. They taught and practiced universal priest-
hood and established a network of friends from city to city. A travel-
ing Essene was received at no expense by his brothers wherever he
went. The Essenes practiced nonviolence up to a certain point. They
submitted to the authorities, which they considered to be instituted
by God. When they traveled, however, they carried weapons as protection against robbers.

The Dead Sea Scrolls contain certain documents called *The Zado-
kite Document, Commentary on the Book of Habakkuk,* and *The
Manual of Discipline* that alternate historical narratives and poetic
passages with monastic rules, some of which were already known because of Josephus' descriptions. Among the most remarkable documents
are a series of hymns of thanksgiving written in the first person in
the style of David's psalms. These hymns were probably composed by a
"Teacher of Righteousness," a personage greatly influenced by the
Psalms and Isaiah and convinced of his prophetic vocation of suffering
and victory over merciless enemies.

Indeed, there was much tension between the Essenes and the temple clergy. A "Wicked High Priest," who, according to the Dead Sea
Scrolls, had rejected and persecuted the "Teacher of Righteousness"
(founder of the order?), was probably responsible for this split. The
Essenes offered no ritual sacrifices at the temple and considered
justice and temperance to be the only true sacrifices God requests.
In this respect, their teachings come close to those of the Old Testament prophets and of Jesus Himself.

The manuscript passages that talk about the "Wicked High Priest"
describe him as a person who persecuted the "Teacher of Righteousness" "in order to confuse him by a display of violent temper, desir-
ing to exile him, . . . [and who] wrought abominable works . . .
defiled the sanctuary of God . . . plundered the property of the
needy." Such a description seems to refer to the time of the high
priest Jason, whose errors aroused the Maccabean revolt. Some historians have stressed some resemblances between the "Teacher of
Righteousness" and Jesus. However, the manuscripts do not give the
death of the "Teacher of Righteousness" a redemptive character.
Their silence on this point seems to exclude the possibility of His
being a Christ prematurely.

Another document called *The War of the Sons of Light and the
Sons of Darkness* tells in symbolic form of the Essenes' messianic expectations and the supreme battle between God and Belial (Satan),

which will bring about the final victory of the Sons of Light, God's allies.

These war descriptions seem to imply that some young Essenes, tired of the nonviolence practiced by their order, may have joined the ranks of the Jewish Zealots that engaged in armed rebellion. They thought the hour of the final struggle between Yahweh and the Gentiles had come. The Essenes' participation in the revolt of 66 would explain the destruction of their convent at Qumran by the Romans and the disappearance of their order after AD 70.

John the Baptist's austerity, his preaching in the desert (where he lived as the Essenes did), the baptism of purification he practiced, all seem to indicate Essene influence. Some people have seen in him an Essene who, for some unknown reason, was separated from the Qumran convent to preach a "baptism of repentance," unique and final, in opposition to the perpetual ablutions practiced by monks of the Dead Sea.

Some of the instructions given by Jesus to His disciples recall Essene ordinances. Their influence on Him (probably through John the Baptist) cannot be denied. However, there are many profound differences. Jesus did not encourage His disciples to lead a monastic life. On the contrary, He made them messengers, preachers, and apostles. Jesus more radically nonviolent than the Essenes, even forbidding His disciples to carry a stick in order to defend themselves from robbers during their travels.

The idea of a final battle between the Sons of Light and the Sons of Darkness — a very tempting idea for the Jews of Jesus' time who expected a Messiah[2] — can be found neither in Jesus' teachings nor in the teachings of the apostles. It is not taught either by the Old Testament prophecies or by Revelation, where God's angels alone — not the saints — will be called to fight the demon. The New Testament writers are truly nonviolent men who are expecting the kingdom of God from God alone.

7. The Herodians. This group was not very large. They were the employees and the supporters of Herod Antipas' government. We have already mentioned this king's unpopularity throughout Galilee.

In the Gospels, we see the Herodians making an alliance with the Pharisees to denounce and execute Jesus, although they were traditional enemies of each other. However, one Herodian, Joanna, the wife of Chuza, Herod's steward, provided for Him with her means. Herod himself was more superstitious than he was religious. He feared the prophetic power of John the Baptist and Jesus while simultaneously trying to get rid of them because of the danger their revolutionary message represented for his throne.

8. The Samaritans. Everything has been said about the Samaritans. Thus we will only refer to them briefly. They were not of Jewish origin. They had come from Mesopotamia as colonists to replace the Jews at the time of the Babylonian Exile and had adopted the worship of Yahweh. Upon their return from Exile, the Jews forbade them to participate in the reconstruction of the temple. It is not known when they built the rival temple on Mount Gerizim. At any rate, Samaria was always an obstacle between Judea and Galilee for the Jews. Border incidents were not rare occurrences.

The Samaritans' presence made it difficult for the Herods and the Roman procurators to keep the peace in Palestine.

Josephus tells of three characteristic events:

Under Coponius' administration, Samaritans secretly entered Jerusalem and dumped human bones under the temple's porticoes. From that time on Samaritans were forbidden to enter the temple, now guarded with more vigilance.

Under Pilate, the Samaritans took up arms and Pilate massacred a large number of them on Mount Gerizim.

After Jesus' death, a Jew on the way to Jerusalem for the celebration of the feast of the unleavened bread, was assassinated by the inhabitants of Ginae, a small Samaritan town. Upon hearing the news in Jerusalem the Jews spontaneously rushed to Samaria and massacred the inhabitants of the border towns which they then set on fire. It was necessary for the leading figures of Jerusalem and the governor Cumanus to intervene before peace could be reestablished. All the individuals whom Cumanus arrested were crucified. Eighteen other Jews were decapitated.

Facts such as these must be recalled in order to measure the scope of Jesus' efforts to reconcile the Jews and the Samaritans. (See Appendixes.)

9. The Jewish Nationalist Movement

The preceding chapters have given us a relatively peaceful view of Palestinian history at the time of Jesus. In reality, the Jewish people were seriously engaged in a life-and-death battle for the survival of their national and religious vocation. They were resisting with all their strength the temptations of gradual assimilation by the Greco-Roman world.

The traditional religion of the Romans and the Greeks was already completely decadent. The gods of Rome, who were rather rugged characters, had been neglected in favor of the more subtle Egyptian, Greek, or Oriental divinities with which they were constantly being confused. The educated people no longer considered these divinities to be symbols of one unique and unknowable God. Syncretism was overcoming the fanaticism of preceding centuries. Greek philosophy took upon itself the reconciliation of all the extremes. Philo of Alexandria, also known as the Jewish Plato, was attempting to harmonize Platonic philosophy and the Old Testament. By writing his *Jewish Wars* and *Jewish Antiquities* in Greek, Josephus was bringing Judaism in line with the wisdom in fashion during the first century.

Emperor worship, through which Rome was to try to unify so many diverse religions and give a sense of duty to a crumbling world, was only beginning to form. Rome showed itself tolerant and granted to the peoples of the empire the right to practice their particular cult so long as they agreed to venerate Caesar. But in Rome, even the crowd practiced Oriental mysteries aimed at purifying the soul from sins. Among these, the cult of Mithra was a rival of beginning Christianity.

Judaism had also spread throughout the entire Mediterranean world, where it had made many proselytes. In many cities, such as Alexandria, Damascus, Antioch, Ephesus, Corinth, and even Rome, Judaism had formed sizable communities distinct from the rest of the population. People reproached them for their narrow fanaticism. Local custom prescribed that all the inhabitants share the task of administration and offer sacrifices to the local gods. But the faithful Jews intended to keep their own customs and could not fully participate in the life of the community, bound as they were by their law. For example, they refused to offer libations in honor of the gods. The first Christians merely imitated them on this point.

When friction occurred between the local authorities and the Jews, the latter usually appealed to Caesar to assert their rights. The emperor was wise enough to grant them exemptions and privileges: the right to stop work and to hold gatherings on the Sabbath, the right to worship freely, not to participate in pagan ceremonies, not to pay certain taxes. However, many Jews who belonged to respectable families had acquired Roman citizenship and this raised yet another problem. Rome's subjects were not forced to serve in the army; they could enlist in the auxiliary troops if they so desired. But the Roman citizens had the privilege and the duty to serve in the legions. Thus, by becoming Roman citizens the Jews were binding themselves to military service. However, the practice of the Sabbath and of the alimentary ordinances could not be reconciled. Those among the Jews who were Roman citizens then asked Rome to exempt them from military service. This exemption was granted by Julius Caesar in 47 or 44 BC. By the same edict, Caesar forbade Roman magistrates to raise auxiliary troops in Jewish territory and also exempted the Jews from the tribute during sabbatical years, that is, every seven years.

Some historians have questioned the authenticity of this edict, whose complete text is recorded by Josephus along with some local decrees concerning its application. These historians point out the fact that Jews could be found both in the armies of Herod and in the armies of the surrounding kings. Their arguments are, however, rather weak. No doubt some impious Jews did enroll voluntarily in the king's armies. It is also evident that some patriotic Jews thought it necessary to take up arms in order to free their country. But it is also just as clear that no faithful Jew could perform his military service either in the Roman legions or in the auxiliary troops because of his religious beliefs and practices.

This is probably why Jesus never had to tell His disciples to refuse military service. The silence of the Gospels on this point is easy to explain if one remembers that Jesus' disciples were not Roman citizens. The problem did not concern them. Even those who might have had Roman citizenship would have been exempted by the imperial edict. All pious Jews were conscientious objectors for ritual reasons and Rome treated conscientious objectors with more tolerance than some of our modern democracies!

But Caesar's edict was not always applied with equal success. The

Gentiles were jealous of the *Diaspora* Jews who formed privileged clans in the cities where they lived. When some massacres took place in Alexandria, Philo went to Rome in AD 39 to obtain Caesar's protection.

Under Tiberius, at the time of Jesus, the Jewish population of Rome was thrown out of the city. "The consuls drafted four thousand men for military service," says Josephus, "and sent them to the island of Sardinia; but they penalized a good many of them who refused to serve for fear of breaking the Jewish law" (*Jewish Antiquities*, XVIII, III, S). The theoretical exemption granted to the Jewish "conscientious objectors" by Julius Caesar was not always conceded by his successors.

The situation was most serious not in the *Diaspora* but in Palestine itself, where the Jews constituted a majority. The slightest infringement upon their religious customs could trigger a revolt.

It is hard to know who, among the revolutionary leaders who succeeded each other in Palestine, actually claimed to be the Messiah. We need only recall the intensity of the messianic expectations and the uncertainty of the Messiah's attributes. For the Jews politics and religion were one and the same thing; he who tried to become king was also claiming the title of Messiah. The Hasmonaeans, the legitimate kings, had held the title of prince of Israel and of high priest. The expected Messiah was to be a legitimate king of David's dynasty, both a military religious leader and a restorer of the purity of worship and of national independence.

At the end of Herod the Great's reign, during Jesus' early childhood, messianic agitation began to manifest itself publicly. Despite the uncertainty of dates, it seems that the census by Quirinius (Luke 2:2), the legate of Syria at that time, was the first event to set off an outbreak of resistance. For the Jews, a census was an impious undertaking. Its aim, for the Romans, was to set the tax base. At this time, the Romans required the Jews to take an oath to Augustus. But a pious Jew could not bind himself by an oath. The Essenes absolutely refused all oaths, and Jesus later also forbade the same to His disciples. In the period to which we are referring, six thousand Pharisees refused to swear an oath to Augustus. This act set off a real wave of civil disobedience.

Several years later another event occurred, probably during the time when Jesus' parents were yet in Egypt. Herod was sick. The rumor of his death began to circulate. Herod had placed above the portal of the temple a golden eagle, which constituted a scandal for the Jews since all images, busts, or representation of any living thing were forbidden. Following the advice of two very prominent lawyers, some young men were lowered from the roof of the temple with ropes and in broad daylight, at a time when many people were present in the temple, they demolished the golden eagle with their axes. Forty instigators of the attempt were arrested and brought before the king who had them executed.

Herod died shortly thereafter. Before dying, however, realizing that the Jews would rejoice at his death, he ordered that a sizable number of Judeans be arrested and put to death as soon as he had died, "so that all the families of Judea will weep over me, whether they want to or not!"

According to Herod's will, Archelaus, one of his sons, became king of Judea. We have already mentioned the political agitation which marked his accession to power, but it is necessary to review these events in some detail in order to bring out their religious background.

As soon as he inherited the throne, Archelaus was faced with a serious problem. The inhabitants of Jerusalem were demanding exemplary punishments for the high priest and the administration officials who had been too docile toward Herod's orders and had permitted the executions of the lawyers and youth for destroying the eagle. As Archelaus hesitated an angry crowd gathered. In panic, the king sent out against them his entire army and cavalry. Three thousand Jews were massacred. The others fled to the mountains.

Some time later, Antipas and Archelaus sailed for Rome to seek the emperor's arbitration in the matter of Herod's succession. It is uncertain how long Archelaus' trip lasted. Transportation was very slow at the time and Josephus' chronology is difficult to interpret. Most likely the events we will now recount took place throughout Archelaus' reign, over a period of ten years, from 4 BC to AD 6.

Since Jesus was born around 6, or 7 BC, He lived in a very troubled time until the age of twelve, and its memories certainly influenced his thought.

While Archelaus was in Rome, Varus, legate of Syria, was returning to Antioch after having put down the uprising. He had left in Jerusalem the equivalent of one Roman legion, six thousand men. He had also left in Jerusalem Sabinus (the procurator of Caesar Augustus' possessions) and had ordered him to take the inventory of Herod's wealth.

Sabinus turned out to be unskilled and dishonest and relentlessly undertook the search for the king's treasures. Prompted by an insatiable cupidity, he took the Jewish citadels by force. The pilgrims en route to Jerusalem for the Pentecost organized themselves in three columns and besieged Sabinus and his legion in the royal palace. The porticoes of the temple became the scene of a desperate battle during which the Jews tried to crush the Romans with stones as the Romans seized the treasures of the temple after having set the porticoes on fire and massacred many Jews. Sabinus thus appropriated four hundred talents for himself.

The Jewish troops of Archelaus had first cooperated with the Romans to maintain "legal" order, but when they saw the violation of the temple, they were scandalized and sided with the insurrectionists. In no time, the land had been put to fire and the sword. The messianic expectations of Israel were aroused. In the disorder of the years that followed, men appeared here and there who claimed the title of "liberator," carried by the Maccabees in the past.

Before examining these so-called messiahs, let us recount how the war ended.

Varus was alerted by Sabinus and returned to Palestine with two other legions and their four "wings" of cavalry with them. He came to the aid of the besieged legion in Jerusalem. In all, the Romans had twenty thousand well-trained men. The ten thousand Jews gathered in the mountains did not stand a chance of victory over such an army.

Then Achiab, Herod's cousin, intervened. He succeeded in convincing the ten thousand Jews that their venture was senseless and stood no chance of success. The Jews were wise enough to follow his advice and they capitulated. Varus proved himself generous. He set most of them free, except those members of the royal house who had taken part in the insurrection. As for the people who still tried to resist, Varus treated them with utmost cruelty: two thousand of them were crucified. He also ordered the destruction of Emmaus by fire, a small town where Roman soldiers had been massacred.

It is quite possible that this event was told to Jesus as a child and convinced Him of the futility of the armed insurrection attempts against Rome. When He later told the parable, which might be called "the parable of prudence," He expressed it thus, "What king, going to encounter another king in war, will not sit down first and take counsel whether he is able with ten thousand men to meet him who comes against him with twenty thousand? And if not, while the other is

yet a great way off, he sends an embassy and asks terms of peace"
(Luke 14:31, 32).

o   o   o

It was also during Jesus' youth that the most violent nationalistic
party of all, the Zealot party, was organized. Its founder was a famous revolutionary, Judas the Galilean (or Gaulanite), who with the Pharisee Zadok preached disobedience and refusal to pay taxes to Rome.

A number of violations of the Holy City and of the temple took
place so that the Jews feared a repetition of the sacrilegious act which
had provoked the rebellion of Mattathias in 168 BC.

Judas was the son of a certain Ezechias whom Herod the Great
had subdued with difficulty. He asserted himself as a capable leader.
His first deed was the ransacking of the arsenal at Sepphoris in Galilee, a royal city a few kilometers north of Nazareth. Supplied with all
the arms he and his men had seized, he had proclaimed himself king.
"This school," says Josephus, "agrees in all other respects with the
opinions of the Pharisees except that they have a passion for liberty
that is almost unconquerable, since they are convinced that God alone
is their Leader and Master. They think little of submitting to death in
unusual forms . . . if only they may avoid calling any man master."
This is why they refused to pay tribute to Caesar. [1]

No one knows what happened to Judas the Gaulanite in the end,
but it is known that neither Antipas nor the Romans ever completely
succeeded in eliminating the Zealots. Twenty years after Judas, there
were still a few around. Jesus chose some of His disciples from among
them.

After Judas' death, there were other pretenders to the throne. In
Perea, Simon, one of Herod's ex-slaves, was proclaimed king and
burned the palace in Jericho.

After him, Athronges took the title of king and gathered a large
crowd around him. He and his four brothers "applied themselves vigorously to slaughtering the Romans and the king's men" (Josephus,
Jewish Antiquities, XVII, X, 7).

The Book of Acts, which mentions Judas the Galilean, also refers
to a certain Theudas, [2] who also tried to stir up the people. It is
noteworthy that when the famous Gamaliel, the Apostle Paul's teacher,
referred to Theudas and Judas the Galilean before the Sanhedrin,
he compared them with Peter and John, who were also accused of

sedition. In the eyes of the Sanhedrin, the first Christians were undoubtedly comparable to the patriots who attempted to deliver Israel.

Several years after Jesus' death, the Zealots changed their tactics, went underground, and reappeared under the name of "Sicarii." Concealing daggers under their clothes, they mixed with the crowds during religious feasts and struck down the Jews they suspected of collaboration. "The first to be assassinated by them was Jonathan, the high priest; after his death there were numerous murders daily. The panic created was more alarming than the calamity itself — everyone, as on the battlefield, hourly expecting death. Men kept watch at a distance on their enemies and would not trust even their friends when they approached. Yet even while their suspicions were aroused and they were on their guard, they still fell, so swift were the conspirators and so crafty in eluding detection." [3]

The Zealots and the Sicarii were not the only movements of this kind! "Besides these, there arose another body of villains with purer hands but with more impious intentions. . . . Deceivers and imposters under the pretence of divine inspiration fostering revolutionary changes, they led [the multitude] out into the desert under the belief that God would there give them tokens of deliverance.

"A still worse blow was dealt at the Jews by the Egyptian false prophet. A charlatan who had gained for himself the reputation of a prophet, this man appeared in the country, collected a following of about thirty thousand dupes, and led them by a circuitous route from the desert to the mount called the Mount of Olives. From there, he proposed to force an entrance into Jerusalem and after overpowering the Roman garrison, to set himself up as tyrant of the people. . . . His attack was anticipated by Felix . . . the Egyptian escaped with a few of his followers; most of his force were killed or taken prisoners; the remainder dispersed. . . ." [4]

The Book of Acts mentions this Egyptian. After having arrested Paul during a demonstration in the temple, a Roman tribune thought he had caught the Egyptian: "Do you know Greek?" he asked Paul. "Are you not the Egyptian, then, who recently stirred up a revolt and led the four thousand men of the Assassins out into the wilderness?" (Acts 21:38).

It was in the midst of such turmoil that Jesus' ministry took place. A burning desire for ritual purity and a passionate messianic hope were little by little carrying the people toward the final revolt. It broke out in AD 66, after the procurator Gessius Florus had crucified many Jews to repress the growing restlessness. The intent of this book is, however, not to describe the gradual fall of Jewish messianism into the violence that caused the destruction of Jerusalem. Our aim is to show that another current was also emerging.

10. The Movement of Nonviolent Resistance

Josephus, in his two works, *The Jewish Wars* and *Jewish Antiquities*, vindicates his own behavior at the time of the revolt of AD 66. He recounts how he was caught up in the collective madness and became the insurrectionary governor of Galilee but later disavowed the nationalist movement and joined the Romans beneath the walls of a besieged Jerusalem. He then tells how he challenged the Zealots to give up and rely on Rome's clemency. However, they did not listen to him.

Josephus was nothing more than a false pacifist. The servile tone of his speeches is very displeasing to our ears. His arguments can be summarized as follows: "Since we are weaker, let us not remain obstinate but rather make a compromise with Rome." In France we still recall the painful memories of the collaborators' words who advised capitulation to Hitler with similar arguments. The attitude of some of the other Jewish contemporaries of Jesus was a quite different one because they used a nonviolent resistance. It is difficult to know whether Jesus was influenced by them or whether He inspired them. But it is known with certainty that for fifteen years, from the beginning of Pilate's rule until the end of the proconsulary regime in Judea AD 26 to 41, the Jews seem to have temporarily given up combating violence with violence. Pontius Pilate, however, was not a particularly tender governor. [1]

Immediately after his arrival in Judea in AD 26, a few months before Jesus began His ministry, Pilate made the mistake of bringing into Jerusalem several military ensigns bearing the emperor's effigy. This was a serious offense to the religious customs of the Jews who forbade any representation of the human form. Once they noticed these images, the Jews gathered together, went to Caesarea and begged Pilate to remove the ensigns from Jerusalem. As Pilate refused, they initiated what today we would call a nonviolent demonstration intended to make him change his mind: they lay down on the ground and stayed there for five days and nights.

The next day, Pilate took his seat on his tribunal in the large stadium and called the people together as if he were intending to answer them. At a given signal, his armed troops were to surround the Jews. When they saw these troops massed around them in three rows, the Jews remained silent. Then Pilate declared that they would be slaughtered if they refused to accept Caesar's images and motioned for the soldiers to unsheath their swords. But the Jews threw themselves to the ground together in tight rows, exposed their necks, and claimed they were ready to die rather than violate their faith. Astonished at the sight of such fervent religious zeal, Pilate ordered the ensigns to be immediately taken out of Jerusalem. Jewish resistance had borne its fruits.

Several years later, Pilate was building an aqueduct to Jerusalem and seized the treasure of the temple to finance its construction. This violation aroused much turmoil. To disperse the demonstration Pilate scattered "plain-clothed soldiers" in the crowd. At a given signal, they began to beat the crowd unmercifully, but the crowd offered no resistance. The people let themselves be massacred without panic or weakness.

A similar event took place three years after Pilate's dismissal. It is all the more striking because one can see in such a case how courageous nonviolent resistance can influence the adversary and how providential events, in this situation Caligula's death, can appear as God's response to acts of courage and faith.

Here is the story:

Caligula, Tiberius' successor, reigned only four years, but he was insane. He was the first among the emperors to demand worship as a god while yet alive. He awarded himself triumphs for imaginary victories and gave the title of consul to his horse. In AD 39, Caligula decided to send Petronius, the legate of Syria, to Jerusalem with three legions, to install one of his statues in the temple. To Jewish eyes, such a sacrilegious deed would have been the "abomination of the desolation," similar to the statue of Jupiter which Antiochus Epiphanes had once installed in the temple and whose recurrence had been announced by Jesus. A massive uprising was the only response to such a sacrilege. However, instead of taking up arms the Jews declared themselves ready to die in order to prevent this scandal. They organized something of a nationwide strike, stopped sowing their fields, and remained in Ptolemais before the legate's house for fifty days of passive resistance. Encouraged by their example, King Agrippa, a childhood friend of Caligula's, joined the intercessors. Upset and astounded by such unanimity, Petronius accepted, at the risk of his life, to intercede before Caligula. But Caligula was infuriated by his legate's disobedience and ordered him to commit suicide.

This is where Providence showed its hand. Because of strong west winds the fatal letter reached the governor 27 days after he had received, by another source, the news of the emperor's murder. Thus Petronius' life was saved. The Jews' nonviolent resistance won over to their cause both the king and the Roman governor himself and gained an unexpected victory without bloodshed.

To conclude the second part of this work, we shall summarize the various currents of opinion at the time of Jesus.

On the whole, three tendencies can be distinguished: the collaborators, the abstentionists, and the resistants.

Among the collaborators, the more prominent were the Herodians and the publicans, that is, those who served the occupation power and whose customs they had more or less adopted. They hellenized their language, clothes, entertainment, games, and customs; everything was done according to Greco-Roman fashion.

Among the collaborators, one should also mention the Sadducees and the majority of the Sanhedrin in Jerusalem. They were conservatives, the guardians of worship in the temple, and did not participate in the political and religious awakening of the people. They did not believe in the coming of the Messiah and were not expecting the reestablishment of the kingdom of Israel. They favored the adoption of a *modus vivendi* with the occupation forces.

Among the abstentionists one should mention the Essenes. They had left society to live in the Judean desert. As Sons of Light they put all their hope in the apocalyptic expectation of a final battle that would bring God's victory over the Sons of Darkness. Other people with a similar stance were probably numerous pietists or lawyers immersed in the artificial world of abstract discussions and fussy Pharisees concerned more with avoiding impure contacts than acting for the people.

The Jewish resistants were of three types. The first category of resistants opposed hellenization, and this implied refusal to offer pagan sacrifices, to hold administrative positions in local government, and to do military service. This time of resistance created ghettos in the Mediterranean cities.

The second form of resistance thrived in Israel itself. The Jewish people of Jerusalem and Galilee, with their piety and their devotion were awaiting Israel's deliverance. The Messiah was at the door. Rumors circulated: he is here, he is there; he is Judas the Galilean, he is John the Baptist, Jesus of Nazareth, Theudas the Egyptian prophet.

Some patriots proclaimed themselves king, retreated to the mountains and hid in the caves of the Judean desert, coming out only to ambush the Romans or assassinate the Jews who collaborated with the occupation forces. Some Pharisees followed their example and joined the final revolt in AD 66.

But there was yet a third type of resistant, who placed himself in the tradition of the great prophets and expected the coming of the "servant of the Lord," the "Prince of Peace," meek and humble of heart, the Founder of the kingdom of God on earth. To this group belong John the Baptist's parents, the priest Zechariah and his wife, Elizabeth; Mary, Jesus' mother, and Joseph, her husband; the prophetess Anna and the aged Simeon; and "all those who were looking for the deliverance of Jerusalem," as Luke describes their hope.

Could the religious faith, civic courage, and political realism that the prophets had exemplified be revived? What new prophet would be capable of leading his people toward a far-reaching reform of habits and consciences? Who would rid Judaism of its formalism and its rabbinical literalism and bring it back to its primitive purity? Who would lead a total revolution that would shake off internal slaveries as well as the foreign yoke? These are the questions Jesus answered by proclaiming Himself messianic King and Liberator without violence. It is not unlikely that the splendid movement which pushed the Jews to resist nonviolently Caligula's blasphematory orders nine years after Jesus' death was inspired by the first Christians who at that time already filled Jerusalem and infiltrated even the ranks of the Sanhedrin.

11. The Transformation* of an Election

This chapter attempts to show how Jesus' thought developed from Jewish premises, which were its source.

Even though we have been able to establish that Jesus' social and political program remained unchanged from His first appeals in Galilee to the period which preceded and followed His death, the Gospels depict an enlarging of His religious thought.

What was the nature of this transformation? Unlike the Essenes, Jesus remained faithful until the end to the Jewish form of worship celebrated in the temple at Jerusalem. Though He proclaimed along with the prophets that God delights in mercy and not in sacrifices, He did not, however, exclude sacrifices. "If you are offering your gift at the altar, and there remember that your brother has something against you, leave your gift there before the altar and go; first be reconciled with your brother, and then come and offer your gift," He says in the Sermon on the Mount. The particular genius of Jesus is manifest in this last sentence: He does not abolish the sacrifice, but enlarges its scope.

His attitude toward circumcision is the same. He does not abolish it, but compares it with a physical healing, thus giving it a more human and less ritualistic meaning. [1]

In the parable of the Good Samaritan, Jesus does not criticize the temple. But He does display a severe attitude toward the priests and Levites who were so confined to their dogmatic and ritualistic preoccupations that they ignored a fellowman wounded by the side of the road.

Until the end, Jesus regularly traveled to Jerusalem at the prescribed times to perform His religious duties in the temple, as did every other orthodox Jew.

The accusation mentioned during His trial: "This fellow said, 'I am

---

*Translator's Note: The literal translation of the French word would be "explosion," "shattering," or "bursting." The sense of this chapter is to show that this "explosion" was, however, not destructive but rather enlarged the scope of Jesus' thought beginning with the Jewish notion of election. For that reason I have suggested simply "transformation."

able to destroy the temple of God and to build it in three days,' " was founded on a misinterpretation and borders on absurdity. Certainly He had once said that the Son of Man was greater than the temple, and He had elsewhere prophesied that the temple would be destroyed and that "there [would] not be left here one stone upon another." However, in the tradition of the prophets, Jesus did not desire the destruction of the temple, but its purification. The day of His messianic entry into Jerusalem, His burning zeal for the temple incited Him to drive out the merchants. "My house shall be called a house of prayer; but you make it a den of robbers" and "he would not allow any one to carry anything through the temple" (Matthew 21:13; Mark 11:16).

All this seems to confirm the statement in Chapter I that Jesus, as a Jewish Messiah, wanted to reform the Jewish religion and understood the threefold (religious, social, political) revolution He had come to announce within the context of the Jewish people.

However, the course of events were to lead Him to enlarge His vision. Without ever softening His message or abandoning the concept of election, which characterizes Judaism, He let this election "explode" under the shock of new situations He had not yet encountered at the time He first presented His message.

Before describing this "explosion," let us recall the somewhat limited framework in which Jesus moved and worked at the beginning of His ministry.

1. Attitude Toward the Gentiles

The Jews thought that the descendants of Abraham would be a blessing to all people but that this blessing would necessarily come through the channel of the chosen people. Only after the conversion of the chosen people would non-Jewish nations learn the way to Jerusalem and also convert themselves to the worship of the true God. Jesus shared these views. When He sent His apostles in pairs, He gave them this order: "Go nowhere among the Gentiles." If we bear in mind that the Syrophoenician border was eighteen miles away from Capernaum and that the Syrophoenicians still worshiped, under a veneer of hellenism, such crude gods as Baal, Ashtoreth, and Melkart, the meaning of this command is absolutely unequivocal.

2. Attitude Toward the Samaritans

Jesus shared the Jewish opinions concerning the Samaritans. The Samaritan border was fifteen miles away from the Sea of Galilee. To go to Jerusalem, one had either to cross Samaria or take a lengthy detour along the Jordan or along the Mediterranean. Jesus traveled constantly by foot between Galilee and Jerusalem but, to our knowledge, He went through Samaria on only two occasions. In His first instructions to His disciples, He commanded them, "Enter no town of the Samaritans, but go rather to the lost sheep of the house of Israel."

3. Attitude Toward the Romans

Although none of Jesus' words concerning the Romans has been preserved, it is certain that He had no contact with them. Tiberias, the Greco-Roman city founded by Antipas in AD 17 (Jesus was then approximately 23 years old), was only nine miles away from Magdala, very close to the center of Jesus' activity. But He never set foot in Tiberias. When He went from the shores of the Lake of Galilee to the Jordan, He almost certainly bypassed this impure obstacle, as did all devout Jews.

4. Attitude Toward Women

If we leave the domain of religious and racial prejudices, we find in Jesus still one other reservation. It was not a Jewish custom to keep company with persons of the opposite sex. This is why His disciples were surprised when they found Him one day beside a well in conversation with a woman. Hadn't Jesus said in the Sermon on the Mount, "Every one who looks at a woman lustfully has already committed adultery with her in his heart. If your right eye causes you to sin, pluck it out and throw it away" (Matthew 5:28, 29). Such words reveal a tension which we find in yet another passage where He says: "There are eunuchs who have made themselves eunuchs for the sake of the kingdom of heaven. He who is able to receive this, let him receive it" (Matthew 19:12). Though the word "eunuch" should not be taken literally here, Jesus is certainly alluding to the voluntary celibacy He imposed on Himself in view of His ministry.

Jesus thus shared His people's views concerning non-Jews and women. But He learned from circumstances and found new solutions to the new problems He encountered, as did the prophets of old.

First of all, one must recall the well-known episode of the Syrophoenician woman. Because Jesus was being sought out by the Herodians and the Pharisees, He had taken refuge for some time in pagan territory. For the first time in His life He was outside Jewish country, in a place where idols were not banned and the environment was coarse and immoral. Those who have visited Baalbek, the ancient Heliopolis contemporary with dawning Christianity, and its gigantic temples dedicated to Baal-Sun, to Bacchus, the god of drunkenness, and to Venus, the goddess of sensuality, know that the purity of Jewish worship and customs in this context represented a permanent miracle. They can also imagine the horror Israelites might have felt at the thought of mixing with people who participated in cultic practices such as these.

Jesus must have experienced this feeling of horror when He was a refugee in the district of Tyre and Sidon. "He entered a house, and would not have any one know it," (Mark 7:24). This is where the event which upset Him occurred. A pagan woman whose daughter was cruelly tortured by a demon heard about Him. She threw herself at His feet and cried out: "Have mercy on me, O Lord, Son of David" (Matthew 15:22-28).

Jesus did not think it necessary to answer this plea. He said nothing. A Jew does not have any relations with Gentiles. His disciples were annoyed by the woman's insistence and told Him, "Send her away, for she is crying after us!" Then Jesus, to discourage her, said, "I was sent only to the lost sheep of the house of Israel." These are the same terms He used when giving instructions to His disciples (Matthew 10:5, 6).

But the woman insisted, "Lord, help me!" Then Jesus answered with an expression that probably was a Jewish proverb, "It is not fair to take the children's bread and throw it to the dogs."

What was the significance of this answer? There was certainly nothing insulting about it. It meant in metaphoric form, "I, the Messiah of the Jews, am called to take care of My people. I was not sent to the Gentiles." By speaking in this way, Jesus was expressing the religious convictions He shared with Israel.

But the woman answered Jesus with a bold remark that was to

upset His ideas, "Yes," said she, "yet even the dogs eat the crumbs that fall from their master's table." This remark was full of good sense and courage and it impressed Jesus. Indeed, if there was enough for the children of Israel to eat, and more, how could He keep the Gentiles from taking part in the feast? For this saying, He told the woman, "Be it done for you as you desire. Great is your faith!" And when she got home, she found her child lying in bed, healed.

By breaking into the closed world of the Jewish people, the Syrophoenician woman had unknowingly participated in the foundation of Christianity. On that day, the kingdom of God, in Jesus' eyes, ceased to be a promise reserved for Israel alone. One will not enter into it by birth only, but also by faith; the "violent ones," whose faith can remove mountains, will grasp it.

On several occasions Jesus admired the faith of His listeners and used them as examples. It is remarkable that three times out of eight the non-Jews were the ones who aroused His admiration. This can help us understand how the teaching of salvation by faith thrust itself upon rising Christianity in such strangely pragmatic ways.

Though in a less obvious way a similar change can be observed in Jesus' thinking about Samaritans. When He first crossed Samaria, Jesus, as a Jewish prophet, did not think it fitting to enter the town of Sychar. He sat down outside the town, on the edge of a well, and sent His disciples into town for food. By this well he met a person who had the double disadvantage of being both a woman and a Samaritan.

Jesus asked her for water. After a series of questions and answers about living water, Jesus reminded the woman that "salvation is from the Jews" (John 4:22), but told her about worship in spirit and in truth which was to come. Troubled by these revelations and by Jesus' words about her loose life, the woman understood that she was talking to a prophet and began to ask Him questions about true worship, declaring that she too was waiting for the Messiah. When Jesus told her He was the One she was expecting, she left her water jar and ran into town to tell the people, who in turn came out to meet Jesus.

The conversation by the well-side led to a pressing invitation which the inhabitants of Sychar addressed to Jesus, "Stay with us!" Jesus accepted the invitation and stayed with them for two days. According to the Gospel, "many Samaritans from that city believed." When reading this narrative one wonders if Sychar, in a schismatic land, was not the site of the first Christian church. For the Samaritans told the woman, "It is no longer because of your words that we believe, for we have heard for ourselves and we know that this is indeed the Savior of the world." Were non-Jews then more inclined to recognize Jesus as the Christ than were the arrogant Jewish Messiah-seekers?

The Gospel of John records the admirable words Jesus spoke to the Samaritan and they seem to summarize the new vision He acquired at Sychar: "The hour is coming, and now is, when the true worshippers will worship the Father in spirit and truth, for such the Father seeks to worship him. God is spirit, and those who worship him must worship in spirit and truth" (John 4:23, 24).

Long after this event, Jesus once again went through Samaria. His attitude had changed. Far from refraining to enter the Samaritan cities, He was the one who now asked for hospitality and sent messengers ahead to prepare lodging for Him.

But on that day, the inhabitants of a Samaritan village were the ones who refused Him lodging, because He was on the way to the temple in Jerusalem, a rival of theirs. Nothing is more irritating than to be rejected when one is filled with good intentions. By asking the Samaritans for hospitality, Jesus was showing His friendship toward them. But they chased Him away, like an enemy! James and John took the blow very hard. During their triumphal journey they had had the opportunity to test the miraculous power with which God had endowed them. The Samaritans' resistance exasperated them. They asked Jesus' permission to order lightning to come down and consume those scoundrels. [2]

But Jesus did not give them His authorization to use murderous violence, which some of the more peaceful-minded among us would sometimes like to use to rid the world of evildoers.

The men of the twentieth century have made themselves masters of a force much more fearful than lightning, and they now have the power of destroying entire nations. They are constantly tempted, as were James and John, to destroy the enemies of good. Should we not look to the story of the Samaritan village as a prophecy and a divine warning meant for us?

In any case, Jesus rebuked His misguided disciples, "You do not know what manner of spirit you are of; for the Son of man came not to destroy men's lives but to save them. And they went on to another village" (Luke 9:55, 56). [3]

Jesus' sympathy for the Samaritans continued to grow and gain strength. One day as He was passing by the border between Samaria and Galilee, He healed ten lepers but was saddened by their lack of gratitude. Only one returned, fell on his face, and thanked Him. He was a Samaritan and Jesus exclaimed, "Were not ten cleansed? Where are the nine? Was no one found to return and give praise to God except this foreigner?" (Luke 7:12-19). And He said to the Samaritan, "Rise and go your way; your faith has made you well." This was not only the physical healing of a non-Jew but also his entry into the kingdom of God.

Why then should one be surprised that the Jewish nationalists mistook Jesus for a Samaritan? [4] Nationalists of all times have accused the generous man who stands above their quarrels of belonging to the enemy. Similarly, narrow-minded believers think that prophetic men, whom God inspires with universal visions, endanger the truth they imagine to be theirs alone.

After opening the kingdom of God to Gentiles and Samaritans, Jesus was going to let the Romans also take their important part in building the kingdom. The story of His meeting with the centurion of Capernaum is too well known to be narrated at great length. According to Matthew 8:5-13, the centurion himself came to Jesus, saying: "Lord, my servant is lying paralyzed at home, in terrible distress." But according to Luke 7:2-10, the centurion approached Jesus by means of an intermediary. This is not surprising since the Roman knew that according to Jewish custom a rabbi such as Jesus could have no contact with a pagan like him.

Thus, the centurion who had friends among the Jewish elders of Capernaum, sent them to the prophet as proxies. It seems that the elders themselves had some trouble convincing the Messiah, because, according to Luke, they pleaded with Him urgently and tried to prove that this centurion was not an ordinary Gentile. "He is worthy to have you do this for him, for he loves our nation and he built us our synagogue."

Those of us who have visited the site of Capernaum cannot forget the ruins of this synagogue where Jesus preached on so many occasions. Archaeologists tell us that this is not the one Jesus knew. That one was destroyed and rebuilt. But the location is the same and the stones the centurion gave were certainly reused. Such was the monument a Roman occupant with a tolerant mind had built for the love of the Jewish nation!

As Jesus was approaching his house, the centurion himself, who as we have said, knew perfectly well that it was impossible for a Hebrew to touch a Gentile, repeated, "I am not worthy to have you come under my roof; therefore I did not presume to come to you" (Luke 7:6, 7).

The modesty of Capernaum's centurion has often been pointed out! The question was not one of personal inferiority, but rather a shrewd knowledge of Judaism. Indeed, the centurion did not hesitate to compare himself with Jesus. He, as a soldier, obeyed his superiors without question and submitted to military discipline. On the other hand, his inferiors owed him complete obedience and submission at every moment. Thus it seemed natural to the centurion that a Jewish prophet would heal his servant since He had authority over demons.

Jesus was surprised by the unlimited confidence the Roman had in Him. From this, He concluded: "Not even in Israel have I found such faith. I tell you, many will come from east and west and sit at table with Abraham, Isaac, and Jacob in the kingdom of heaven" (Matthew 8:10,11).

Once again, we witness a genuine religious revolution. At the very hour when the Jewish people were about to exclude themselves from the kingdom of God, non-Jews were entering by faith into the kingdom, reserved until then for descendants of Abraham. Jesus concluded with sadness, "The sons of the kingdom will be thrown into the outer darkness; there men will weep and gnash their teeth." And to the centurion, Jesus said, " 'Go; be it done for you as you believed.' And the servant was healed at that very moment" (Matthew 8:12, 13).

Neither Matthew nor Luke tells us that Jesus then went to the centurion's house. According to Matthew He entered Simon Peter's house and healed his mother-in-law. Nor do these Gospels mention the centurion's conversion. To our knowledge Jesus did not summon the man in order to tell him, "Your faith has saved you," or "Follow Me," as He told His new disciples. The officer most likely continued to practice his Roman religion [5] and go about his military duties.

How did women enter the kingdom of God?

There is a considerable jump from the severity of the Sermon on the Mount to the reception Jesus gave to the women who followed Him in His travels, received Him in their homes, and accompanied Him to His execution. Some of these women even provided financial assistance for Him. Jesus accepted this help without worrying about public opinion.

Surprisingly enough, the more virtuous women, such as His mother or sisters or His apostles' wives, were not always the ones to enter the intimate circle of the disciples. Jesus painfully alluded to the necessity for His followers of breaking with their respectable families. On the other hand, there was a whole group of women who entered the narrow door to the kingdom and were scorned by every-one else: sick ones who touched His robe, abandoned widows, and even prostitutes. Jesus, who exhorts us to be careful how we look at women, allowed Himself to be touched by a prostitute! And touched in what way! Tears to wet His feet, a head of hair to wipe them, kisses to revere them, a broken alabaster vase to pour out very expensive perfume.

Simon the Pharisee who had invited Jesus for a meal that day was scandalized. His attitude may be justified. How many suspicions must have crossed His mind, the least of them being, "If this man were a prophet, he would have known who and what sort of woman this is who is touching him, for she is a sinner" (Luke 7:39).

But in the somewhat alarming enthusiasm of the prostitute, Jesus was to discern one of the principal virtues of the kingdom of God, the one He places even above faith because it resembles God most, namely, love. We do not know the nature of the woman's love for Jesus. Had she seen in Him the Messiah, the Savior of the world, the Son of God who was capable of purifying her? Or, more probably, had she been overwhelmed upon meeting for the first time a genuinely pure Man who treated her like a sister or a friend?

The text does not reveal these secrets. Whatever the case may be, her tears were not only tears of admiration, but also tears of repentance mixed with the passionate expression of a desire for for-giveness. This is how Jesus interpreted her deed. The traditional cate-gories of "pure" and "impure" were totally upset. Simon, with his pure hands, was the one who became impure because he needed only a little forgiveness and felt only a little respect and a little thank-fulness for the Savior of mankind. The prostitute, on the other hand, was the one who became pure. She was purified by Christ because vir-tue, in God's eyes, is to be transformed by faith. Through Jesus, the woman had seen God and had become attached to Him. For her also, Jesus pronounced the great word of eternal life, "Your faith has saved you; go in peace" (Luke 7:50).

o   o   o

Thus, from one stage to another, we see Jesus' thought expanding until it had become universal. But we must always remember that Jesus' universalism does not mix with all the concepts, all the beliefs, and all the religions of the ancient times in the melting pot of tolerance. Jesus did not abolish the divine banquet where, according to Jewish tradition, Abraham, Isaac, and Jacob are seated. He simply invited to this banquet those on the outside who responded to His invitation by showing love and faith in God.

Until the very end Jesus claimed to be the Jewish Messiah. He never renounced His privilege of being the Anointed One of the Lord, but He had destroyed the wall which separated the holy God from the non-Jews. Thus He became the "new and living way" by which all men, from the Orient and the Occident, have access to the kingdom of God.

By acting in this way, He removed every pretext for the use of violence from the community of His disciples, who were to become the church.

III. REVOLUTIONARY NONVIOLENCE AND HUMAN INSTITUTIONS

12. Sabbatical Revolution Versus Human Tradition

Those among Jesus' contemporaries who, above all others, should have recognized Him as the Messiah were the Pharisees. Indeed as an orthodox Jew, Jesus wanted to bring the people back to an integral practice of God's law, as did the Pharisees.

Jesus shared almost all the Pharisees' convictions. Like them, He was expecting the kingdom of God to come soon. Like them, He made no distinction between this coming and the restoration of the Jewish state; like them, He believed in demons and angels; like them, He believed in the resurrection. From an ethical standpoint, the similarity was also very great: like the Pharisees, Jesus was a convinced believer in the Sabbath. He went to the temple as they did. Hillel the Pharisee was the first to formulate the famous Golden Rule which Jesus later reformulated, "Do not do unto others what you would not want for yourself." How then did the break occur which was to retard the coming of the kingdom of God?

In reality, it was Jesus who took the offensive by making severe judgments against the Pharisees. They refused to act in harmony with the Jubilean summons, although they appeared to practice the law with great zeal. They were avaricious and would not give up their usurious exploitation of the poor. They were proud and would not abandon their prominent seats. They were authoritarian and would not allow a Galilean peasant to teach them. They were hypocrites and hid their intentions behind noble appearances.

But to the extent that the Pharisees did not repent upon hearing Jesus' call, they felt offended by His requirements. In fact, they felt so deeply offended that they put the entire responsibility for the misunderstandings that separated them upon Him.

What then were their grievances against Jesus? There were four of them:

1. Jesus violated the Mosaic law and taught others to do likewise.
2. Jesus did not belong to a rabbinical school. He therefore had no authority to interpret the Scriptures.
3. Jesus was threatening the holy institutions of Judaism.
4. The political agitation Jesus created was endangering the Jewish people.

1. Jesus Violated the Mosaic Law and Taught Others to Do Likewise

To keep the people from hellenization, the Pharisees had multiplied the ritual barriers that made mixed marriages and the mingling of races impossible. This was especially necessary in Galilee where the racial boundary lines were not so clear as in Judea.

We have already seen how much the Pharisees feared that the "crowd who do not know the law" [1] would submerge the nucleus of faithful Israelites. The schools of the scribes therefore tried as conscientiously as at all possible to specify all possible implications of the law of Moses with commentaries and commentaries upon commentaries that were later to become the *Talmud* and the *Mishna*. These traditions, "the tradition of the elders," were aimed at preserving the purity of the people, but they soon became more important than the law itself. This was the tradition Jesus attacked. The Pharisees who equated law and tradition thought they were facing, in Jesus, a dangerous adversary of the Mosaic law itself.

2. Jesus Did Not Belong to a Rabbinical School

In Jesus' time, custom dictated that a rabbi, though famous, should found his teaching upon the commentaries of the rabbis of the preceding generation. This method is still employed today whenever religious inspiration reaches a low point or sclerosis takes hold of a once-living doctrine. So the Pharisees immersed themselves in the study of the *Torah* and carefully remembered the elders' commentaries, with the hope of someday earning the right to add their own commentaries to those of their masters.

Jesus, however, had studied the Scripture until He was 30 years old. He was well acquainted with the law and the prophets and quoted them constantly, although He had never attended a rabbinical school. His first speeches stupefied His audience by their originality and freedom of interpretation of the Scriptures. "He taught them as one who had authority," says the Gospel, "not as their scribes" (Matthew 7:29).

This question of authority was at the heart of the clashes between Jesus and the Pharisees. Quite obviously, Jesus drew His authority from God Himself, and bypassed all the rabbis, even Moses. When the scribes questioned Him about the origin of His authority, Jesus refused to answer. Had He said, "It comes from men," He would have had to show what we would today call a university degree, which He did not have. Had He answered, "From God," His enemies would have accused Him of blasphemy and would have killed Him before His time (Matthew 21:23-27).

So Jesus turned the question around by asking them from whom they thought John the Baptist received his authority to baptize. If they had answered, "From God," the Pharisees would have been forced to change their ways. If they had answered, "John is a common man. His baptism is a fraud," the people themselves would have revolted against the Pharisees, because they thought John the Baptist was a prophet.

As good tacticians, the Pharisees did not answer Him, and Jesus, for His part, also refused to answer them. Thus the question of authority remained unanswered and painfully wedged between Jesus on the one hand and the Pharisees on the other until the denouncement of the final drama.

3. Jesus Was Threatening the Holy Institutions of Judaism

We have mentioned the temple in a previous chapter. The priests thought Jesus was threatening it. Besides the temple, the leaders thought they could see the Galilean prophet questioning the entire structure of the political, ritual, and ethical institutions of the Jewish people. Every nation is inclined to equate the values to which it holds with the institutional shell aimed at protecting them. Consequently, its leaders are tempted to use lies to defend truth, violence to protect peace, and persecution to save charity! For the Pharisees, the drama was even more acute because they were conscious of representing the people chosen by God to be His witness in history. They were convinced that Jesus was shaking the Jewish institutions, the guardians of the divine absolute. When John the Baptist said, "God is able from these stones to raise up children to Abraham" (Matthew 3:9), they thought he was putting Israel's election into question. And when Jesus stated in the temple, "Before Abraham was, I am" (John 8:58), the scandal was so great, they took up stones intending to kill Him.

4. The Political Agitation Jesus Created Was Endangering the Jewish People

The chief priests and the Pharisees showed genuine political judgment when they gathered in council and asked, "What are we to do? For this man performs many signs. If we let him go on thus, everyone will believe in him and the Romans will come and destroy both our holy place and our nation" (John 11:47, 48). They were sincere when they decided to put an end to the young prophet's activities by any means. They truly believed they were saving their people.

The Gospel of Matthew tells us that Pilate, though not a Jew, realized that they had delivered Him up because of envy.

Until Jesus appeared, the Pharisees' influence had met no rival! "They are as matter of fact, extremely influential among the towns folk; and all prayers and sacred rites of divine worship are performed according to their exposition. Their power over the mass is such that they are heard, even when they speak against the king and the high priest." [2]

Now the miracles and speeches of Jesus were winning the people away from this influence. Nothing is more alarming for those in power than the success of a newcomer. The Gospel of John reports that the Pharisees said to one another, "You see that you can do nothing; look, the world has gone after him" (John 12:19).

Besides that, Jesus was not "very accommodating." A certain passage from the Sermon on the Mount concerning nonresistance to evildoers might lead us to believe that He was the passive victim of the Pharisees' plot. This was not the case. He was the One who began the struggle. We will now follow step by step the stages of a conflict where Jesus constantly took the initiative.

Those who are not familiar with the Gospel see Jesus as the stereotyped apostle of passive nonresistance in the face of wicked men. What would happen to us, they say, if we let the wicked do as they pleased, as Jesus tells us? But to understand Jesus, one must read the Sermon on the Mount as a jubilean speech, aimed at restoring the purity of divine law by destroying the human traditions Jesus considered to be evil. On that basis turning to "civil disobedience," Jesus and His disciples systematically began to violate all these disastrous traditions, one by one, opposing them with deliberate conscientious objection, aimed at breaking the cast that enclosed the truth.

The events that followed those of Nazareth, mentioned at the beginning of the book, will give us a chance to see how Jesus went about breaking sharply with the customs that enslaved His contemporaries.

We left Him in the synagogue at the time He was assuming the role of the Messiah. His speech was poorly received. He was too well known in His own town to begin recruiting His disciples there. Those who had heard Him, exclaimed, "Where did this man get all this? . . . Is not this the carpenter, the son of Mary and brother of James and Joses and Judas and Simon, and are not his sisters here with us?" (Mark 6:2, 3)."No prophet is acceptable in his own country," Jesus said later during the discussion that followed. "A prophet is not without honor, except in his own country, and among his own kin, and in his own house" (Mark 6:4).

What could He do? Give in? Should not sacred institutions be obeyed first? Is there something higher than the church, home, and country? Haven't they been instituted by God for the good order of this world?

But Jesus did not submit Himself. On the contrary, He took the offensive so vigorously that it embarrasses today's reader of the passage. People shout: "What we have heard you did at Capernaum, do here also in your own country" (Luke 4:23). They dare Him to perform miracles. The Gospel of Matthew seems to acknowledge defeat by saying, "And he did not do many mighty works there because of their unbelief" (Matthew 13:58). Luke gives a different explanation — Jesus did not want to perform miracles in Nazareth, but He did give an unpatriotic speech calling Elijah and Elisha to witness! Neither of them, He said, did any miracles in their own country because of the wickedness of their fellow countrymen. Indeed, many people in Elijah's day were suffering because of the long famine of three and a half years, but the widow of Zarephath, in Sidon, was the only one for whom Elijah provided flour and oil. There were many lepers in Israel at the time of Elisha, but Naaman the Syrian, a Gentile, was the only one whom the prophet healed (Luke 4:25-27).

Thus, Jesus completed His break with the inhabitants of Nazareth. He had attacked their pride as members of the chosen people and was going to suffer the consequences of His audacity. After He narrowly escaped death for the first time, He left His childhood town never to return.

He soon broke with His family as well. At first, it had been favorable to Him. The Gospel of John pictures Jesus going down to Capernaum with His mother, brothers, and disciples. But this harmony did not last. Tension probably developed when Jesus started selecting His apostles. He called Simon and Andrew, James and John, the Sons of Zebedee, but omitted His brothers. From that time on, when Mary or her sons wanted to communicate with Jesus, they had to wait outside and have an intermediary request an audience with Him. At any rate, this is what happened one day when the crowd was pressing particularly close around Him.

The untimely interventions of His mother and brothers had certainly made this break necessary. Jesus said later, speaking from experience, "He who loves father or mother more than me is not worthy of me" (Matthew 10:37). The day His mother wanted to see Him, He said something that certainly must have hurt His family very deeply, "Who is my mother, and who are my brothers? Here are my mother and my brothers! For whoever does the will of my father in heaven is my brother and sister and mother" (Matthew 12: 48-50). The reason for His separation from His family is clear: they had not yet agreed to do God's will; so Jesus could not be subject to them. He had founded a new family and gathered around Him only those who wanted to do God's will.

Jesus' brothers thought He had become insane, and one day a group of them came to seize Him. At Capernaum they found some scribes from Jerusalem who confirmed their opinion, "He is possessed by Beelzebul and by the prince of demons he casts out the demons" (Mark 3:22), which means, in today's language, "He is a lunatic; He is mad."

Till the time of the cross, the jealousy of Jesus' brothers did not diminish; instead it took a different form. They gave up trying to keep Him from acting and tried to make Him do imprudent things. Some Gospel commentators think there were Zealots among Jesus' brothers. They thought He was excessively timid and may have eventually agreed with Judas. They may have tried to accelerate the course of events by forcing Jesus to take the leadership of a nationwide insurrection. If the uprising failed, it would mean that He was not the Messiah. If it succeeded, they would then join Him. Therefore they said to Him, "Leave here and go to Judea, that your disciples may see the works you are doing. For no man works in secret if he seeks to be known openly. If you do these things, show yourself to the world" (John 7:3-5). But Jesus did not follow their advice and refused to go to Jerusalem at that time.

Now that we understand the reasons that pushed Jesus to free Himself from His home village and His family, it is easier to grasp the motives that drove Him to break with the tutelage of the scribes and Pharisees.

The first conflict arose over the forgiveness of sins, and it was an important one. The Pharisees had been impressed by the physical healings Jesus performed. But one day He also meant to heal souls. A paralytic had been let down to Him through the roof and Jesus had said, "Man, your sins are forgiven you" (Luke 5:20). The Pharisees were scandalized because, as they saw it, God alone could grant the forgiveness of sins. They had set up between God and man a kind of accounting, and in this system, only acts of penance and offerings could cover the violations of the law and allow someone to receive the absolution of his faults.

In Jesus' eyes, sin was utterly different. It was a grave illness that attacked man in his soul, just like the paralysis from which the body of the man before him was suffering. God in His loving, fatherly power wanted to restore (Matthew 9:2 uses the verb *aphiemi*) man's spiritual wholeness, as well as his physical health. Jesus was endowed with this power; He was the hand of God, the healing Messiah. He expected only one thing from the sick man: faith, that is to say, confidence. The believer should not hesitate in defying conventions to confide in Him! Whereas the Pharisees held to the rules, to the accounting system, and to the human institution, Jesus was announcing a meeting between two beings enamored of each other: the God of "the restoration of all things" and the sick man, ill both in body and soul. A compromise between Jesus and the Pharisees was no longer possible.

The second conflict arose in the following manner. Jesus was at the time recruiting apostles. The choice of the first four does not seem to have aroused any criticism. They were respectable people, of good reputation, fishermen on the lake, who owned their boats and their nets: Peter and Andrew, and their cousins, James and John, who worked for them. "Follow me, and I will make you fishers of men" (Matthew 4:19).

But the choice of the fifth apostle raised a wave of reprobation. In Capernaum, there was a man people avoided. He was neither a leper nor a Gentile. Worse yet, he was a publican to whom the government had leased the customs rights for the city's port where the freight from Syria was loaded onto boats. Levi had become rich and had gathered around himself a crowd of rather shady characters. His house was open to all, his place was noisy, and the people who came drank hard. This is precisely the man Jesus noticed one day sitting at the tax office. He chose him as His fifth disciple. Jesus did not give a long speech; He merely said, "Follow me!" and Levi obeyed (Luke 5:27).

This sensational choice could have inspired the population. Rabbi Akiba had also been an *Am-haerez* before becoming a famous lawyer. Unfortunately, things did not go smoothly that night. To celebrate his new vocation, Levi invited Jesus and His disciples to a feast and Levi's friends joined them. They began to eat and drink. The Gospel does not tell us about any excesses, but there was nothing sad about that evening. Now, the whole city knew the reputation of Levi's usual friends. The scribes from among the Pharisees motioned for some of Jesus' disciples to come out. They still had some regard for the prophet of Nazareth and they wanted to help Him out of a scrape. "Why does he eat with tax collectors and sinners?" they asked the disciples (Matthew 9:11). We will return to the answer Jesus gave them at the end of the chapter.

Some time after this incident, the third conflict arose. On this occasion Jesus did not confront the Pharisees, but some of His best friends. John the Baptist's role as forerunner of Jesus, as the prophet in the desert who preached the imminence of the Messiah's coming, is well known. He who thought he was not worthy of untying Jesus' sandals had seen in Him the Messiah he had announced.

Now John the Baptist led an even more austere life than the Pharisees. He dressed in animal skins and lived on wild honey and insects, whereas Jesus and His disciples showed no such signs of austerity. They formed a joyous group. We can imagine them going through the streets of the Galilean cities, chatting joyfully, in no way affecting the stern expressions on the faces of John's disciples. John the Baptist, in his prison, had been troubled by this and his disciples began to doubt that Jesus was the Messiah. As His friends, they did not gossip behind His back like hypocrites because they were tied by a common messianic expectation. They approached Jesus and asked, "Why do we and the Pharisees fast, but your disciples do not fast?" (Matthew 9:14). Jesus constantly astonished His contemporaries!

The fourth conflict was deliberately willed by Jesus in the manner of demonstration in civil disobedience. On the Sabbath the Jews were forbidden to do any work. In particular, they could neither harvest, nor thresh, nor winnow, nor clean the harvest, nor grind the grain, nor carry food from one house to another. All Palestinians, except the most rebellious *Am-haerez*, kept the Sabbath. Anyone who violated this holy law was supposed to go to Jerusalem and offer a special sacrifice for his sin.

One Sabbath day Jesus passed through a ripe grainfield. His disciples tore off the heads of grain, rubbed them in their hands, and ate them — all with Jesus' consent. By doing this, they were simultaneously violating all six of the legal prescriptions mentioned above! The Pharisees were shocked and said, "Look, your disciples are doing what is not lawful to do on the Sabbath" (Matthew 12:2).

Why? We are still wondering about it today. Was it all that important for Jesus to defy His environment, to associate with shady characters, to adopt easygoing manners, to dissociate Himself from pious folk, to authorize His disciples to violate the Sabbath? Was it really necessary for Him to jeopardize the success of His gigantic undertaking, the establishment of God's kingdom, by irritating Jewish opinions on mere details? Would it not have been wiser for Him, who wanted to give the Sabbath its original meaning, to conform temporarily to the accepted customs, gain a good, serious reputation, and then to try to reform the institutions of Judaism from the inside?

No! Jesus truly had the soul of a revolutionary. His answers to the "whys" of His contemporaries are quite revealing: I have come to create new institutions. Do you think I will tear the new garment of my teaching in order to patch the worn-out robe of your old practices? Certainly not! Because the new patch would tear the old cloth and make the hole worse, and my new garment would be lost. And this wine of my kingdom, filled with ferment, do you think I will pour it into the old wineskins of your traditions? Of course not! My doctrine would burst your customs. The wine would spill and be lost as well as your wineskins. "New wine is put into fresh wineskins, and so both are preserved" (Matthew 9:16, 17; Luke 5:36-39).

These words are unequivocal. Jesus had come not only to change hearts but to restore Israel. He had to change institutions as well as hearts in order to restore God's justice in the world. If the institutions were not changed, they would smother under their weight the noblest souls that had been momentarily awakened to the call for a better world.

Let us listen to Jesus' other answers: Why is it that My disciples do not fast? Ask Me, rather, why they should fast. Is there anything sad about the kingdom of God? Is it not similar to preparing for a wedding? We are walking toward the house where the banquet is being served. Moreover, the bridegroom is in the nuptial procession. In the name of what ill-natured spirit do you want to prevent the bridegroom's companions from rejoicing? (Luke 5:34, 35).

The most revealing reply is a response to the Pharisees who accused His disciples of violating the Sabbath: You criticize them for eating when they are hungry? What was the purpose behind the institution of the Sabbath? Do you think God created man to be bound by one thousand and one sabbatical ordinances? Is the Sabbath a severe punishment God invented in order to torture human beings? No! The Sabbath was made for man (Mark 2:27). It is a day of liberation, a wonderful gift of God to man so that he may rest, along with his wife, his son, his daughter, his servants, and even his beasts of burden (Deuteronomy 5:14, 15).

Since His adversaries still insisted, Jesus cut the controversy short by a final argument. One day, He reminded them, David was hungry and He did not hesitate to break a law that was considered sacrosanct. He ate the bread of the Presence, which was consecrated by God and reserved for priests alone, and even gave some to his companions. Now I am the Son of Man, David's descendant, announced by the prophets and come to accomplish the law of Moses. I am greater than the temple. As Son of Man, I am even the Master of the Sabbath (Matthew 12:5-8).

These words that Jesus used to proclaim His royalty, His messiahship, and His jubilean right to free the old institutions from the stifling cast that had changed their meaning would seem haughty if they were not modified by the explanations He gave to those who reproached Him for His evil company. The Son of Man, the Master of the Sabbath, the descendant of David, He said, enjoys being around publicans and sinners, not to adopt their life-style and to get drunk, but because they are sick. Is the doctor reproached for his contacts with sick people? Would you want Me to turn away from those who need Me most for fear of catching some ritual impurity or for fear of public opinion? No! I have come for them, for those who are sick in their souls. They are looking for Me, but you, who consider yourselves healthy, think you do not need Me. And since you do not need Me, I have not come to call you, but those who want to be healed (Matthew 9:12, 13).

In these words we see the profound motive that impelled Jesus to restore the Mosaic institutions to their original purity. They had been given by a God whose prime concern is man. God is love. He wants man to be treated with respect. That is why the Messiah took the risk of losing His life at the hands of tradition's defenders in order to take care of the sick, the weak, and the least of His brothers.

13. The Temptations of Violence and of Abstention

At this point, we must interrupt our development in order to summarize the alternatives facing Jesus. He had gone too far to turn back. He was proclaiming the kingdom of God, inaugurated by a Jubilee. This Jubilee was upsetting human tradition and putting the Mosaic law back into practice. His adversaries were trying to kill Him in order to prevent a dangerous revolution. He had only two alternatives: violent resistance to the enemies or a flight into the desert — the Zealot temptation or the Essene temptation.

1. The Zealot Temptation

The Zealots were preparing themselves to wage a war of liberation against Rome. They were extremist Pharisees and had used their daggers sometimes against the occupation forces, sometimes against their fellow-countrymen whom they suspected of moderation or collaboration. After having assassinated those who favored collaboration with Rome one by one, they finally succeeded in sweeping the entire nation into a generalized war in AD 66.

Now we know that there were Zealots among Jesus' disciples: Simon, called the Zealot, and probably Judas Iscariot. [1] Jesus had been tempted by the solution of force. Even before His public ministry, He had struggled with such a temptation. From a high mountain He saw in spirit "the kingdoms of the earth and the glory of them," and the tempter said, "All these I will give you if you fall down and worship me." Of course, this passage is not referring to the physical meeting of two persons, but rather to the Messiah's inner struggle. Jesus knew the miraculous power He possessed would have allowed Him to dominate the world if He used the means every conqueror used: military power, money, prestige and glory. But He rejected this possibility: "Be gone, Satan! for it is written, 'You shall worship the Lord your God and him only shall you serve!' "

Parenthetically, the vision of bread seems to have played a certain role in this first temptation. God's bread would have made it possible to feed the hungry of the world. This vision seems to have haunted Jesus until the end because it inspired the institution of the Lord's Supper.

One day in Galilee, as the Passover (the feast of unleavened bread) was approaching, Jesus took pity on the hungry people of the crowd and miraculously fed them. The Zealots were enthusiastic. They were convinced they had at last found the Messiah. They wanted to vanquish Jesus' resistance and take Him away to make Him King. But Jesus overcame this second temptation to power. He escaped and withdrew to the mountain to be alone (John 6:14, 15).

A third time the same temptation harassed him during a journey in Trachonitis in the area of Caesarea Philippi. Simon Peter was overjoyed at the spiritual discovery he had made, "You are the Christ, the Son of the living God" (Matthew 16:16). Jesus answered by announcing that He would be put to death and that He would not resist His enemies because this death was part of God's plan (Matthew 16:21, 22).

Peter then said aloud what a secret voice had been whispering to the Messiah; he took him aside and began to scold him, "God forbid, Lord! This shall never happen to you," which very likely meant: "We, Your disciples, will not allow this to happen; we will fight for You"; or "Do not let Yourself be murdered! Let us retreat into the Judean Mountains, among the Zealots or the Essenes, where the police cannot reach us." Jesus' impatient reaction reveals the dramatic nature of His own inner struggle. He answered the tempter as He had previously on the mountaintop, "Get behind me, Satan! You are a hindrance to me; for you are not on the side of God, but of men" (Matthew 16:23).

But despite this new moral victory, Jesus was still faced with the temptation to use violence. It can be felt in the ultimatum He gave to the cities of Israel. Change your ways or My disciples will shake the dust of their shoes against you, or in the curses He spoke against Capernaum, Chorazin, and Bethsaida after they had rejected Him (Matthew 10:14, 15; 11:20-24).

To the extent that Jesus was announcing the kingdom of God on earth and proclaiming the Jubilee, He clashed with the obstacle all revolutionaries encounter: the spiteful and violent reaction of the conservatives, the guardians of the old institutions and privileges. As a young revolutionary, Jesus saw that the success of His undertaking was being jeopardized. If He wanted to keep it from failing, it may be necessary to abbreviate the long and difficult pilgrimage of justice in history and impose the kingdom of God on the rebellious by force.

Such a decision would have been made for the good of all, even of His enemies. After the establishment of the kingdom, they would have been the first to join Him and congratulate Him for His energetic initiative. [2]

It is therefore not surprising to find the word "hate" in Jesus' vocabulary when He talks about the necessary separations. One day He turned to the crowd that was following Him and said, "If any one comes to me and does not *hate* his own father and mother and wife and children and brothers and sisters, yes, and even his own life, he cannot be my disciple" (Luke 14:26).

We can sense that He was on the verge of making a warlike decision when He exclaimed, "I came to cast fire upon the earth; and would that it were already kindled! I have a baptism to be baptized with; and how I am constrained until it is accomplished! Do you think I have come to give peace on earth? No, I tell you, but rather division; for henceforth in one house there will be five divided, three against two and two against three; they will be divided, father against son and son against father, mother against daughter and daughter against her mother, mother-in-law against her daughter-in-law and daughter-in-law against her mother-in-law" (Luke 12:49-53).

Another very revealing statement is the famous quotation concerning the violent ones who will take over the kingdom of God: "From the days of John the Baptist until now the kingdom of heaven has suffered violence, and men of violence take it by force" [3] (Matthew 11:12).

As the conclusion of the drama rapidly drew nearer, Jesus faced an increasingly intense inner struggle. One day as the scribes and Pharisees were harassing Him with their loaded questions, He vented his indignation: "Woe to you, scribes and Pharisees, hypocrites!" (Matthew 23:13). This passage is too well known to be quoted in its entirety. We shall mention only the words where Jesus seems to call divine vengeance upon the reactionaries who obstruct the road to the kingdom of God: "Therefore I send you prophets and wise men and scribes, some of whom you will kill and crucify, and some you will scourge in your synagogues and persecute from town to town, that upon you may come all the righteous blood shed on earth, from the blood of innocent Abel to the blood of Zechariah, the son of Barachiah, whom you murdered between the sanctuary and the altar. Truly, I say to you, all this will come upon this generation" (Matthew 23:34-36).

The parables Jesus used during the last week He spent in Jerusalem almost all conclude with violence. Some tenants revolt against the heir of the vineyard and Jesus said, "He [the master] will put those wretches to a miserable death" (Matthew 21:41); some people who had been invited to attend the wedding feast of the king's son refused the invitation: "The king was angry and he sent his troops and destroyed those murderers and burned their city" (Matthew 22:7). Later, the same king told his servants, "Bind him [the man who had no wedding garment] hand and foot and cast him into the outer darkness; there men will weep and gnash their teeth" (Matthew 22:13).

But, people say, these are only parables, Oriental imagery used to make an impression on the listeners and bring them to repentance. But to destroy corrupt customs that turned the temple into a "den of robbers," to force His contemporaries to take a stand in favor of the kingdom, Jesus took a whip of cords and chased out those who sold and bought in the temple. He overturned the tables of the money-changers and the seats of those who sold pigeons and said, "My house shall be called a house of prayer; but you make it a den of robbers" (Matthew 21:13).

Thus the temptations to use violence accompanied Jesus until His death. A few hours before His arrest He went so far as to reverse His earlier instructions concerning absolute poverty and meekness. "But now, let him who has a purse take it, and likewise a bag. And let him who has no sword sell his mantle and buy one." And they said: "Look, Lord, here are two swords." And He said to them, "It is enough" (Luke 22:36-38). Beyond the help of these two paltry human weapons, Jesus was counting on the help of twelve legions of angels which God held in reserve, ready to intervene at the first call to deliver Him from His adversaries, had He only willed it.

It was only after an intense inner struggle, after the genuine moral agony at Gethsemane, that Jesus finally rejected resorting to violence and gave up the idea of using His disciples' swords. One must not see in Jesus a theorist of nonviolence. Jesus finally overcame violence by a succession of day-to-day decisions and a series of redemptive acts. He freely chose on every occasion the road of nonviolence rather than that of armed defense. [4]

Jesus' nonviolence is therefore not the extra-historical dream of some mystic trying to forget the concrete realities of this world and ignore the wickedness of men. It is a step-by-step exploration through the obstacles, the mountain passes, the snares and the cliffs of history. Jesus has carved a new path into the hardness of human realities, a path He trod first, carrying on His shoulders all the requirements of the kingdom of God: social justice, transformation of institutions, commitment to truth, individual regeneration. These are the materials He found around Him among men. This is the wood, the stones, and the sand with which He built the kingdom of God on earth as in heaven.

Consequently, the chastisement deserved by the hypocrisy of the Pharisees, the jealousy of the Sanhedrin, the cowardice of Pilate, and the weakness of the crowd fell back on Him. Jesus deliberately chose to be crucified for being responsible for the apparent failure of God's kingdom. His voluntary sacrifice was not a capitulation, because, since that day, no man, no nation, no party, no head of state, whether a believer or an unbeliever, can forget Christ. No one can ignore the fact that he is nailing God Himself to the cross with his injustices and his crimes.

2. The Temptation of Abstention

If Jesus was tempted to commit violence, it is also true that several times He was on the verge of giving up all public activity in order to retire to the desert and form a community of the faithful.

Several reasons incited Him to it. One must not forget that He began His ministry when He was approximately thirty years old, after having been baptized by John the Baptist, who was a prophet from the desert, under the strong influence of the Essene monks. Like the Essenes in their *Manual of Discipline*, John the Baptist reechoed Isaiah's call: "A voice cries: 'In the wilderness prepare the way of the Lord, make straight in the desert a highway for our God.' " Like the Essenes who expected the coming of two Messiahs (Aaron and Israel), John the Baptist also expected the coming of the Messiah he was announcing.

However, John the Baptist indiscriminately baptized all those who came to him with a repentant mind, whereas the Essenes formed a closed congregation and considered themselves to be the "penitents of the desert," the "Sons of Light," struggling against the "Sons of Darkness," whom they also called "Children of Belial."

Jesus was sympathetic with the ministry of John the Baptist. Like him He lived a long time in the desert, but He did not participate to the same extent in the ascetic practices of the Essenes.

He recruited His disciples among men whom the Essenes would have considered impure. He did not advise them to practice the ablutions, the fasts, the separation from women, or the communal living in the desert.

The Gospel, however, reveals a certain anguish on the part of Jesus. He dedicated Himself completely to the crowds in order to accomplish His mission of salvation in favor of the destitute, but simultaneously, He seems to have been overcome by a nostalgia for solitude from time to time, and also by the desire to form a small faithful community away from the world, to wait for the glorious return of the Son of Man.

Once He let impatient words slip from His mouth, which revealed His inner struggle. The incident occurred as He was going down the mountain, the day after the Transfiguration. With Peter, James, and John as witnesses, He had communicated with the invisible world. And after coming down into the midst of the crowd, He heard the complaint of a man whose son was epileptic, "I brought him to your disciples and they could not heal him." Jesus grew impatient with the powerlessness of His disciples and the unending requests of the crowd and exclaimed, "O faithless and perverse generation, how long am I to be with you? How long am I to bear with you?" (Matthew 17:17).

With this same aversion for the crowd, He enjoined His disciples not to give holy things to dogs, and not to throw pearls before swine "lest they trample them under foot and turn to attack you" (Matthew 7:6).

One day Jesus used very strange words, whose importance we tend to forget, to explain to His disciples why He spoke in parables. It is thought today that parables were meant to present the profound truth of the kingdom in a more accessible form. But, strangely enough, the crowd seems not to have understood one of the more simple ones, the parable of the sower, and Jesus concluded by telling His listeners, "He who has ears to hear, let him hear" (Matthew 13:9). After the crowd had dispersed, His close friends and the Twelve questioned Him, "Why do you speak to them in parables?" And Jesus answered with these mysterious words, "To you has been given the secret of the kingdom of God, but for those outside everything is in parables; so that they may indeed see but not perceive, and may indeed hear but not understand; lest they should turn again, and be forgiven" (Mark 4:10-12). And he added: "Do you not understand this parable? How then will you understand all parables?" Here again one feels Jesus' impatience with "those outside."

A little later, the Gospel of Mark says, "With many such parables he spoke the word to them, as they were able to hear it; he did not speak to them without a parable, but privately to his own disciples, he explained everything" (Mark 4:33, 34).

Such texts seem to place Jesus much closer to the Essenes than one would think at first glance. He too was trying to gather around Him a small group of disciples to whom He gave secrets the crowd was not able to receive.

Our surprise at this attitude of Jesus can be somewhat attenuated if we reread the Old Testament passages that refer to the "eyes that see not" and the "ears that hear not."

Some 740 years before Jesus, the prophet Isaiah had received the following instructions from God: " 'Make the heart of this people fat, and their ears heavy, and shut their eyes. . . . Then I said, 'How long O Lord?' And he said: 'Until the cities lie waste without inhabitant, and houses without men, and the land is utterly desolate . . . like a terebinth or an oak, whose stump remains standing where it is felled, a holy posterity will be reborn of this people" (Isaiah 6:10-13).

After having experienced, like Isaiah, the incomprehensible indifference of His people, Jesus was prophesying, like Isaiah, that the majority of His listeners would not be converted, but hardened by His message. However, their hardness of heart would not catch God unawares because God uses failures and transforms them into victories. Like the holy posterity that was to come from the Jewish people after the destruction of Jerusalem, the disciples to whom Jesus disclosed the secret of the kingdom of God would be the first elements of a new people.

Thus the uneasiness we felt earlier has been somewhat dispelled. Nevertheless, Jesus still seemed to oscillate between a widespread call to the crowd on the one hand ("Nothing is covered that will not be revealed, or hidden that will not be known. What I tell you in the dark, utter in the light; and what you hear whispered, proclaim on the housetops" (Matthew 10:26, 27); and an initiation reserved only for a small group of elect: "The gate is narrow and the way hard that leads to life, and those who find it are few" (Matthew 7:14).

The Gospel of Mark describes Jesus as forbidding His disciples the demons He expelled, and the people He healed to announce that He was the Messiah (Mark 1:34; 3:12; etc.). Had He been hindered in

His activities by the indiscretion of a leper He had healed? This is most likely the case because "Jesus could no longer openly enter a town, but was out in the country; and people came to him from every quarter" (Mark 1:44, 45). He also was afraid of being mistaken for a military messiah, such as the Jews were expecting, and He preferred to withdraw to the desert in order to avoid this confusion (John 6:14, 15).

Jesus liked to go to the desert to pray. Sometimes He went there alone, sometimes He went with His disciples to give them rest and to teach them. Indiscrete crowds of people often followed them there (Mark 3:7-12). Jesus would then give in to their persistence and teach them while healing the sick.

But the desert became both a refuge and a temptation to Him, especially at the end of His ministry, when Jesus moved the focus of His ministry from Galilee to Judea. He had lived in a village beyond the Jordan, and in Aenon near Salim, not far from the place where John the Baptist had baptized him. It was there that Jesus' disciples had baptized for the first time, after the manner of John the Baptist (John 3:22, 23).

Toward the end of His ministry, Jesus came back to this same area, in the footsteps of His forerunner whom Herod had decapitated, as if He were attempting to return to the beginning of His ministry. A few days earlier in Jerusalem He had openly proclaimed that He was the Christ. The Jewish authorities had tried to seize Him in order to stone Him, but He had escaped from their hand and had come to Aenon (John 10:40, 41). Most likely, He was tempted to remain there permanently, far from the struggles of history, because "many came to him . . . and believed in him there" (John 10:41, 42). Was it not better to give up trying to convert the mass of the people who rejected Him, in order to gather the "remnant" of the faithful Jews in the desert?

After having interrupted his retreat to perform the miracle that upset Jerusalem, the raising to life of Lazarus at Bethany, Jesus once again disappeared because the Sanhedrin had threatened Him with death. "Jesus therefore no longer went about openly among the Jews, but went from there to the country near the wilderness, to a town called Ephraim; and there he stayed with the disciples" (John 11:54).

However, the last act of the drama was drawing near. A more pressing call than that of founding a small faithful sect was summoning

Jesus to Jerusalem. He had to go to the temple and affirm His prerogatives as messianic King. [5]

Jesus' Entry into History

Most people today see Jesus as if He had refused to play a historical role. The thoughtlessness of this idea is amazing. People want to imagine Him as a mere sublime "yogi," sheltered from the world, living on the shores of eternity, an ascetic who would have invited His disciples to follow Him in solitude in order to teach them an ideal having no connections whatsoever with the concrete problems of this world. [6] The exceptional nature of His holiness is extolled to more easily evade the duties of discipleship.

To justify this type of evasion, people often quote Jesus' answer to Pilate, who was questioning Him about His kingdom: "My kingship is not of this world; if my kingship were of this world, my servants would fight, that I might not be handed over to the Jews; but my kingship is not of this world" (John 18:36).

Thus, people generously concede to the partisans of nonviolence that Jesus was nonviolent since He did not permit His disciples to shed blood for His protection. This is self-evident. But they immediately go on to say that the kingdom of God, of which Jesus is the champion, is a purely spiritual kingdom, completely unrelated to the realities of this world. Thus as Christians the disciples of Jesus must not bear arms, but as citizens of the state, they must participate in the armed defense of the community. [7]

Such an interpretation of His words shows a lack of acquaintance with Jesus. Indeed, in John's Gospel, "not to be of the world (*cosmos*)" in no way means that one belongs to a disincarnate kingdom.

In his "high priestly prayer" (John 17), Jesus, referring to His disciples, said: "The world has hated them because they are not of the world, even as I am not of the world. In 15:19, He told His disciples, "If you were of the world, the world would love its own; but because you are not of the world, but I chose you out of the world, therefore the world hates you." "Not to be of the world" (*cosmos*) does not imply an evasion from the world, but a nonconformity to the *cosmos* in which we live, and this provokes hate from those who surround us.

"When I was with them [my disciples]," He said in His prayer,

"I kept them in thy name — and none of them is lost. . . . I do not pray that thou shouldst take them out of the world, but that thou shouldst keep them from the evil one" (John 17:12, 15).

Thus it is clear that the Messiah had "both feet on earth," where He wanted His kingdom to be physically present in the person of His disciples.

But what is the relation between Christ's kingdom, which is not of this *cosmos*, and the *cosmos* itself, to which the Roman Empire, represented by Pilate, belonged?

Evidently, the old scheme of the chosen people was constantly present in Jesus' mind. His kingdom is made up of the elect, the ones He called His "servants" in His answer to Pilate. Like the soldiers of a prince, they could be called upon to fight for Him. But Jesus has another mission for them, because His kingdom has another origin than the kingdom of this world: "My kingship is not of this world" (John 18:36). [8]

What will be the mission of the Messiah's servants? They will continue Jesus' ministry in the world: "As thou didst send me into the [*cosmos*], so I have sent them into the . . . [*cosmos*]" (John 17:18). Certainly, the mandate the disciples received in the world will not be easy to carry out in the world because the world has not received the light of God which came into the world (prologue of John's Gospel). "If they persecuted me, they will persecute you," however, "if they kept my word, they will keep yours also" (John 15:20).

It is because the deeds of the *cosmos* are evil that men prefer darkness to light (John 3:19). "For God so loved the world that he gave his only Son. . . . God sent the Son into the world, not to condemn the world, but that the world might be saved through him" (John 3:16, 17). This sentence contains all of redemption, a redemption meant not only for individual man, but also for the entire world. The sovereignty of the prince of this *cosmos* (the power of darkness) over the world is only transitory. "The ruler of this world is judged" (John 16:11). "In the world you will have tribulation; but be of good cheer, I have overcome the world" (John 16:33).

Thus the reality which Jesus opposes to the *cosmos* is not the disincarnate kingdom of ideas, but God's very act. The Messiah came from God and returns to God after having planted the kingdom of God in the *cosmos*. He will come back, because His final aim is to save the *cosmos*. The kingdom will be fulfilled on earth as in heaven.

In this way Jesus overcame His enemies without using the violent methods common to the kingdoms of this world. To inaugurate His triumph as a peaceable King, He entered Jerusalem five days before the Passover, free from the temptations of both violence and abstention. Followed by the long procession of His nonviolent disciples, Jesus made His entry into history on that same day, into the history of each nation and of each century, until the day when His victory in the *cosmos* will be complete.

14. Jesus' Nonviolence or the Discovery of the Person

The preceding chapters have shown the reasons that impelled Jesus to overturn the Jewish institutions of His day. He wanted to enable Israel to fulfill its role as the chosen people. The cast of human traditions had to be broken and the truth set free so that Israel's election could become accessible to all nations.

The preceding chapters have also shown that Jesus' conflict with the guardians of the Jewish institutions was so acute in Galilee, that humanly speaking, He was faced with two options: war — with the Pharisees first, then with the Romans, which would have greatly pleased the Zealots — or withdrawal from the world, which would have greatly pleased the Essenes. Jesus, however, chose a third road, that of His nonviolent entry as the Messiah into Jerusalem, His capital city.

But nonviolence alone was merely a framework. In this chapter, we shall attempt to discover the content Jesus wanted to give His nonviolent action.

The Redeemer, the Subject of Nonviolence

Jesus had given up violence without, however, abandoning the struggle. With this in mind, He had substituted the announcement of His death for the expectation of His immediate accession to the throne. His death would then be followed by a return on the third day: "Jesus began to show his disciples that he must go to Jerusalem and suffer many things from the elders and chief priests and scribes, and be killed, and on the third day be raised" (Matthew 16:21).

Christian theology since the Apostle Paul has given numerous explanations for Jesus' death. This is not the place to list them. One should notice, however, that Jesus Himself was extremely reserved on the subject. The four Gospels contain practically no theology of the crucifixion. The most explicit passage is found in John 6. According to the writer, Jesus employed the following words concerning the "living bread," which certainly come close to Christian communion or the breaking of the bread as it was practiced during the second century:

"I am the living bread which came down from heaven; if anyone eats this bread, he will live forever; and the bread which I shall give for the life of the world is my flesh" (John 6:51).

But the first three Gospels are much more sparing in their comments. In Matthew 16:24 and its parallels (Mark 8:34; Luke 9:23), Jesus invites His disciples to follow Him, soon after the announcement of his own death: "If any man would come after me, let him deny himself and take up his cross and follow me!" So the cross, which implied refraining from all violence, was not meant for the Redeemer alone; it is one of the signs of the kingdom of God. Every Christian is a "cross-bearer."

Elsewhere Jesus uses the word "ransom," around which He builds another general rule: "Whoever would be great among you must be your servant, and whoever would be first among you must be slave of all. For the Son of man also came not to be served but to serve, and to give his life as a ransom for many" (Mark 10:43-45). In this passage, the idea of ransom brings to mind two figures. The first is the person who serves others to the point of losing his life (cf. the good shepherd in the Gospel of John) and the other is the person who exchanges his life for the life of a prisoner (the *goel* of the Old Testament).

Quoting from the prophet Isaiah (chapter 53), the Gospel of Matthew attributes healing of sickness and of sin to an exchange similar to the one made by the *goel*, the Servant of the Lord: "That evening . . . He healed all who were sick. This was to fulfil what was spoken by the prophet Isaiah, 'He took our infirmities and bore our diseases'" (Matthew 8:16, 17). This passage is well worth quoting in its entirety because it can shed some light on the profound thought of Jesus: "Surely he has borne our griefs and carried our sorrows; yet we esteemed him stricken, smitten by God, and afflicted. But he was wounded for our transgressions, he was bruised for our iniquities; upon him was the chastisement that made us whole, and with his stripes we are healed" (Isaiah 53:4, 5).

The Redeeming Event of Capernaum

Taking into account the Old Testament references to the Redeemer's role, we shall retrace our steps and consider an exceptionally important event which took place in the synagogue at Capernaum

(Matthew 12:1-14; Mark 2:23; 3:6; Luke 6:1-11). According to Luke, this event took place after the series of clashes which we described in chapter 12. They had been provoked by the proclamation of the Jubilee and had put Jesus on the verge of a violent conflict with the Pharisees.

The young prophet's popularity was so great in Capernaum that the Pharisees felt they were being supplanted in their own synagogue. It was, of course, customary for a distinguished guest on the Sabbath to be invited to read the Scripture and comment upon it. On this particular Sabbath, Jesus Himself seems to have led the service. He was the One who taught while the scribes and Pharisees stood by. They were there only as observers and critics. But their opposition was in no way platonic. Irritated and jealous as they were, they decided to keep Jesus from making the people stray from their healthy religious observances. They had probably made contacts with Herod's police to prepare for the prophet's arrest (Mark 3:6). These proud adversaries of Hellenism and Antipas had stooped rather low by requesting the intervention of their worst enemies, the Herodians! Thus the scribes and Pharisees in the audience were watching Jesus attentively. They hoped to catch Him in the very act of breaking the Jewish law, to have Him indicted and condemned to death.

Jesus was perfectly aware of this situation. He was in the process of risking His life and thereby compromising the future of God's kingdom on earth. There was still time for Him to either take up arms or withdraw from the struggle by avoiding a confrontation with His adversaries.

The alternative between violence and abstention must be faced by reformers at every historical turning point and there never seems to be a third choice. Jesus, however, was going to find the third way and thus eliminate the merciless alternative for all His disciples.

The Common Man, Object of Nonviolence

Let us notice first of all the nature of the object that allowed Him to make the choice. It was a human being, a man with a withered hand. Still today when the problem of the "lesser evil" is discussed, the human being as an individual is always overlooked. People say, "Our nation is about to be exterminated; or the future of our civilization, of our moral values, of true religion is threatened; or yet, our institutions violate human rights and to save human rights, we must temporarily forget our scruples and use violence, sacrificing men to destroy unjust structures, and thus saving the poor from oppression."

The revolutionaries, from their point of view, say, "The misery of the hungry is so deep, the liberation of the exploited so urgent, and the requirements of justice so exacting, that we are forced to choose violence rather than resignation; the sacrifice of millions today is preparing for 'a better tomorrow.' " For centuries both progressive and the reactionary camps have been "temporarily" choosing violence, "temporarily" shedding the blood of millions of victims in the name of a better future. [1]

Because each side speculates about "what would happen if we let the enemy win" they mercilessly sacrifice man, whether friend or enemy, this common man to whom Jesus referred as our neighbor. And every generation is faced with new options time after time considered to be so important that it repeatedly believes itself compelled to use violence. Once the crisis has passed, the following generation can hardly recreate the climate that engendered such wars. In the middle of the twentieth century, we are incapable of imagining the collective emotions that led to the war of succession in Spain, or the Crimean War, or even World War I!

It is all the harder for us to imagine what the problems of Hellenism, of Roman occupation, or of the preservation versus the rejection of traditional Sabbath forms meant for Jesus. However, if one considers that today's struggles for the salvation of democratic freedom, for national independence, for the abolition of colonialism, or for social justice are extremely important, how much more important the struggle for the kingdom of God must have seemed to Jesus. He undoubtedly saw it as the only real "ultimate struggle" of history.

The seriousness of the situation could have incited Him to "temporarily" forget the plight of this man with his withered hand in the synagogue. His name was never preserved. The people of Capernaum were probably used to him. He was probably one of those unimportant poor people who beg at the doors of religious gatherings, a man who was unable to work because of the condition of his hand. The Gospel does not even tell us that he asked to be healed. He was simply sitting there. As Jesus was speaking, He could have glanced over the audience and ignored that withered hand. But the Messiah had started a campaign of deliberate disobedience of false sabbatical interpretation. He wanted to break the bars of the rabbinical prison, and the opportunity before Him was exceptional.

He knew, however, that the eventuality of a scandal might cause His own arrest and death. This was no objection! Jesus would not back out. Let the tyranny of Judaism perish — and with it His own chances of success! A new form of justice had to prevail. This totally new justice would be founded upon the ransom that Jesus was going to pay for the life of a man.

Then Jesus called to the sick man, "Come and stand here." He wanted everyone to see what was about to happen. Why didn't He avoid the scandal at the last moment? Why didn't He whisper in the man's ear, "As you can see, the circumstances are not very favorable today? Come and see me tomorrow morning at Simon Peter's house and I will heal you." Had not the sick man been waiting for years? Could he not wait one day longer? No! Jesus wanted to act on the spot not only because of the sabbatical revolution, but also in the name of something more important. The man stood before Jesus and Jesus said, "Stretch out your hand." The man stretched out his hand and his hand was healed.

Thus, on that day, voluntarily, officially, in a Jewish "church," before hundreds of witnesses, Jesus had violated the rabbinical traditions that regulated the Sabbath. [2] This crime deserved the death penalty, because it is written in the Book of the Exodus: "Every one who profanes it [the Sabbath] shall be put to death; whoever does any work on it, that soul shall be cut off from among his people. . . . Whoever does any work on the sabbath day shall be put to death" (Exodus 31:14, 15).

The scribes and the Pharisees immediately left and made a complaint to Herod's police. Justice was to follow its course, the complaint was to reach Jerusalem, and several months later, the criminal would be executed (Mark 3:6; 8:15; 12:13). [3]

Now we can answer the question: For what reason, or better, for whom, did Jesus do this? The one for whom He had sacrificed everything was standing in the middle of the synagogue. Who was he? An important figure on whom the future of humanity depended? No, he was only a man, a "common man," whom Jesus had taken out of his anonymity and had placed at the center of all things and for whom He had "exchanged" His life.

Who was this poor man's *goel*? Who was the brother or the cousin offering himself voluntarily as a ransom for him? Was He the anonymous soldier of Yahweh's army, the one everyone gladly sacrifices for a noble cause? No! He was the central figure of human history, God's Messiah, who had come with the prodigious ambition of establishing God's kingdom on earth.

Redemption, therefore, is not a metaphysical theory. It took place on a specific day in the history of mankind. One person was saved; another risked His own life. Jesus was the *goel* who redeemed the man with the withered hand by substituting His glorious condition for a miserable destiny.

Jesus' career was a succession of redemptive acts of this kind, and they all led to a cross.

Jesus' primary preoccupation outweighed His respect for Abraham, Moses, and the temple, as well as the urgency of a religious, social, and political revolution. It also preempted the establishment of a messianic kingship in Israel and the necessity of establishing *hic et nunc* the kingdom of God on earth. This one preoccupation was the lot of a human being, the healing of a sick hand! [4]

The Two Foundations of Nonviolence

Let us return to the event at Capernaum and listen to Jesus Himself explain to His furious or marveling listeners why He violated the Sabbath.

a. The Redemptive Act. The first motive is given in Mark's (3:4) account: "Is it lawful on the sabbath to do good or to do harm, to save life or to kill?" With these words, Jesus was clearly stating the problem of the institution's role. He was not abolishing the Sabbath; rather He was justifying it: "The sabbath was made for man." But, on the pretense of protecting man against the corruption of the Gentiles, the Sabbath had become a means of enslaving man to inhuman rules. Jesus was solemnly recalling to the people's memory that the Sabbath has no other aim than doing good to man. The Sabbath day, the sabbatical year, and the year of Jubilee are meant only to reestablish justice and give the weak their place in society.

Because it was a Sabbath day, the Messiah had to do good on that day. *Good could not wait to be done.* To put it off would have been a crime. God can never wait. [5] The Sabbath is there to do His will. This is the day that the suffering man must be made whole.

We always think we only have the choice between violence and cowardice. But for Jesus, the real choice takes place at another level. One must choose between doing good to the human being placed in one's path, or the evil which one might be doing by mere abstention. For Him, there is no "no-man's-land," enabling us to portion our attitudes, to do a little good to our neighbor without taking the risk of becoming involved for his sake, or to do him a little harm while still remaining charitable.

In the synagogue, Jesus had to choose between good and evil done to a neighbor. He refused to measure the far-off consequences of His action. His explanation is in no way obscure, "To do good is to save a person; not to do him good is to kill him." To save someone is to restore that person physically and morally. To neglect and postpone this restoration is already to kill. Although the man with the withered hand was not in danger of losing his life, Jesus could not neglect his sickness. He had come to save the entire person, and that immediately. [6]

b. The Uniqueness of Every Man. Jesus' second argument concerning the function of the Sabbath is found in Matthew (12:12). It is an argument *a fortiori* which He liked to use: He appeals to rustic common sense. Everyone who has lived in the country knows that cattle cannot go without eating or drinking on Sunday. Every peasant, no matter how pious, is tied down by his duties toward his animals. [7]

The Pharisees themselves who were sometimes farmers took care of their cattle which represented all their wealth. No ritual prescription could oppose a requirement of this type. But Jesus goes one step further. The peasant of his example owns only one sheep. We find here the framework of the parable of the good shepherd for whom his one lost sheep is worth as much as the ninety-nine safe ones. But in this case, the shepherd owns only this one sheep. In the synagogue, Jesus looked at the beggar with his hand and saw him with the eyes of a God who would only possess one man in the world. God's love centers totally on each man as if he were the only one.

Jesus, the Messiah, the arm of God, has only one sheep. His only wealth. But this sheep is wounded; it is fallen into an abandoned pit. Jesus appeals to the common sense of His listeners. You who own only one sheep, would you let it die because it is the Sabbath? Of course not! It would not be in your interest. Your kind heart would also prompt you to save it. The Sabbath does not oppose these things! And turning to the Pharisees, He says, "Of how much more value is a man than a sheep!"

Thus on a Sabbath day in the synagogue at Capernaum, Jesus founded the modern world by showing that in God's eyes, man is unique and comes before anything else. The sacrosanct tradition will be violated, the Messiah will be condemned to death, and He will rise again. The kingdom of God will take a different form, but the future will center around the newborn child of history: the person.

The True Dilemma

At the beginning of this book we stated that nonviolence was the framework of the ethic of the Sermon on the Mount, but what was its object? In the synagogue of Capernaum, Jesus gave an object and a body to His ethical teaching, namely, our neighbor.

It was also on that day that Jesus laid the indestructible foundations of Christian nonviolence, by limiting His disciples to the only true dilemma every conscience must face:

> To do good or to do harm, that is
> To save or to kill. [8]

By choosing to save man at the price of His life, Jesus forever joined two facts: redemption and nonviolence. Because Jesus is the Redeemer no one can any longer save by killing or kill to save. Life alone, life given, not life exacted from others, can save a man's life.

True Christian Solidarity

However, because Jesus was ready to give His life as a ransom for men, He did not require His disciples to sacrifice themselves then and there. He could certainly see that they would die as martyrs, but only at the time God would choose (Mark 10:39). He was giving His life so that His disciples might live: "While I was with them I . . . guarded them and none of them is lost. . . ."

A few hours after speaking these last words, Jesus was arrested in the Garden of Gethsemane. The Roman cohort and the temple officer said, "We are looking for Jesus of Nazareth." Jesus answered, "I told you that I am he; so if you seek me, *let these men go*," and the writer added: "This was to fulfil the word which he had spoken, 'of those whom thou gavest me, I lost not one!' "(John 18:7-9).

This comment throws a new light on the meaning Jesus gave to the words "to lose" and "to save." He did indeed mean both the physical and the spiritual life of His disciples.

The deep interest Jesus showed in caring for His disciples and His mother to the very end rids the passion story of any false heroism. [9] This interest is matched only by Jesus' care for the *crowd* that lamented Him: "Daughters of Jerusalem, do not weep for me, but weep for yourselves and your children" (Luke 23:28); for *a man who came to arrest Him*: He healed his ear (Luke 22:51); for *His companion of execution*: "Truly I say to you, today you will be with me in Paradise" (Luke 23:43); for *those who were crucifying Him*: "Father, forgive them, for they know not what they do" (Luke 23:34).

By demonstrating genuine Christian heroism, Jesus invalidates any argument in favor of a Christian heroism that would manifest itself in the bloody solidarity of battlefields.

15. Was Jesus Mistaken About the Date?

Many of Jesus' own sayings refer to the second coming of the Son of Man as if it were an imminent event.

These same texts prove that the Gospel tradition is quite ancient. The first three Gospels are entirely built around the hypothesis of an impending return of the Son of Man. Jesus thought He would return before the death of some of His disciples (Matthew 10:22, 16:28). If the Gospel tradition were merely a liturgy written after the death of the last apostles for worship use, as some people have suggested, it is hard to understand why the church of the second century would have retained, without modification, Jesus' words concerning His second coming that had not taken place. Indeed, these texts point out to the second century Christians that Jesus may have been mistaken about the date of His return. By handing down to us the Synoptic documents, the church admitted that Jesus was not omniscient. It also unwittingly proved to the scholars of centuries to come that the Synoptic tradition goes back to Jesus Himself and that His words were scrupulously transmitted to us.

The Imminence of the Kingdom

Let us recall the most striking of these words: In Matthew 10:23, we read, "Truly I say to you, you will not have gone through all the towns of Israel before the Son of man comes." This passage seems to indicate that at the beginning of His ministry, Jesus did not even foresee that His death would occur before His glorious accession to the throne. Matthew 16:28 also implies a return in a very short time: "Truly I say to you, there are some standing here who will not taste death before they see the Son of man coming in his kingdom."

One might think that words such as these were spoken at the beginning of Jesus' ministry and that He may have later modified His views. But some of the parables Jesus told at the very end of His ministry show that He still believed in the imminence of His return, even though He was facing death. Among these, we find the parable of the dishonest steward, upon which we have already commented, the parable of the talents, the parable of the pounds, the parable of the wise and foolish maidens, and the parable of the marriage feast. All of these parables foresee a very short delay between the departure of the "master of the house" and his return: the duration of a journey, the space of a night, the time necessary to prepare a feast or send out the invitations. The servants who bring their accounts to the master are the very ones to whom the master had entrusted his capital before leaving (parables of the dishonest steward, of the talents, and of the pounds). The guests who refuse to take part in the messianic feast and are punished are the very ones who were invited (the narrow gate, the marriage feast, the foolish and wise virgins).

Besides these parables, there were numerous exhortations to vigilance. When Jesus says: "You know neither the day nor the hour," He is not trying to reassure His disciples by saying, "There is no hurry"; rather He is reminding them that they must always be on the alert, "You do not know on what day your Lord is coming . . . the master of that servant will come on a day when he does not expect him, and at an hour he does not know. . . . Watch therefore, for you know neither the day nor the hour. . . . Take heed to yourselves lest your hearts be weighed down with dissipation and drunkenness and cares of this life, and that day come on you suddenly like a snare; for it will come upon all who dwell on the face of the whole earth. But watch at all times, praying that you may have strength to escape all these things that will take place and to stand before the Son of man" (Matthew 24; 25; Luke 21:34-36).

These exhortations were not meant for us. They were obviously addressed to Jesus' listeners, who were called to persevere throughout these violent but short trials which were to come before the imminent return of the Son of Man.

In a previous chapter, we referred to the question the disciples asked Jesus when He announced they would receive the baptism of the Holy Spirit: "Lord, will you at this time restore the kingdom to Israel?" (Acts 1:6). This question shows that the disciples were firmly expecting the coming of the kingdom of God within the framework of the kingdom of Israel, after the death and resurrection of Jesus.

Twenty years later, the Apostle Paul (2 Thessalonians 2:1-12) still found it necessary to calm the overexcited Thessalonians' expectations, "We beg you not to be quickly shaken in mind or excited . . .

to the effect that the day of the Lord has come . . . for that day will not come, unless the rebellion comes first, and the man of lawlessness is revealed . . . who exalts himself against every so-called god or object of worship . . . proclaiming himself to be God. . . ."

These words reecho Jesus' utterance in Matthew 24:24, 33, "False Christs and false prophets will arise and show great signs and wonders, so as to lead astray, if possible, even the elect. . . . So . . . when you see all these things, you know that he [the Son of Man] is near, at the very gates."

Time Expands

Some fifty years later, the situation had changed considerably. The apostles had died, the Son of Man was yet to come, and doubts began to arise among the Christians of the second generation. Unbelievers began to laugh at their vain expectation.

These are the words of the author of the Second Epistle of Peter: "Scoffers will come in the last days [1] with scoffing, following their own passions and saying: 'Where is the promise of his coming? For ever since the fathers [the faithful of the first generation] fell asleep, all things have continued as they were from the beginning of creation. . . .' But do not ignore this one fact, beloved, that with the Lord, one day is as a thousand years, and a thousand years as one day. The Lord is not slow about his promises as some count slowness, but is forbearing toward you not wishing that any should perish but that all should reach repentance" (2 Peter 3:8, 9).

This interesting passage shows the budding Christian theology attempting to explain to the believers the tardiness of the kingdom of God. Gentiles were changing their way of life at a rapid pace. God then wanted all men to repent. When all would be converted, the judgment would take place in a better context than if it should come immediately.

The rest of the passage also reveals to us that as the writer of the epistle saw it, this new delay in the coming of the kingdom would be brief. He employs Jesus' theme of the robber coming at night and states, "The day of the Lord will come like a thief and then the heavens will pass away with a loud noise and the elements will be dissolved with fire, and the earth and the works that are upon it will be burned up." And he adds, "Since all these things are thus to be dissolved, what sort of persons ought you to be in lives of holiness and godliness, waiting for, and hastening the coming of the day of God. . . ! But according to his promise we wait for new heavens and a new earth in which righteousness dwells."

These words allow us to understand the type of transition that second-generation Christians experienced in going from a chronological concept of an imminent kingdom of God on earth to a juxtaposition of earthly and heavenly realities. Indeed, if the material elements are doomed to destruction, the new heaven and the new earth will be a totally new creation, with no relation to the real world. Consequently, one can neglect the body and care for the eternal, the soul. Thus Christianity gradually became reconciled with the neoplatonic concepts of spirit and matter that were very popular at the beginning of the first century.

But nineteen centuries later, the Christian faith is still plagued by the victory of Greek philosophy over Jesus' Jewish thought. The idea of a historical establishment of the kingdom of God sounds as foreign to our rationalistic ears as it did to the Greek contemporaries of Jesus. Such a doctrine can be accepted by faith alone. It cannot be worked out rationally because reason finds a dualism of spirit and matter rather easy to grasp. Thus the rationalism of the second century church shrank Christian hope for this world down to almost nothing. This earthly world was destined to vanish. The church tended to underestimate the historical, political, and social problems. The earth was a "valley of tears" where God was putting man through various trials, an arena of testing where God could sort out the good and the bad, the saved and the damned, the candidates for heaven and those for perdition.

Consequently, war, injustice, sickness, and poverty were no longer considered to be obstacles to the kingdom of God. They were trials God sent believers before receiving them in heaven. The Christian was to accept them without understanding God's mysterious intentions in allowing such things to happen. Resignation was the prized virtue, a virtue for which every Christian was to strive during his journey in the valley of tears. By eliminating the pride of life and the desires of the flesh, the believer would go straight to paradise.

Moral Relativism, a Consequence of Expanded Time

But as God cannot require everyone to die to himself (this would cause the end of all creation), he allows ordinary Christians to be content with the commandments that hold for everyone, that is, to conform to the natural order of things as created by God. Obedience to the natural order means essentially performing the "duties of one's station. "The child, the adolescent, the husband, the wife, the citizen, everyone according to his profession (also instituted by God), the farmer, the factory worker, the employer, the employee, the magistrate, the police officer, the military man, the diplomat, all will conscientiously perform the duties of their station. The world, although it is imperfect and sinful, is not completely abandoned by God. At every level of life, God has placed human authorities with ecclesiastical authorities in charge of maintaining the order He has instituted. If everyone does his humble job, all will be well.

This is why the Roman Catholic Church and the church that grew out of the Reformation in all sincerity recommend obedience to the magistrate, who, according to Romans 13, bears the sword in the name of God to carry out His vengeance, and whom one should not resist for fear of resisting the order God instituted.

The history of Christianity in Europe has, alas, shown the fallacy of such ideas. After the fall of the Roman Empire, and its schism into antagonistic countries, each prince went on believing he carried the sword in the name of God. The result of this belief caused general anarchy, continuous civil wars, crusades, persecutions against heretics, and religious wars. Each prince imposed upon his subjects the religion of his choice: *Cujus regio, ejus religio.* Had not Paul said, "He who resists the authorities resists what God has appointed"?

The eighteenth century tried to instill tolerance into the chaos of regimes that all claimed to be instituted by God. But the eighteenth century did not meet its expectations. To stop tyranny, the "tolerant" people began to use the guillotine. Since then parliamentary and authoritarian regimes have succeeded each other. Christians have been relying on false traditions and ignoring the gospel; so they have continued to obey the authorities for conscience' sake. The atrocities of two world wars between Christian peoples have shown the absurdity of blind obedience to orders. [2]

The positive outcome of these atrocities has been the church's hesitation to teach as it did in the past that governing authorities come from God. But then the church stops there. It does not yet dare to go back to the nonviolence of Jesus Christ and the first Christians. "Since you are not sure about your duty," it tells its members, "be submissive to the authorities. It is the solution with the fewest risks; you will be in the framework of "the duties of your station," and, "the path to follow will be completely outlined."

So the Christian submits himself. He is a good father, a good citizen, a good worker, a good soldier. No one mentions to him the imminence of God's kingdom with its religious, social, and political implications. Tormented consciences are provided with magnificent shelters of euphoric international conferences, subtle theological discussions, splendid liturgies, and the vague hopes mentioned in religious hymns.

We must be courageous enough to say flatly that the ethic of the "duties of station" is nothing less than contemporary resurrection of the pharasaic ethic. Time has substituted man-made tradition for the kingdom and justice of God. Today's "Christian citizen kits" are very well equipped, whether they be Russian, German, French, or American. Like their Jewish ancestors, today's Christian citizen scrupulously tithes mint and dill and cummin but neglects the weightier matters of the law: justice, mercy, and faith. He too is a "blind guide."

It is not at all surprising then that the masses are loosing interest in the church. Its teaching is irrelevant if it has no clear answer to the problems of today's world. The church has restricted itself to three secondary tasks: It gives society honest citizens who carry out the duties of their station. It comforts the poor whom society neglects. It consoles the dying for whom medical science has given up hope. [3] Faith for most Christians today amounts to overcoming man's fear in the face of life and death. And sometimes, it does not even go this far! The shepherd and the peasant used to fear nature's threat and its unpredictability. They then resorted to the church. But modern man knows no fear, because his technology and his comfortable houses protect him from nature. He even likes to take risks and gamble with death out of love for speed. He believes in the earthly life, in the attainment of well-being, in modern technology, and in the ever more interesting historical events. Sometimes he worships his country. Sometimes he serves socialism or national independence. At night, when he goes to bed, he no longer prays for his salvation, but sometimes he asks fate to help him win the sweepstakes. He no longer awaits a kingdom of God that he no longer needs, but he grows impatient because man has not yet succeeded in landing a man on Mars.

Let us stop criticizing modern man. He was not the one who abandoned the church. Rather the church was the one to give up answering the questions he is asking. Here are some of these questions: What will be the outcome of the population explosion: famine or war? What would happen to humanity if atomic war broke out? If a totalitarian regime took over, what would be the future of my country, of my language, of my civilization, and of the moral values they represent? What is the goal of modern science? Will technology free humanity from hunger and ignorance or will it enslave man to the computer? What can I do with my limited material and intellectual resources and my dependence upon society for my livelihood? What can I do to provide for the future of my children, to better society, to prevent war, and to contribute to the establishment of justice and peace?

To each of these questions the church gives nothing but vague and wordy answers. Yet all one needs to do is read the gospel with naive eyes to see that the problems facing a Jew of the first century were similar to those facing modern man. "What will happen to humanity," this Jew was wondering, "if Rome crushes all these nations under its material power? What will happen to the Jewish people if the worship of the emperor destroys faith in the true God? What will happen if Israel's divine calling becomes the laughingstock of the wise men of our day? Will Greek culture bring an era of eternal peace or will it dash the world into chaotic immorality? What can I as a Jew, limited by my human resources and my dependence upon the society that gives me my daily bread, do to become an instrument of God and prepare the way for the coming of the Messiah?"

To these questions of his contemporaries, Jesus had given a concrete answer, "The kingdom of God is imminent, repent, believe the good news." He proclaimed the jubilean revolution and the restoration of Israel by arousing the enthusiasm of the oppressed and the faith of the poor.

But twenty centuries have gone by. History has expanded and unfolded in a process which to nineteenth-century man seemed unending.

Time Contracts

Then suddenly, in the twentieth century, history stops its treading. Time once again contracted, stimulated by an unknown force in which some see the hand of God. In Jesus' time, Israel could feel the end of the Jewish state approaching, identified it with the end of the world, and thought in apocalyptic terms. Similarly, Western civilization can vaguely feel that its end is near, though it is still at the height of its splendor. The doctrine of imminence once again becomes real. The rationalistic philosophies of the "good old days" are losing their brilliance in the distance. The shelters of traditionalism, liturgy, or mysticism are beginning to look like escape mechanisms. Youth thirsts for action. Action for what purpose? It does not know. But one must go faster, higher, farther; one must produce more or destroy, no matter what the cost. Destroy what? Unjust structures? No one knows exactly how.

Popular novels are filled with the apocalypse of modern times. Adolescents literally devour science-fiction literature. Their imagination carries them sometimes toward artificial evasion, sometimes toward the hope of imminent earthly happiness, sometimes toward the expectation of man-made catastrophies that may annihilate humanity.

In such a context one should wonder whether imminence of the kingdom is not about to become once again a reality.

"It is a myth!" say the rationalists. The return of the Son of Man never did happen and never will. But what do they know about it? History is moved by myths, not by reason; i.e., the myth of the *laissez-faire* in the eighteenth century, the myths of the "triumph of science," and "perpetual progress" of the *Grand Soir* [4] in the nineteenth century, the myths of the unescapable advent of socialism or of the *Herrenrasse* in the twentieth century. And since we are guided by myths, would it not be better to be guided by a constructive rather than a destructive one? Above all, a myth based on a revelation from God is far better than a myth invented by man to justify his superiority complex.

But after all, what is a myth? Is it necessarily a lie? A myth gives us in symbolic form a certain vision of human existence and its goal. It is founded on concrete historical facts. Man, proud of his scientific knowledge of reality, is far from knowing what space, time, life, and ideas are. He must be content with being a man, and he can understand his origin or his end in no other way than in the form of a myth.

Over against a senseless modern myth that would put the human race in competition with the Creator Himself, there is what we will provisionally call the myth of the God of goodness, who has chosen witnesses among men to prepare on earth the coming of a kingdom of justice and truth and love. This myth dies hard. It always comes back throughout history in different forms, especially following hopeless massacres where man outdid himself in criminality. Are not the League of Nations of the past, the socialist International, and the United Nations today reflections — very dim, of course, but nonetheless very moving ones — of man's hope for a kingdom of God?

Truly the expectation of the kingdom of God is the mysterious guide of history. Economic factors and technological discoveries are merely used by human hope to build a better future. Why then should we refuse to recognize the revealed origin of the hope for the kingdom of God? Why should we refuse to admit that Christ taught it to us? When one must choose between nothingness and the kingdom, how can one choose anything but the kingdom?

The Parable of the Two Eyes

Physiology tells us that with only one eye we perceive all objects in the same plane. This can easily be verified by closing one eye; the awkwardness of our gestures shows that we have lost our sense of depth. But nature gave us two eyes, and the distance between them enables each eye to perceive objects from a slightly different angle. If one closes and opens each eye alternately in front of a series of objects spaced in depth, we soon become aware of this fact. If we concentrate on an object near to us, we have to cross our eyes slightly to avoid a double image. If on the other hand we look from a distance through the bars of a gate, for example, the objects in the foreground will form double images. Our brain corrects this double image on our retinas by "forgetting" the splitting of the foreground objects which become annoying when we are conscious of them. Psychologists tell us that one eye has of itself no sense of depth, but that the effort of the oculary muscles (which make our eyeball converge) allows the brain to reconstitute the depth of the different planes.

Now the effort of our oculary muscles is coordinated by our nervous system to the efforts of our motor muscles. A newborn child has no sense of depth, but he has two eyes. As soon as he can grasp objects and walk, he learns to see "correctly" and move among the obstacles around him without bumping into them.

Let us now try to apply this to the problem of behavior. Let us assume that man has two eyes, two visions of the world, an *exterior* vision that enables him to perceive the sensible world, reality "as it is," and an *interior* vision which reveals to him the kingdom, reality "as it should be."

Man is like a child who cannot yet superimpose the two images. Each image is flat. Indeed, the world "as it is" has no depth; it is a sequence of phenomena with no rhyme or reason, without origin or end. Similarly the world "as it should be," the kingdom, is flat. Isolated from the sensible world, it remains an "ideal" without substance, because ideas need the support of matter to become realities.

Now adult man should be capable of seeing reality with stereoscopic vision. His eyes and his spirit should be able to superimpose these two images of the world. Each of these images would at the same time gain relief, depth, and a meaning that monoculary vision cannot give.

Jesus Christ is the Adult Man, the normal man whose vision has completely superimposed the world as it is and the kingdom of God, thus gaining a depth vision into the nature of things, of the origin and the end of humanity.

So Jesus was not mistaken about the date after all, when He said, "The kingdom of God is at hand, repent, believe the good news." He was only expressing the correct vision of the world, His own.

But if Jesus was not mistaken, who then is? Was the second and third generations of Christians, the entire church, and our own generation who in its weakness is letting time expand once again because it can no longer make the world "as it is" coincide with the world "as it should be." In the absence of a correct vision of the world, history is nothing but the repetition of chaos.

How will our generation ever regain a correct vision of the world, unless it makes the "musculary" effort necessary to gain a stereoscopic vision of the world: the kingdom of God is at hand, let us repent and believe the good news?

The gospel cannot be written either as a scientific analysis of fact or as a theological or philosophical doctrine. To see the world correctly in relief and depth is not to write up a declaration of faith; it is to act by faith. The superposition of the two images of the world happens whenever a man submits himself to Christ, forgets the determinisms that bind him and acts in the world and in the present, according to the coming kingdom of God.

16. Jesus and Gandhi, or Can the Sermon on the Mount Be Put into Practice?

We have intentionally reserved the discussion of the "Sermon on the Mount" and its application for the last chapter.

Jesus' well-known words, "You have heard that it was said, 'An eye for an eye and a tooth for a tooth.' But I say to you, Do not resist one who is evil.[1] But if anyone strikes you on the right cheek, turn to him the other also" (Matthew 5:38, 39) have continuously divided Christians. Indeed, a minority states: "These words are categoric; we must put them into practice, whatever the cost." But the majority answers: "Jesus is expressing Himself in paradoxes, like the Orientals. Experience shows that the power of the wicked is great on earth. Sometimes one must resist them with weapons. If everyone gave his coat to the robber who stole his cloak, the order God wants in the world would be abolished. The Christian must give the state a hand in order to preserve order."

The majority is right insofar as nonviolence cannot be made into an article of law, apart from faith. Nonviolence can only overcome evil on earth if it is the act of God's power on earth, working through men. Nonviolence if it is a mere abstention from evil may even encourage crime. But the majority is wrong if it denounces pacifists and conscientious objectors on the grounds of wanting to bypass God's redemptive power in attempting to gain salvation by keeping their hands clean.

The coming of Gandhi, whose life and teaching surprisingly resemble that of Jesus, has restated the whole problem of nonviolence when majority theology thought it had already answered the question negatively. In fact, Gandhi was not announcing a religion of works but the religion of love.

Some nonviolent Christians make easy preys for the attacks of a certain Christian theology. In their eyes, nonviolence is the common denominator of all the great religions. They venerate Gandhi as much as they do Christ and dream of a universal religion where all conflicting viewpoints would be reconciled.

In reacting against their syncretism, official theology discards Gandhi because he overlooks the fact of sin and the need for divine grace. With Gandhi, it dismisses a nonviolence whose roots, it claims, are not Christian. Now we hope to have shown in this book the incorrectness of such a theory. Nonviolence finds its roots not only in Jesus' action but in the Mosaic principles of the Old Testament itself.

We will now try to outline briefly the similarities and differences between Gandhi and Jesus, from a historical, as well as a theological and ethical viewpoint. Then we will more clearly see to what degree their teachings complete or contradict each other.

The Historical Viewpoint

Gandhi, like Jesus, belonged to a nation oppressed for several generations by a foreign power. The British Empire, like the Roman, used the old method of dividing in order to rule, perpetuated old quarrels between princes and provinces, and either instated or overthrew the docile petty kings whenever they needed to do so. In India there were collaborators, as there were among the Jews in Jesus' days, who had adopted their master's culture to the point of forgetting their national language. But there were also patriots who found in their religion and in their national traditions a burning thirst for independence. The British, like the Romans, generally showed themselves tolerant toward local custom and worship as long as it did not disturb the peace. Armed revolts sprang up in India, as in Palestine, but they were promptly crushed.

Gandhi, like Jesus, lived among "collaborators," as well as among partisans in a war of independence. Both Gandhi and Jesus could have sheltered themselves in an abstentionist spiritualism. Both opened the way to a new concept of freedom.

Both leaders stressed the moral and spiritual conditions of liberation rather than precipitating the liberation itself. They demanded more from themselves than from their disciples, more from their disciples than from their people, more from their people than from their adversaries. Both were men of prayer. They never identified their message with the political platform of a given party, but they preferred to remain on the sidelines, as the inspirators and counselors of everyone. They both commented authoritatively upon the holy books of their religion, and sent messages to cities and towns to proclaim repentance, a radical change in the way of life, the end of social injustice, and the abolition of a hypocritical cast system. Their violent death shows a final similarity. Gandhi, like Jesus, died blessing his assassins.

But here the analogy stops. Gandhi had a political aim. He wanted to unify his people and liberate them from the foreign yoke. To reach his goal, he used one method, the *satyagraha* (power of truth) and put it to work through *ahimsa* (nonviolence). After twenty-five years of struggle, he reached his goal and obtained national independence. From a human standpoint, he succeeded.

From a human standpoint, on the contrary, Jesus failed. Moreover, His aim was not the same as Gandhi's. Jesus wanted to prepare, then inaugurate the kingdom of God on earth. His nonviolence was not a means to reach this end,[2] but rather an obedience and a witness to God, who is love and who alone will establish His kingdom on earth. It is true that if the Jewish people had listened to Jesus, the course of history would have been different. Likely national liberation with persecution would have been a result of this obedience. But Israel rejected Jesus' calls and preferred the way of violence, which led to the destruction of the Jewish state.

On the other hand, Jesus was not facing a huge multitude of politically ignorant peoples with different languages, as Gandhi was. Rather, as the Messiah who had come to accomplish the prophecies, He was confronting a nation that had been unified for centuries. He could either be recognized by the entire nation, as the Messiah, or be rejected as an impostor by the nation as a whole. The latter event took place, and Jesus' failure would have been radical and definitive if His only aim had been the national liberation of Israel.

But Jesus had inherited a deeper message from the Jewish prophets: (1) national liberation will not occur so long as the people are unfaithful to God; (2) because of the Jewish people's unfaithfulness, God will call together from the Orient and the Occident a universal people, formed by all those who will answer God's call.

Thus Jesus' failure on the national level transformed His act into a universal one. His plan is still developing today and its final completion gives direction and meaning to human history. For the present, it has already given rise to a multitude of volunteers in the world, namely, the church, insofar it is faithful to its mission.

Only the future will reveal Gandhi's place in history. The task he had chosen to carry out, the liberation of India, is finished. Many among his disciples are today members of the Indian government. In coming to power, they had to make compromises with military violence and industrial techniques that their master abhorred. Until now, no universal people, no "church" has sprung up from Gandhi's work. Will the Christian church understand that neither state nor political party can ever accept Gandhi's heritage, and that only a faithful church as the universal people of Christ constantly regenerated by the grace of God and liberated from compromise can continue the task of the Indian prophet?

The Theological Standpoint

Jesus' theology was Jewish and He expressed it in the fundamental paradox which generates action. If God is all powerful, nothing that happens is outside His will. But if God is good, He cannot be the author of evil and death; on the contrary, He is fighting them until the final victory.

Thus Jesus' moral monotheism led to a pragmatic dualism. We use the term "pragmatic" because Jesus, who struggled with evil, did not "believe" in evil as some medieval theologians. However, the reality of evil, of the frightening influence it has over the world and of the power it possesses over the children of God, posed the problem of violence for Jesus in a much more acute way than for the Hindus. As He saw it, evil truly was an enemy of God, and a dangerous one, to be fought at any cost. Only the bloody struggle of the cross and redemption was to overcome this enemy and submit it to God's order.

Gandhi, however, repeatedly stated in his writings that the necessity of a bloody struggle fought by God in His Son was incomprehensible to him. His Hindu mind saw evil, as well as good, as a manifestation of the divinity. It is therefore useless to combat it.

In his autobiography Gandhi tells how he was reached by Christian propaganda in South Africa and how he tried as sincerely as possible to acquire faith in Christ as his Savior. Unfortunately, this encounter took place with sectarians who insisted only on the problem of his personal salvation. So Gandhi wrote: "I do not seek redemption from the consequences of my sin; I seek to be redeemed from sin itself, or rather from the very thought of sin. Until I have attained that end, I shall be content to be restless."[3]

Gandhi's great spiritual sensitivity is fully revealed in this quotation, and at the same time, all that separates him from Christianity.

He did not believe in the reality of evil outside himself. Evil was in himself as a consequence of his own ignorance, his own desires, his own egoism. This is the Hindu doctrine. Had he overcome these inner obstacles and dissipated these illusions, the problem of external evil would no longer exist. So Gandhi projected into the outside world his optimistic views about evil as an inner illusion that contemplation can dissipate. On the contrary, for Jesus, who was freed from the problems of inner evil, evil was an objective obstacle, outside Himself, that should be fought with utmost energy.

So Gandhi gave up trying to become a Christian and began to search in Hinduism for the teachings that had moved him so deeply in the Gospels. The following words describe the result of his research: "A drop in the ocean partakes of the greatness of its parent although it is unconscious of it. But it is dried up as soon as it enters upon an existence independent of the ocean. We do not exaggerate when we say that life is a mere bubble. Our existence as embodied beings is purely momentary; what are a hundred years in eternity? But if we shatter the claim of egotism, and melt into the ocean of humanity, we share its dignity."[4]

"To me God is Truth and Love. . . . God is the source of light and life, and yet he is above and beyond all these. God is conscience. He is even the atheism of the atheist. . . . He is a personal God to those who need his touch . . . He simply IS to those who have faith. He is long-suffering. He is patient, but he is also terrible. He is the greatest democrat the world knows. He is the greatest tyrant ever known. We are *not*. He alone *Is*."[5]

It is evident that in this context the problem of evil did not face him as it faced Jesus. For the Hindus, God is at once Brahma, the immutable Essence, Vichnu the Creator, and Siva the Destructor; creation and destruction are two complementary principles that make possible the reincarnation of beings until their final reabsorption in God.

Hindu nonviolence thus stems from belief in the illusory character of all appearances, even the transitory appearance of the human being. Christian nonviolence, on the contrary, grows out of the unique worth of each human being in God's sight. "Why kill the evildoer?" asks the Hindu. "It will merely hasten his reincarnation. Violence is useless and aberrant. It belongs to the world of illusory passions that delay the return of all beings to God."

"I cannot kill the evildoer," says the Christian. "By shortening his earthly life, I am running the risk of taking away an opportunity for him to repent and be reconciled with God."

But if Hindu nonviolence is based on the beliefs described above, why was Gandhi a man of action, whereas his fellow believers have traditionally been passive? The answer is that Gandhi was particularly devoted to the god Krishna.

Usually, a Hindu will choose one name from among the thousand names of God, that is, from among the thousand aspects of God, and he will become more attached to this particular aspect. Krishna is the semi-historical and semi-legendary hero of one of India's sacred books, the *Bhagavad-Gita*. Gandhi chose it as his bedside book, and commented upon it for his disciples.

In the *Bhagavad-Gita*, Krishna, one of the incarnations of Vishnu, is portrayed as the divine coachman of prince Arjuna's chariot on the eve of a battle between Arjuna and one of his usurping parents. Arjuna has doubts about carrying through his murderous deed, but Krishna finally makes him decide in favor of war, at the end of a long dialogue: ". . . there is none that can destroy that changeless being. It is those bodies of the everlasting, imperishing, incomprehensible body dweller that have an end, as it is said. Therefore fight, O thou of Bharata's race. He who deems this to be a slayer, and he who thinks this to be slain, are alike without discernment. This slays not, neither is it slain. . . . For to be born sure is death, to the dead sure is birth; so for an issue that may not be escaped thou dost not well to sorrow. . . . This body's tenant for all time may not be wounded, O thou of Bharata's stock, in the body of any beings. Therefore thou dost not well to sorrow over any born beings. Looking like wise on thine own law, thou shouldst not be dismayed; for to a Knight,[6] there is no thing more blest than a lawful strife."[7] As one can easily see, the *Bhagavad-Gita* is not a nonviolent book!

Its inspiration has been compared to the Psalms of David. Like the Christians who do not hesitate to transpose David's struggles with his enemies onto the spiritual level, the modern interpreters of the *Bhagavad-Gita*, among them Gandhi, give a symbolic meaning to the battle of Arjuna. It is in reality the struggle between good and evil. Arjuna is the hero of the altruistic act, done for God, without hope of gaining something in the process.[8] Hindus like to compare this altruistic deed of Krishna with the redeeming deed of Jesus on the cross.

Through his devotion to Krishna, Gandhi reintroduced into his faith a certain pragmatic dualism reminiscent of Christianity without ever offsetting the fundamental philosophical equilibrium of Hinduism. "God," says Gandhi, "is continuously acting; He never rests. . . . However, His tireless activity is the only true rest."

Jesus also found His rest in God. He withdrew to be near to Him, in solitude, to regain strength through prayer and to prepare for action. But the God of Jesus is a personal and acting God, the God of the Jewish prophets, who cannot rest as long as the scandal of sin and death lasts. From this Hebrew tension between the God of justice, who requires the destruction of sin and the punishment of the guilty, and the God of love, who does not want the least of His children to perish, from this contradiction sprang redemption. In the best sense of the word, redemption is a drama, that is, an action that has happened in time, a unique event that marked a date in the history of humanity.

From a Hindu perspective, however, time is illusory; everything is already accomplished in God. From a Christian perspective, time is real. There was a period before redemption, a time of struggle between God's love and justice. Then there was an hour of decision when God's justice and love were reconciled by Jesus' sacrifice on the cross. And now we live in a temporary period conditioned by the redemptive act and placed under the responsibility of men who obey God's call until the coming of the Messiah's reign.

The Ethical Standpoint

It is now easier to compare Gandhi's nonviolent ethic with that of Jesus. Our criterion will be the passage from the Sermon on the Mount, "You have heard that it was said, 'An eye for an eye and a tooth for a tooth!' But I say to you, do not resist one who is evil. But if anyone strikes you on the right cheek, turn to him the other also."

How did Gandhi think this commandment was to be put into practice? He saw it as a game of chess. "Nonviolence is not a resignation from all real fighting against wickedness. On the contrary, the nonviolence of my conception is a more active and real fight against wickedness than retaliation whose very nature is to increase wickedness. . . . I seek entirely to blunt the edge of the tyrants' sword, not by putting up against it a sharper-edged weapon, but by disappointing his expectation that I would be offering physical resistance. The resistance of the soul that I should offer would elude him. I would at first dazzle him and at last compel recognition from him, which would not humiliate but uplift him."[9]

In short, Gandhi is accepting the challenge of the enemy because he knows he is a better player than the enemy and in the end he will win. It is true that Gandhi's adversary were the British and that the British have a sense of "fair play." Nevertheless, Gandhi's fundamental optimism did not lead him astray. His nonviolence stimulated the energies of the Indian people and finally overcame British colonialism. From a more general standpoint, Gandhi showed that the Sermon on the Mount can in many circumstances be politically effective. The demonstration of such an effectiveness in the age of automation and the atomic bomb is one of the great moral victories of the twentieth century.

To claim that Jesus in the Sermon on the Mount was proposing a Gandhian-type "chess game" would be a distortion of the texts. He certainly did not give up the possibility of changing his enemies' hearts. But the motive for his nonviolence is elsewhere; namely in God Himself, a God who for centuries has dealt with a thankless people and who has continuously shown His love for the good and the wicked alike by sending sun and rain. To be "the sons of the Most High" (Luke 6:35), we must be loving, and therefore nonviolent, without hoping to necessarily overcome the enemy. Jesus stated in one of the beatitudes, "Blessed are those who are persecuted for righteousness' sake" without promising any other earthly successes than the final coming of the kingdom of God. In the same line of thought as the Sermon, one finds the words: "If any man would come after me, let him deny himself and take up his cross and follow me." This self-denial to which Jesus refers is not the ascetic discipline Gandhi prescribed for his disciples to prepare them for nonviolent combat,[10] but rather something deeper. It is a preparation for the possible failure of their attempts and for physical death when the enemy will think he is the victor. God alone will change the cross of His Son into a victory.

One should not, however, exaggerate the gospel's pessimism. In Jesus' mind, God always triumphs and he may triumph immediately when faith is found on earth among men of good will. But the final victory comes after, not before, the cross. On a different level, one could say that Jesus sees nonviolence as inseparable from small groups of men of faith who live by God's grace and whose function on earth is to be God's witnesses of the cross and redemption. These groups are the salt of the earth, the light of the world, the city on a mountain-top.

However, the opposition between Jesus and Gandhi should not be carried to an extreme. In Gandhi's mind nonviolence is also a witness, an unconditional obedience to God who is truth and love. And if one believes that the Gospel of John reveals one facet of Jesus' thought which the three other Gospels ignore, one will discover a certain concept of the eternal truth of God existing before Jesus' coming and independent of time, a concept that seems very similar to Gandhi's *confession of faith:*

"You have asked me why I consider that God is Truth. In my early youth I was taught to repeat what in Hindu scriptures are known as one thousand names of God. But these one thousand names of God were by no means exhaustive. We believe, and I think it is the truth, that God has as many names as there are creatures and therefore we also say that God is nameless and since God has many forms we also consider Him as formless, and since He speaks to us through many tongues we consider Him to be speechless and so on. . . . I would say with those who say God is Love: 'God is Love.' But deep down in me I used to say that though God may be God, God is Truth above all. I have come to the conclusion that for myself God is Truth, but two years ago I went a step further and said Truth is God. And I came to that conclusion after a continuous and relentless search after Truth which began nearly fifty years ago. I then found that the nearest approach to Truth was through Love."[11]

Law and Grace Are Allies

Certainly Christians can only regret the misunderstanding that separated Gandhi from evangelical faith and his lack of understanding of God's redemptive plan in Christ, but they should be exceedingly thankful for the "ethical revolution of the twentieth century" he initiated.

Gandhi has proved that Jesus was right when He gave the Sermon on the Mount. Therefore he must be looked upon as Jesus' ally or auxiliary. He has destroyed the false arguments of all those who had been trying for centuries to prove that Jesus' ethic was not made for this earth, or that it was reserved for individual saints. He brought this ethic down to the town square and even to the battlefield. If it is relevant there, it has all the more reason to be relevant for private life.

Why then do today's Christians hesitate so much when it comes to putting this ethic into practice? The reason is that Christians in both East and West are now participating in the power structure. They have adopted an ethic of compromise with honors, power, money, and war, and they cannot free themselves from it. "We are putting the doctrine of grace through faith into practice," they say, "not grace through works. The Apostle Paul is our master."

Are they sure the Apostle Paul would claim them as his own? The grace Paul preached is given to those who, like him, have tried to obey God in all things by imitating Christ. It is only on account of their courageous struggle that Paul tells them: "Take heart; it is your faith that saves you, not your inner or outward success."

God has nothing to say to those who have given up following Christ before even starting, and have settled down in a comfortable mediocrity to which they give the name of "salutary tension." Grace will never reach these people because they don't really need grace to gain their salvation. Theirs is a salvation through compromise.

Thus Gandhi can be considered as an ally of divine grace. By showing us that voluntary dispossession and love can be put into practice on earth, he makes us once again face our sin. If the teachings of Gandhism prevailed in the church, Christians would once again see their sin; they would truly repent and the power of divine grace would come over them again. But if the church turns its back on Gandhism, its ethical teaching will be lost in the intricacies of mediocre casuistry and its members' behavior will fall into pharasaic moralism.

However, Mahatma Gandhi, who so providentially came to the church's aid, also needed Christ to be saved. Indeed, the dangers of moralism are threatening his disciples, as well as the followers of Jesus. Nonviolence has become a fad in some circles, and this fact may cause the great moral awakening started by Gandhi to stray into "techniques of nonviolence" which is a new religion of "works." These techniques, of course, should not be ignored. They can be used to obtain good results after all, but with the risk of forgetting that nonviolence is above all a witness to God. Should nonviolence become a mere method to "gain the whole world," it would quickly be used by political parties for ends of dubious integrity. And then what would be left of it?

Nonviolent Christians therefore must continuously remember, as everyone else should, that evil is no illusion. It cannot be eliminated by inner discipline or by silent demonstrations. God Himself could not economize on redemption. Are we stronger than God? Have we found a cure-all that would allow us to bypass the cross of Christ?

Gandhi, who did not understand redemption, knew he was a sinner and bemoaned the imperfection of his deeds. He was cut to the heart when the liberation of India coincided with bloody struggles between Hindus and Muslims and finally resulted in the schism of the country. Should nonviolent Christians be more superficial than Gandhi?

If history is not moving toward the kingdom of God, the liberation of India is just another chapter without sequel. Of course it made manifest one of the aspects of divinity, but it was followed by other events which some Hindus may also look upon as divine, since their divinity is destructive as well as constructive.

But if, on the contrary, history is dominated by two events that unfold in time — the redemption accomplished by Christ on the cross and the final coming of the kingdom of God — then Gandhi's work, this imperfect, nonviolent liberation of one nation, will appear as one of the premonitory signs of the kingdom. Through it, men are also called to repentance, to faith in the God of redemption, and to hope in the final victory of Christ.

17. Conclusion

From its very beginning in the world, the nonviolence which the disciples of Jesus Christ inherited from their Master posed the problem of church-state relations. The early church bore very little resemblance to what the Christian church has become today. However, like our church of today, it was conditioned by the dependence of its members upon society, by the average mediocrity of their personalities, and also by their burning faith in Jesus Christ. The states with which they dealt were the Jewish and Roman states, both very different from our national states today, but whose function was also to curb crime and to work for the common good.

Despite the considerable changes in the notions of church and state throughout the centuries, Christian thought still tries to find in the Bible a revealed definition of the church and the state, by studying, for example, the thirteenth chapter of Paul's Epistle to the Romans. We think, however, that this research is useless, because it begins with the wrong method. This error becomes apparent as soon as theology refers to "the church" and "the state" as if there were only one church and only one state in the world as in apostolic times.

To be strictly objective, one should refer to the *churches* (separated everywhere into national churches and into numerous denominations) and to the *states* (trying to keep interior order, but divided into hostile governments that use their "right" to wage war with each other). If we adopt this terminology, it soon becomes obvious that the rules of submission to Caesar as they are deduced from Romans 13 are inadequate for our day.

Should one then give up trying to search for a social ethic in the Bible? Far from it! But one should face the problem with a different method. The Bible relates "slices of history": the history of Israel among the nations, the history of Jesus among the Jews, the history of the apostles among the Gentiles. Each of these "slices" contains some form of revelation: the revelation of the relations that should exist between God and His people on the one hand, between God's people and the world — and the society in which they find themselves — on the other.

Thus biblical revelation neither defines the nature of God nor the nature of society, which would permit an *a posteriori* definition of their relation. Rather, it gives an *a priori* definition *of their relations*, which leaves both the nature of God and the nature of man very much in the dark.

When Jesus tells His disciples, "You are the salt of the earth, you are the light of the world, you are the eye of the social body, you are my witnesses," He is not teaching us the "arithmetic" of the kingdom of God, that is, the art and technique of performing operations on numbers, on absolute values (which "God" and "the state" cannot understand). Rather, He is revealing to us the "algebra" of the kingdom of God, that is, the science of "functions and relations" between unknown values. Thus, any speculation concerning the church and the state, taken as absolute values, is not scriptural and is doomed to failure. Moreover, the study of the gospel has shown us the relativity with which Jesus looked upon man-made institutions. In this view they are instruments of God only insofar as they are open to the kingdom of God.

The algebraic formulas found in the Scripture still give us an exact revelation of God's will for His people. Though they do not give us the values of the unknowns, they allow us to explore and clear out large sections of the jungle of human society where we live.

Let us review some of these formulas:

First Formula: Jesus' nonviolence finds its roots in the Jewish concept of a *chosen people with a mission among the nations*. This formula is still valid for the church in the twentieth century.

Second Formula: The ethic of the chosen people does not allow for a divorce between justice and forgiveness. *Justice and forgiveness follow each other in time*, just as the Sabbath follows the six days of the week. For the chosen people, the Sabbath is the premonitory sign of the final reestablishment of all things. Jesus wanted to restore the sabbatical and jubilean ethic in Israel. Consequently, the awakening He started had a revolutionary character, from both a religious and a social standpoint. This formula is valid for the church of the twentieth century.

Third Formula: Jesus' ethic differs from that of the Essenes in that it does not grow out of a pessimistic view of the world. It does not propose asceticism; neither does it demand escapism from the world. It does not oppose an "ethic of absolutes" to life in flesh; rather, it states, in the Sermon on the Mount, that *a behavior governed by the love of God is possible in the world*. This formula is valid for the church of the twentieth century.

Fourth Formula: Jesus' nonviolence does not grow out of a pantheistic, optimistic, or utopian view of the world; it comes from a precise evaluation of the terrible power of evil. It becomes manifest in *the very act of redemption by which God, and God alone, overcame the power of evil by using it for His glory.* The church of the twentieth century is a witness to this as was the first century church.

Fifth Formula: Jesus had a political program: the reestablishment of Israel by means of which the chosen people would become the light of the nations. The church of Jesus Christ in the twentieth century is the new Israel, formed by those who have come from the East and West and respond to Jesus' call. The church of the twentieth century has inherited the political program of Jesus. *It must again and again repent and reform itself according to Jesus' sabbatical and jubilean program* and carry out its function: announcing the coming kingship of the Christ over the world and inaugurating it with visible signs.

Sixth Formula: Jesus never abandoned His political program. His nonviolence is not founded upon the weakness of a God who has given up doing justice. Jesus is announcing the imminent judgment. But because of the chosen people's disobedience and the sacrifice of His Son, *God is delaying His judgment and showing His love for the man He created in granting Him an opportunity for salvation.* This salvation, of which the church is both the beneficiary and the messenger, is meant for all individuals and all nations.

Seventh Formula: During the delay Jesus inaugurated by His sacrifice, God always saves; He never kills. He places the human being as a person, whether good or evil, at the center of human history. Man must be healed. By inventing the person, Jesus has revealed to us that we are capable of understanding the Person of God, who is our Father. *The object of nonviolence, the fabric of which it is knit, is the human being as person, always unique in the sight of God's person, since the unique Son of God sacrificed His life for this person.* Once again this formula is valid for the witness of the church in the twentieth century.

o   o   o

Two more considerations concerning the role of nonviolence in history are as follows.

To our knowledge, all the religious, philosophical, or political doctrines that affirm the inevitable use of violence also admit that it is secondary. It is only a means of reaching an end: justice and peace. But peace is nonviolence. Thus all men agree that nonviolence is the final end of history.

Consequently, those who abandon nonviolence as the supreme goal of human endeavor are not exhibiting a sense of history, as it is commonly thought, by accepting participation in the necessary "involvements" in order to do one's human duty. On the contrary, they are bypassing history, freezing history, betraying history, insofar as they abandon its supreme goal. They are taking history back centuries to a pre-Christian or extra-Christian period. Woe to humanity on the day when the church will have given up being the salt of the earth and will have capitulated to the violent ones!

The function of the church of Jesus Christ in the twentieth century is to draw history out of the mire by proving that nonviolent action is the visible expression of redemption, the only means chosen by God to bring about justice and peace. Should those who are predicting a collective suicide of humanity by the use of nuclear weapons be right, it may even be necessary to save history by tearing humanity away from a premature death, contrary to God's will.

Our last remark concerns the awareness of history. Economic, physiological, and sociological factors certainly determine history, as the body determines the spirit. But even though the human being is determined by his body, he exists only in his *awareness* of existing. So much the more, human history exists only in its awareness of existing. A history unaware of itself would not exist.

Now, the locus of historic awareness is the individual. It is true that the individual is the product of his heredity, that he is shaped by his environment, and that he gains a consciousness of history by means of the books and monuments that recall it. It is nonetheless true that an awareness of history is always gained on an individual level. History is continuously thought over by individual beings, as a musical phrase composed by some past genius must be replayed by a musician to become alive again.

Thus it is important that each of us acquire as correct a view of history as possible, that is, as close as possible to Jesus Christ's view of history.

Footnotes

Preface

1. There is a direct proportion between the tendency of Christians to intellectualize all moral issues and the degree to which they have become a part of the bourgeois establishment.

2. The word "atom" means "that which cannot be cut."

3. Angelology and demonology were the knowledge of angels and demons, originated in Persia.

4. The German exegete Friedrich Hauck supported the same point of view in his *Evangelium des Lukas*, Leipzig, 1934.

Chapter 1

1. Some authors claim that the word "Pharisee," whose root is PRS, can also be interpreted as PARSI which means Persian. The Pharisaic sect would then have had a Persian origin, which would explain its dualistic belief in God and Satan, in angels and demons.

2. In the four Gospels, the notion of a paradise after death sometimes takes the place of the eschatological notion of the kingdom of God on earth as in heaven. When the messianic hopes were dampened after the destruction of Jerusalem, the Christians rapidly began seeing the earth, where they were persecuted, as a valley of tears, a place of trials on the road to heaven. This sometimes resulted in a regrettable lack of concern for the future of humanity on this earth.

3. The history of Creation and of the Fall, we are told, comes from a Sumerian myth. Granted! It is all the more remarkable that the Jews with their particular outlook were able to derive a thoroughly ethical story from a crass legend.

4. The "offense" that God's Word inflicts upon natural man is the only starting point of a life renewed by God's grace.

5. A Western traveler to Moscow returned home with the following anecdote which underlines a certain analogy between Christ's thinking and the creative finalism of sovietism. The traveler, pointing out to his Russian guide the shattered facades of some old houses along a muddy and hole-infested road, asked, "Is this not the proof of the ineffectiveness of your political regime?" The Russian replied, "Those houses are there to be rebuilt. Come back five years from now and you will see new apartment buildings on the same spot."

Jesus was asked one day, "Why is this man blind?" He answered, "That the works of God might be made manifest in him", or, in today's language, so that he might be healed (John 9:1-3).

6. Despite the increasing leniency of our customs, and perhaps partly because of this leniency which complies with evil and opens from time to time enormous gaps of injustice, our civilized society resorts to "blood vengeance" in its most inhuman form. It assumes the right to inflict appalling collective punishments upon entire nations declared guilty of "violating God's law." No risk is too great for restoring the injured "immanent" justice. The soldier, modern "avenger of blood," is given all the arms deemed necessary to save God's honor. While carrying out his sacred task, he tarnishes his hands with the blood of others, but he remains innocent in God's eyes, whose works he executes. His body finally rests in the "field of honor."

Chapter 2

1. We have put in parentheses several words which are found in Luke's text, but which are not found in the text of Isaiah 61, quoted by Jesus.

2. To better understand the following discussion, the reader should consult the Old Testament texts which institute the sabbatical year: Leviticus 25 (which describes the Jubilee in detail); Exodus 21:2-6; 23:10-12; Deuteronomy 15:1-18; 31:9-13; Ezekiel 46: 16-18; Jeremiah 34:8-17; Leviticus 26:34-38, 43; 2 Chronicles 36:20, 21.

3. The French version to which the author is referring translates *ratsah* by "pay the debt of their iniquity." The King James Version reads, "They shall accept of the punishment of their iniquity" (translator's note).

4. Cf. the section concerning the *goel* at the end of chapter 1.

5. Cf. Ezekiel 45:7, 8; 46:16-18.

6. This idea of "investment" is found in certain parables of Jesus. Matthew 25:14-30; Luke 20:9, 10. In conformity with the jubilean principle this investment is limited in time. Once the delay has passed, man must return his capital to God, the sole Owner.

7. There is a certain similarity between this passage and Jesus' prophecy against Jerusalem and the cities of Galilee. Six centuries later, Israel's leaders still were disobeying the same ordinances. Their refusal to repent was to bring about a similar chastisement.

8. Nehemiah 5:1-13 is particularly interesting for our study not only because it recounts the stirring celebration of the Jubilee, but also because it describes the process by which the poor of Israel were forced to pawn their fields, vineyards, and houses in order to receive wheat or pay their taxes during a period of famine and how they were forced to turn their children into slaves when they could not meet the demands of their creditors. Jesus describes this same process in His parable of the unforgiving servant.

Chapter 3

1. S. W. Baron, *Social and Religious History of the Jews* (Columbia University Press, N.Y., 1952), chap. VIII, "Social Troubles."

2. The very existence of the *Prosboul* proves that, contrary to certain authors' affirmations, there was in Israel at the time of Jesus a strong current of opinion in favor of a strict application of the Jubilee's second provision, that is the periodic remittance of debts.

3. *Mishnah, Gittin IV,* 3.

4. Babylonian *Talmud, Gittin.*

5. Cf. Exodus 22:26: "If ever you take your neighbor's garment in pledge, you shall restore it to him before the sun goes down; for that is his only covering, it is his mantle for his body; in what else will he sleep? And if he cries to me, I will hear, for I am compassionate."

6. Certain Muslim countries still live under the system of *Hamsin* according to which the sharecropper owes his master four fifths of his harvest! The poverty of the Indian peasant is also caused by the exactions of the *Zamindars,* the usurers in charge of collecting taxes and rents. The Chinese revolution more recently abolished a similar system. Palestine in Jesus' time suffered under the same type of oppression.

7. The socialization of the means of production is yet too recent to take preference over free enterprise. It has been producing spectacular results in some countries. But one does not know if it will paralyze individual initiative as time goes on. Free enterprise on the other hand encourages initiative and permits the rapid creation of a pro-

176

ductive capital. But this system also leads to the accumulation of capital in the hands of a minority, to the exploitation of the worker, and to unbridled competition which degenerates into wars. The exploitation of workers has become less visible now in the West than 50 years ago but has been expanded to an intercontinental scale. The hyperindustrialized continents draw their extreme prosperity from the wealth of a cluster of underdeveloped regions on their periphery.

The large foreign companies who invest their capital in underdeveloped regions (oil, mines, canals, dams) are also draining off dividends for their stockholders when the profits should be going to the inhabitants of these regions. Foreign companies are very effective in promoting rapid industrialization, but the concessions granted them should be only short-term ones. A periodic redistribution of capital would avoid the cruel injustices and bloody revolutions such concessions cause. Think of the Suez Canal, of oil in North Africa and the Middle East, of copper and uranium mines in tropical Africa and Latin America, etc. (Translator's note: Last sentence was added by the author in preparation of English edition.)

8. Exodus 22 also has a jubilean connotation. It orders "restoration" or "restitution" of alienated property. The Hebrew verb meaning "to restore" is *Shalam* from which the substantive *Shalom* (peace) derives. According to Moses, there is no peace without "restoration or without justice."

Chapter 4

1. Cf. end of chapter 1.

2. However, when the Zealots wanted to carry Him off to make Him king (probably as war leader) or when people tried to put Him in the role of a judge (*krites*), He objected. We will later examine the causes of this refusal.

3. *Kerygma* means proclamation of a message by the king's heralds.

4. These remarks lead us to the distinction between the eschatological and apocalyptic in Jesus' thought. Eschatology, knowledge of the "last things," is strongly rooted in history. It prolongs on earth and in a concrete and near future the election of the Jewish people, from which it cannot be separated. In our time, one cannot yet formulate eschatological thoughts apart from either the ancient Israel or the new Israel, the church. The future of the two Israels can be imagined only on earth where God's people must be a witness to the nations. The hardships announced by the prophets are always temporal ones, followed by a reestablishment of Israel on earth, where justice will reign from then on.

Apocalyptic thought, on the other hand, originates from the expectancy of a total destruction which will affect not only the earth, but also the universe and will be followed by a new creation. The mingling of these two concepts is evident in Matthew 24.

5. Cf. the other "You said so" which Jesus pronounced before the Sanhedrin (Matthew 26:47-68).

6. According to Roman custom, a small sign called *titulus* was to indicate the reason for a criminal's execution.

7. God.

8. The last of the pagan kings preceding the coming of the Son of Man.

9. The empires of the Babylonians, of the Medes, of the Persians, and of Alexander's Greeks according to Daniel. Jesus probably added the Roman Empire or the kingdom of the Herodian dynasty to the list.

10. The Messiah, King of Israel.

11. Cf. Luke 22:18, "I shall not drink of the fruit of the vine until the kingdom of God comes."

12. "Hosanna to the King of David! Blessed is he who comes in the name of the Lord" (Matthew). "Blessed is the kingdom of our father David that is coming!" (Mark). "Blessed is the King who comes in the name of the Lord" (Luke). "Blessed is he who comes in the name of the Lord, even the King of Israel" (John).

Chapter 5

1. Cf. also Isaiah 56:1, 2, 4-7; 58:13, 14; 66:23.
2. Jacob, too, was in a historical situation; his concern was not to come under his brother's vengeance and he overcame the angel. The angel at the ford of Jabbok is not the God of the absolute, but the God of Israel. The struggle with the angel continues today for each one of us, not on ethical grounds, but on the grounds of doubt, faith, and grace.

Chapter 6

1. Later Jesus would say, "Be sons of your Father who is in heaven; for he makes his sun to rise on the evil and the good, and sends rain on the just and the unjust" (Matthew 5:45).
2. This term refers to God as the "avenger" of His oppressed people, whom He liberates by redeeming it (cf. end of chapter 1).
3. Cf. end of chapter 1.
4. Several times throughout history, great religious movements that started with the unique preoccupation of being faithful to God, degenerated into violence and civil war: (a) Muhammad, who had been forced to flee from Mecca on the 16th of June 622, gave up his earlier patience and began to attack the caravans of his enemies. (b) Luther in 1525, fearing the excesses of the revolted peasants, abandoned the nonviolence of his beginnings and advised the princes to use violence against them. He also ordered the believers to support the princes. (c) Coligny in 1562, shocked by the news of the Vassy massacre and tired of seeing his defenseless fellow believers imprisoned, tortured, and assassinated, decided to take up arms and thus opened the era of religious wars.

Jesus, on the other hand, seeing that His earthly work was about to be destroyed by His adversaries, refused to be carried away into armed resistance. The early Christians and some Protestant groups of the 16th century were the only ones who followed their Master in the path on nonviolence.

Chapter 7

1. In one of Jesus' parables upon which we commented in Chapter III, He alludes to the succession crisis that marked Archelaus' coming to power: "A nobleman went into a far country to receive kingly power and returned. . . . But his citizens hated him and sent an embassy after him, saying: 'We do not want this man to reign over us' " (Luke 19:12, 14). This narrative undoubtedly refers to Archelaus' unsuccessful trip to Rome between AD 4 and 6, that is, when Jesus was ten or twelve years old.
2. We have seen how the creditor and sometimes the king himself could have his insolvent debtor sold, along with his wife, children, and possessions until the debt had

178

been paid. Jesus tells about one of these sales, which He probably saw with His own eyes.

3. Cf. Chapter I.

Chapter 8

1. Hillel, the kindly Pharisee who was satisfied, it is said, with a few pennies to support his family, seriously wondered whether the *Am-haerez* even had a conscience.

2. The Jehovah's Witnesses sect practices conscientious objection today, but is ready to take up arms on the day of the supreme battle between Yahweh and Satan.

Chapter 9

1. The gospel tells us how some of Jesus' listeners tried to make Him say that one should refuse to pay tribute to Caesar. By agreeing with them, Jesus would have sided with the Zealots. Did He not say as they did, "Neither be called master, for you have one master, the Christ"?

2. Theudas lived under procurator Fadus around AD 46.

3. Josephus, *Jewish Wars*, II, XIII, 3.

4. *Ibid.*, 4, 5.

Chapter 10

1. The violence and blunders of Pilate caused him to be recalled to Rome by Vitellius. He was unable to justify himself, as we have already seen.

Chapter 11

1. John 7:22-24.

2. Jesus was accustomed to their fits of anger and had nicknamed them "Boanerges," or "sons of thunder."

3. This pithy remark and the decision to go elsewhere define exactly, both theologically and pragmatically, what Christian nonviolence is.

4. John 8:48: "Are we not right in saying that you are a Samaritan and have a demon?"

5. This would explain why Jesus did not tell him to give up his military profession.

Chapter 12

1. John 7:48, 49.

2. Josephus, *Jewish Antiquities*, XVIII, I, 3.

Chapter 13

1. The word "Iscariot" may be a deformation of the word *sicarii*, the Latin equivalent of "Zealot." Traditionally, "Iscariot" has been said to mean "a man of Karioth" (ish-Karioth), citizen of Karioth. However, it is assumed, there is no city with this name.

2. All revolutionaries must fight on two fronts: the exterior one, against the enemies of their people, and the interior one, against the reactionaries who oppose revolution. In Jesus' mind the interior front came first because He believed with the prophets that God would liberate His people as soon as they would obey His voice.

3. Whatever the interpretation one chooses to give these words, they still reveal Jesus' sympathy for "men of violence." According to some, they mean that Jesus thought only men with a violent character could force the door to the kingdom of God and become its heroes. Jesus' disciples would be called to constitute a band of combatants who would fight for Israel's independence like the Zealots.

According to others, these words are on the contrary a warning against those who want to establish the kingdom of God by violence, but they would also reveal a profound irritation toward the "luke-warm" who think that one can enter the kingdom of God without effort.

4. Christian nonviolence does not come from a pantheistic theory or moral pragmatism. It is the "way of the cross" (*via crucis*) that the disciple must follow after his Master. The passion of Jesus Christ is the defining element of Christian nonviolence.

5. No motive other than this proclamation of His messiahship can explain Jesus' return to Jerusalem. This is proof of the fact that He truly considered Himself to be the Messiah.

6. Today's nonviolent conscientious objectors are often criticized for their "angelism." "If you want to break with this world," they are told, "go live on a desert island." But Christ's kingdom, which they are trying to serve, must be present in the world like a leaven of life.

7. Luther developed this theory known as the "doctrine of the two kingdoms."

8. In Greek this means literally: "My kingdom is not of this source." In other words, my kingdom does not have the same origin as the kingdoms of this world. This passage brings to mind the scene where Jesus looked upon the kingdoms of this *cosmos* and their glory, but refused to conquer them with the means proposed by the tempter.

Chapter 14

1. Today, either to liberate the world from the exploitation of capitalism or to free it from the danger of communism, people on both sides are beginning to think that the destruction of humanity by the atomic bomb may well be the lesser of two evils!

2. Cf. the *Shabbath* tractate of the *Mishnah*, XXII, paragraph 6: "They may anoint or rub their stomach but not have themselves kneaded or scraped . . . they may not set a broken limb. If a man's hand or foot is dislocated he may not pour cold water over it, but he may wash it after his usual fashion and if he is healed in this way, he is healed."

3. We have already mentioned the collision between the Sanhedrin and the Romans at the time of Jesus' trial. If Jesus had chosen violence, He would have set off, on one hand, a civil war, and on the other hand, a war of national liberation.

4. By acting in this way, we do not think that Jesus gave up His religious, social,

and political revolution; He did not "stray" from the path God had intended for Him to follow. Most revolutionaries deviate from the primary aim — man — out of concern for efficiency. Jesus did not deviate by giving up the violent defense of His kingdom. He chose man and by choosing man, He gave His kingdom an importance such as no political movement before and after Him ever had, an importance such that a new civilization was going to grow out of it.

To limit Christianity to a preaching of individual salvation would betray Jesus because the individual who has been redeemed by his *goel*, Christ, is also the material for a new religious, social, and political fabric willed by God.

5. The unfaithfulness of Christians becomes obvious in view of their priorities. The economic and political necessities cannot wait, they say; God, however, has plenty of time. But in Jesus' eyes, God cannot wait! The economic and political necessities whose importance He does not underestimate will be served better if God comes first.

6. Elsewhere in the Gospel, as well as in this case, Jesus makes no distinction between body and soul; to save is to heal at once the entire human being, body and soul. To kill is to destroy the entire human being, body and soul. One cannot kill the body to save the soul, or kill the soul to save the body. The famous words: "Whoever seeks to gain his life will lose it, but whoever loses his life will preserve it," do not mean that one can save one's soul by hurling one's body into death. It is not the sacrifice of the body that counts, but the unlimited dedication of our entire being, body and soul, to a cause more important than our life. The cause Jesus proposes is a person: Himself, and the cause for which He gave His life was also a person, the other man. And I too am one of those "other men" for whom He gave His life willingly.

7. "Bundles of straw, bundles of branches, and bundles of young shoots may be removed from their place if they were put in readiness before the Sabbath as cattle fodder; if not they may not be removed" (*Shabbath* tractate of *Mishnah*; XVIII, 2).

8. The false dilemma can be stated as follows: to use violence or to allow the wicked to do as he pleases; to use the sword or to be a coward.

9. Jesus never advocated the tyrannical heroism of group solidarities. Peter thought he could "give his life" for Jesus (John 13:37), "Lord, why cannot I follow you now? I will lay down my life for you." But Jesus put him back in his place: "The cock will not crow till you have denied me three times."

Chapter 15

1. This proves that the author thought the last days preceding the Messiah's return were still quite near.

2. The Nuremberg trials, atrocities committed by Christian nations in Algeria and Vietnam (Calley trial) have also underlined the absurdity of blind obedience to orders.

3. Rapid progress in modern social security, hospital care, medicine, and surgery is shrinking the area of life where the church still has some usefulness.

4. The final revolution which will abolish capitalistic exploitation and make men good, because competition and the state will have vanished forever.

Chapter 16

1. The Greek text uses the verb *anthistemi*, which means "to face someone for a fight," and should be translated: "Do not fight evil with the same weapons."

2. For Gandhi, nonviolence was also more than a means toward his end. It was also

a witness to God; but Gandhi placed his spirituality in the service of an immediate political end. This, Jesus did not do.

3. From *My Experiments with Truth* (London: Phoenix Press, 1949), p. 104.

4. From *Yeravda Mandir* (Ahinedabad: Navajivan Press, 1935), p. 68.

5. From *Young India*, March 5, 1925, p. 81.

6. The warrior, the *kshatriva*, belongs to one of the four castes of Hinduism. His function, instituted by God, is to fight for the good, somewhat like the knights of the Middle Ages.

7. From *Bhagavad-Gita*, II, 17-19, 27, 30, 31.

8. "Action alone is thine. Leave thou the fruit completely alone," says *Bhagavad-Gita*.

9. From *Young India*, Oct. 8, 1925, p. 346.

10. Gandhi called his disciples to what he called "voluntary suffering": a absolute truth, a pledge of chastity, a pledge of poverty, a pledge of no possession.

11. From *Young India*, Dec. 31, 1931, p. 427.

Appendix I
Texts Related to Chapter 8

JOSEPHUS, JEWISH ANTIQUITIES
Book XVIII, chapter 11
Date: AD 8 (Jesus is 15 years old)

During the administration of Judaea by Coponius, who, as I have said, had been dispatched with Quirinius, an event occurred which I shall now describe. When the Festival of Unleavened Bread, which we call Passover, was going on, the priests were accustomed to throw open the gates of the temple after midnight. This time, when the gates were first opened, some Samaritans, who had secretly entered Jerusalem, began to scatter human bones in the porticoes and throughout the temple. As a result, the priests, although they had previously observed no such custom, excluded everyone from the temple, in addition to taking other measures for the greater protection of the temple.

JOSEPHUS, JEWISH ANTIQUITIES
Book XVIII, chapters 1, 2, 3
Date: circa AD 35

The Samaritan nation too was not exempt from disturbance. For a man who made light of mendacity and in all his designs catered to the mob, rallied them, bidding them go in a body with him to Mount Gerizim, which in their belief is the most sacred of mountains. He assured them that on their arrival he would show them the sacred vessels which were buried there, where Moses had deposited them. His hearers, viewing this tale as plausible, appeared in arms. They posted themselves in a certain village named Tirathana, and, as they planned to climb the mountain in a great multitude, they welcomed to their ranks the new arrivals who kept coming. But before they could ascend, Pilate blocked their projected route up the mountain with a detachment of cavalry and heavy-armed infantry, who in an encounter, with the firstcomers in the village slew some in a pitched battle and put the others to flight. Many prisoners were taken, of whom Pilate put to death the principal leaders and those who were most influential among the fugitives.

When the uprising had been quelled, the council of the Samaritans went to Vitellius, a man of consular rank who was governor of Syria, and charged Pilate with the slaughter of the victims. For, they said, it was not as rebels against the Romans but as refugees from the persecution of Pilate that they had met in Tirathana. Vitellius thereupon dispatched Marcellus, one of his friends, to take charge of the administration of Judaea, and ordered Pilate to return to Rome to give the emperor his account of the matters with which he was charged by the Samaritans. And so Pilate, after having spent ten years in Judaea, hurried to Rome in obedience to the orders of Vitellius, since he could not refuse. But before he reached Rome Tiberius had already passed away.

Vitellius, on reaching Judaea, went up to Jerusalem, where the Jews were celebrating their traditional feast called the Passover. Having been received in magnificent fashion, Vitellius remitted to the inhabitants of the city all taxes on the sale of agricultural produce and agreed that the vestments of the high priest and all his ornaments should be kept in the temple in custody of the priests, as had been their privilege before. At that time the vestments were stored in Antonia — there is a stronghold of that name — for the following reason. One of the priests, Hyrcanus, the first of many by that name, had constructed a large house near the temple and lived there most of the time. As custodian of the vestments, for to him alone was conceded the right to put them on, he kept them laid away there, whenever he put on his ordinary clothes in order to go down to the city. His sons and their children also followed the same practice.

JOSEPHUS, JEWISH WAR
Book II, chapter 12
Date: circa AD 50

Next came a conflict between the Galilaeans and the Samaritans. At a village called Gema, situated in the great plain of Samaria, a Galilaean, one of a large company of Jews on their way up to the festival, was murdered. Thereupon, a considerable crowd assembled in haste from Galilee with the intention of making war on the Samaritans; meanwhile, the notables of the country went off to Cumanus, and entreated him, ere any irreparable mischief was done, to repair to Galilee and punish the perpetrators of the murder, as that was the only means of dispersing the crowd before they came to blows. Cumanus, however, treating their request as less important than other affairs on his hands, dismissed the petitioners without any satisfaction.

When the news of the murder reached Jerusalem, the masses were profoundly stirred, and, abandoning the festival, they dashed off to Samaria, without generals and without listening to any of the magistrates who sought to hold them back. The brigands and rioters among the party had as their leaders Eleazar, son of Deinaeus, and Alexander, who, falling upon the borders of the toparchy of Acrabatene, massacred the inhabitants without distinction of age and burnt the villages.

Cumanus, taking with him from Caesarea a troop of cavalry known as "Sebastenians," now set off to the assistance of the victims of these ravages; he made prisoners of many of Eleazar's companions and killed a yet larger number. As for the rest of the party who had rushed to war with the Samaritans, the magistrates of Jerusalem hastened after them, clad in sackcloth and with ashes strewn upon their heads, and implored them to return home and not, by their desire for reprisals on the Samaritans, to bring down the wrath of the Romans on Jerusalem, but to take pity on their country and sanctuary, on their own wives and children; all these were threatened with destruction merely for the object of avenging the blood of a single Galilaean. Yielding to these remonstrances the Jews dispersed. Many of them, however, emboldened by impunity, had recourse to robbery, and raids and insurrections, fostered by the more reckless, broke out all over the country.

Manuscripts of the Dead Sea:
Manual of Discipline

Everyone who is admitted to the formal organization of the community is to enter into a covenant in the presence of all fellow-volunteers in the cause and to commit himself by a binding oath to abide with all his heart and soul by the commandments of the Law of Moses. . .

. . . He that so commits himself is to keep apart from all froward men that walk in the path of wickedness; for such men are not to be reckoned in the covenant. . . .

. . . God regards as impure all that transgress His word. No one is to have any association with such a man either in work or in goods, lest he incur the penalty of prosecution. Rather is he to keep away from such a man in every respect, for the Scripture says: "Keep away from every false thing."

. . . "Desist from man whose breath is in his nostrils, for as what is he reckoned?" All that are not reckoned in the Covenant must be put aside, and likewise all that they possess. A holy man must not rely on works of vanity, and vanity is what all of them are that have not recognized God's Covenant. All that spurn his word will God blast out of the world. All their actions are as filth before Him, and He regards all their possessions as unclean.

. . . When these men exist in Israel, these are the provisions whereby they are to be kept apart from any consort with froward men, to the end that they may indeed "go into the wilderness to prepare the way," i.e., do what Scripture enjoins when it says, "Prepare in the wilderness the way . . . make straight in the desert a highway for our God." (The reference is to the study of the Law which God commanded through Moses to the end that, as occasion arises, all things may be done in accordance with what is revealed therein and with what the prophets also have revealed through God's Holy Spirit.)

". . . In this time the men of the community shall form a sanctuary apart for Aaron, unified with the Saint of Saints, and a house of community for Israel, those whose conduct is pure" (direct translation from French).

Extracts from the Manuscripts of the Dead Sea:
The Sons of Light and the Sons of Darkness

On the trumpets for marshalling the battle they shall write: "The marshalled squadrons of God are able to wreak His angry vengeance upon all the Sons of Darkness."

On the trumpets of assembly for the infantry, when the gates of war are opened for them to go out to the enemy line, they shall write: "A reminder of the vengeance to be exacted in the Era of God."

On the trumpets of carnage they shall write: "The force of God's power in battle is able to fell all the perfidious as slain men."

On the trumpets of ambush they shall write: "The hidden powers of God are able to destroy wickedness."

On the trumpets of pursuit they shall write: "God has smitten all the children of Darkness. He will not turn back His anger until He has consumed them."

. . . On the standard of Merari they are to write: "Offering unto God," together with the names of the chiefs of the Merarites and those of the commanders of its thousands.

On the standard of the thousand they are to write: "God's anger is vented in fury against Belial and against all that cast their lot with him, that they have no remnant"; together with the name of the commander of the thousand and of its hundreds.

On the standard of the hundred they shall write: "From God comes the power of battle against all sinful flesh."

. . . All of these shall pursue the enemy to annihilate him in the battle of God unto his eternal extinction. And the priests shall blow for them on the trumpets of pursuit, and they shall fall upon the enemy to pursue him unto destruction. And the horsemen shall keep chasing them back into the thick of the battle until utter destruction is achieved. And while the enemy are falling slain, the priests shall go sounding the signals from a distance; they shall not go into the midst of the slain lest they be defiled by their impure blood; for the priests are holy and they are not to defile the oil of their priestly anointment with the blood of vain heathen.

. . . Today is the day which he has fixed to reverse and make stumble the prince of the kingdom of perdition and he will send his eternal help to the side he has redeemed by the power of an angel whom he has made full of glory to rule over his empire; Michel who dwells in light eternal, will bring to Israel the light in joy, peace and benediction to the party of God in order to exalt among the gods, the rule of Michel and the dominion of Israel over all flesh. Justice will rejoice in high places and all of the sons of his truth will be content in eternal knowledge. And you, sons of his Alliance, be strong in the crucible of God until a sign from his hand fills his crucibles with his mysteries in order that you may resist.

> Arise, O warrior!
> Take thy captives, thou man of glory;
> and reap thy spoil, O valiant!
> Set thy hand upon the neck of thy foemen,
> and thy foot upon mounds of the slain.
> Smite the nations that assail thee,
> and let thy sword devour guilty flesh.
> Fill thy land with glory
> and Thine inheritance with blessing.
> Be a multitude of possessions in Thy fields,
> silver and gold and precious stones in Thy palaces.
> Zion, rejoice exceedingly,
> and shine forth, O Jerusalem, with songs of joy,
> Let thy gates be continually open,
> that the wealth of the nations may be brought unto thee;
> and let their kings minister unto thee,
> and all that oppressed thee make obeisance to thee,
> and lick the dust of thy feet!
> O daughter of my people,
> ring out your songs of joy!
> Put on your finery.

Appendix II
Texts Related to Chapter 9

JOSEPHUS, *JEWISH WAR*
Book I, chapter 23
Golden eagle affair at the end of Herod the Great's reign
4 BC (Jesus is 3 years old)

There were in the capital two doctors with a reputation as profound experts in the laws of their country, who consequently enjoyed the highest esteem of the whole nation; their names were Judas, son of Sepphoraeus, and Matthias, son of Margalus. Their lectures on the laws were attended by a large youthful audience, and day after day they drew together quite an army of men in their prime. Hearing now that the king was gradually sinking under despondency and disease, these doctors threw out hints to their friends that this was the fitting moment to avenge God's honor and to pull down those structures which had been erected in defiance of their fathers' laws. It was, in fact, unlawful to place in the temple either images or busts or any representation whatsoever of a living creature; notwithstanding this, the king had erected over the great gate a golden eagle. This it was which these doctors now exhorted their disciples to cut down, telling them that, even if the action proved hazardous, it was a noble deed to die for the law of one's country; for the souls of those who came to such an end attained immortality and an eternally abiding sense of felicity; it was only the ignoble, uninitiated in their philosophy, who clung in their ignorance to life and preferred death on a sick-bed to that of a hero.

While they were discoursing in this strain, a rumour spread that the king was dying; the news caused the young men to throw themselves more boldly into the enterprise. At mid-day, accordingly, when numbers of people were perambulating the temple, they let themselves down from the roof by stout cords and began chopping off the golden eagle with hatchets. The king's captain, to whom the matter was immediately reported, hastened to the scene with a considerable force, arrested about forty of the young men and conducted them to the king. Herod first asked them whether they had dared to cut down the golden eagle; they admitted it. "Who ordered you to do so?" he continued. "The law of our fathers." "And why so exultant, when you will shortly be put to death?" "Because, after our death, we shall enjoy greater felicity."

These proceedings provoked the king to such fury that he forgot his disease and had himself carried to a public assembly, where at great length he denounced the men as sacrilegious persons who, under the pretext of zeal for the law, had some more ambitious aim in view, and demanded that they should be punished for impiety. The people, apprehensive of wholesale prosecutions, besought him to confine the punishment to the instigators of the deed and to those who had been arrested in the perpetration of it, and to forgo his anger against the rest. The king grudgingly consented; those who had let themselves down from the roof together with the doctors he had burnt alive; the remainder of those arrested he handed over to his executioners.

JOSEPHUS, *JEWISH ANTIQUITIES*
Book XVIII, chapter 1
Judas the Galilean and Saddok
4 BC - AD 6 (Jesus was between 3 and 12 years old)

Quirinius, a Roman senator who had proceeded through all the magistracies to the consulship and a man who was extremely distinguished in other respects, arrived in Syria, dispatched by Caesar to be governor of the nation and to make an assessment of their property. Coponius, a man of equestrian rank, was sent along with him to rule over the Jews with full authority. Quirinius also visited Judaea, which had been annexed to Syria, in order to make an assessment of the property of the Jews and to liquidate the estate of Archelaus. Although the Jews were at first shocked to hear of the registration of property, they gradually condescended, yielding to the arguments of the high priest Joazar, the son of Boethus, to go no further in opposition. So those who were convinced by him declared, without shilly-shallying, the value of their property. But a certain Judas, a Gaulanite from a city named Gamala, who had enlisted the aid of Saddok, a Pharisee, threw himself into the cause of rebellion. They said that the assessment carried with it a status amounting to downright slavery, no less, and appealed to the nation to make a bid for independence. They urged that in case of success the Jews would have laid the foundation of prosperity, while if they failed to obtain any such boon, they would win honour and renown for their lofty aim; and that Heaven would be their zealous helper to no lesser end than the furthering of their enterprise until it succeeded — all the more if with high devotion in their hearts they stood firm and did not shrink from the bloodshed that might be necessary. Since the populace, when they heard their appeals, responded gladly, the plot to strike boldly made serious progress; and so these men sowed the seed of every kind of misery, which so afflicted the nation that words are inadequate. When wars are set afoot that are bound to rage beyond control, and when friends are done away with who might have alleviated the suffering, when the raids are made by great hordes of brigands and men of the highest standing are assassinated, it is supposed to be the common welfare that is upheld, but the truth is that in such cases the motive is private gain. They sowed the seed from which sprang strife between factions and the slaughter of fellow citizens. Some were slain in civil strife, for these men madly had recourse to butchery of each other and of themselves from a longing not to be outdone by their opponents; others were slain by the enemy in war. Then came famine, reserved to exhibit the last degree of shamelessness, followed by the storming and razing of cities until at last the very temple of God was ravaged by the enemy's fire through this revolt. Here is a lesson that an innovation and reform in ancestral traditions weighs heavily in the scale in leading to the destruction of the congregation of the people. In this case certainly, Judas and Saddok started among us an intrusive fourth school of philosophy; and when they had won an abundance of devotees, they filled the body politic immediately with tumult, also planting the seeds of those troubles which subsequently overtook it, all because of the novelty of this hitherto unknown philosophy that I shall now describe. My reason for giving this brief account of it is chiefly that the zeal which Judas and Saddok inspired in the younger element meant the ruin of our cause.

JOSEPHUS, *JEWISH ANTIQUITIES*
Book XVIII, chapter 1
The Zealots

As for the fourth of the philosophies, Judas the Galilaean set himself up as leader of it. This school agrees in all other respects with the opinions of the Pharisees, except that they have a passion for liberty that is almost unconquerable, since they are convinced that God alone is their leader and master. They think little of submitting to death in unusual forms and permitting vengeance to fall on kinsmen and friends if only they may avoid calling any man master. Inasmuch as most people have seen the steadfastness of their resolution amid such circumstances, I may forego any further account. For I have no fear that anything reported of them will be considered incredible. The danger is, rather, that report may minimize the indifference with which they accept the grinding misery of pain. The folly that ensued began to afflict the nation after Gessius Florus, who was governor, had by his overbearing and lawless actions provoked a desperate rebellion against the Romans.

JOSEPHUS, *JEWISH ANTIQUITIES*
Book XVII, chapter 10

Then there was Judas, the son of the brigand chief Ezekias, who had been a man of great power and had been captured by Herod only with great difficulty. This Judas got together a large number of desperate men at Sepphoris in Galilee and there made an assault on the royal palace, and having seized all the arms that were stored there, he armed every single one of his men and made off with all the property that had been seized there. He became an object of terror to all men by plundering those he came across in his desire for great possessions and his ambition for royal rank, a prize that he expected to obtain not through the practice of virtue but through excessive ill-treatment of others.

Disturbances caused by various agitators.
Date: Gratus was procurator in Judea
From AD 15 to 26 (Jesus was 22 to 33 years old)

There was also Simon, a slave of King Herod but a handsome man, who took pre-eminence by size and bodily strength, and was expected to go farther. Elated by the unsettled conditions of affairs, he was bold enough to place the diadem on his head, and having got together a body of men, he was himself also proclaimed king by them in their madness, and he rated himself worthy of this beyond anyone else. After burning the royal palace in Jericho, he plundered and carried off the things that had been seized there. He also set fire to many other royal residences in many parts of the country and utterly destroyed them after permitting his fellow-rebels to take as booty whatever had been left in them. And he would have done something still more serious if attention had not quickly been turned to him. For Gratus, the officer of the royal troops, joined the Romans and with what forces he had went to meet Simon. A long and heavy battle was fought between them, and most of the Peraeans, who were disorganized and fighting with more recklessness than science, were destroyed. As for Simon, he tried to save himself by fleeing through a ravine, but Gratus intercepted him and cut off his head. The royal palace at Ammatha on the river Jordan was also burnt down by some rebels, who resembled those under Simon. Such was the great madness that settled upon the nation because they had no king of their own to restrain the populace by his pre-eminence, and because the foreigners who came among them to suppress the rebellion were themselves a cause of provocation through their arrogance and their greed.

Then there was a certain Athronges, a man distinguished neither for the position of his ancestors nor by the excellence of his character, nor for any abundance of means but merely a shepherd completely unknown to everybody although he was remarkable for his great stature and feats of strength. This man had the temerity to aspire to the kingship, thinking that if he obtained it he would enjoy freedom to act more outrageously; as for meeting death, he did not attach much importance to the loss of his life under such circumstances. He also had four brothers, and they too were tall men and confident of being very successful through their feats of strength, and he believed them to be a strong point in his bid for the kingdom. Each of them commanded an armed band, for a large number of people had gathered round them. Though they were commanders, they acted under his orders whenever they went on raids and fought by themselves. Athronges himself put on the diadem and held a council to discuss what things were to be done, but everything depended upon his own decision. This man kept his power for a long while, for he had the title of king and nothing to prevent him from doing as he wished. He and his brothers also applied themselves vigorously to slaughtering the Romans and the king's men, toward both of whom they acted with a similar hatred, toward the latter because of the arrogance that they had shown during the reign of Herod, and toward the Romans because of the injuries that they were held to have inflicted at the present time. But as time went on they became more and more savage (toward all) alike. And there was no escape for any in any way, for sometimes the rebels killed in hope of gain and at other times from the habit of killing. On one occasion near Emmaus they even attacked a company of Romans, who were bringing grain and weapons to their army. Surrounding the centurion Arius, who commanded the detachment, and forty of the bravest of his foot-soldiers, they shot him down. The rest were terrified at their fate but with the protection given them by Gratus and the royal troops that were with him they made their escape, leaving their dead behind. This kind of warfare they kept up for a long time and caused the Romans no little trouble while also inflicting much damage on their own nation. But the brothers were eventually subdued, one of them in an engagement with Gratus, the other in one with Ptolemy. And when Archelaus captured the eldest, the last brother, grieving at the other's fate and seeing that he could no longer find a way to save himself now that he was all alone and utterly exhausted, stripped of his force, surrendered to Archelaus on receiving a pledge sworn by his faith in God (that he would not be harmed). But this happened later.

And so Judaea was filled with brigandage. Anyone might make himself king as the head of a band of rebels whom he fell in with, and then would press on to the destruction of the community, causing trouble to few Romans and then only to a small degree but bringing the greatest slaughter upon their own people.

JOSEPHUS, *JEWISH ANTIQUITIES*
Book XX, chapter 5
Theudas
Date: Fadus was procurator from AD 45 to 48

The Book of the Acts makes allusion to Theudas (Acts 5:36)

During the period when Fadus was procurator of Judaea, a certain impostor named Theudas persuaded the majority of the masses to take up their possessions and to follow him to the Jordan River. He stated that he was a prophet and that at his command the river would be parted and would provide them an easy passage. With this talk he deceived many. Fadus, however, did not permit them to reap the fruit of their folly, but sent against them a squadron of cavalry. These fell upon them unexpectedly, slew many of them and took many prisoners. Theudas himself was captured, whereupon they cut off his head and brought it to Jerusalem. These, then, are the events that befell the Jews during the time that Cuspius Fadus was procurator.

JOSEPHUS, *JEWISH WAR*
Book II, chapter 12
Sedition in AD 48-52

Under the procurator Cumanus' administration disturbances broke out, resulting in another large loss of Jewish lives. The usual crowd had assembled at Jerusalem for the feast of unleavened bread, and the Roman cohort had taken up its position on the roof of the portico of the temple; for a body of men in arms invariably mounts guard at the feasts, to prevent disorders arising from such a concourse of people. Thereupon one of the soldiers, raising his robe, stooped in an indecent attitude, so as to turn his backside to the Jews, and made a noise in keeping with his posture. Enraged at this insult, the whole multitude with loud cries called upon Cumanus to punish the soldier; some of the more hot-headed young men and seditious persons in the crowd started a fight, and, picking up stones hurled them at the troops. Cumanus, fearing a general attack upon himself, sent for reinforcements. These troops pouring into the porticoes, the Jews were seized with irresistible panic and turned to fly from the temple and make their escape into the town. But such violence was used as they pressed round the exits that they were trodden under foot and crushed to death by one another; upwards of thirty thousand perished, and the feast was turned into mourning for the whole nation and for every household into lamentation.

This calamity was followed by other disorders, originating with brigands. On the public road leading up to Bethhoron some brigands attacked one Stephen, a slave of Caesar, and robbed him of his baggage. Cumanus, thereupon, sent troops round the neighbouring villages, with orders to bring up the inhabitants to him in chains reprimanding them for not having pursued and arrested the robbers. On this occasion a soldier, finding in one village a copy of the sacred law, tore the book in pieces and flung it into the fire. At that the Jews were roused as though it were their whole country which had been consumed in the flames; and, their religion acting like some instrument to draw them together, all on the first announcement of the news hurried in a body to Cumanus at Caesarea, and implored him not to leave unpunished the author of such an outrage on God and on their law. The procurator, seeing that the multitude would not be pacified unless they obtained satisfaction, thought fit to call out the soldier and ordered him to be led to execution through the ranks of his accusers. On this the Jews withdrew.

JOSEPHUS, *JEWISH WAR*
Book II, chapter 13
Riots preceding the revolt
of AD 66 — Terrorist methods of the Sicarii
Felix was procurator from AD 52-58

Nero appointed Felix to be procurator of the rest of Judaea. Felix took prisoner Eleazar, the brigand chief, who for twenty years had ravaged the country, with many of his associates, and sent them for trial to Rome. Of the brigands whom he crucified, and of the common people who were convicted of complicity with them and punished by him, the number was incalculable.

But while the country was thus cleared of these pests, a new species of banditti was springing up in Jerusalem, the so-called "sicarii," who committed murders in broad daylight in the heart of the city. The festivals were their special seasons when they would mingle with the crowd, carrying short daggers concealed under their clothing, with which they stabbed their enemies. Then, when they fell, the murderers joined in the cries of indignation and, through this plausible behavior, were never discovered. The first to be assassinated by them was Jonathan the high-priest; after his death there were numerous daily murders. The panic created was more alarming than the calamity itself; every one, as on the battlefield, hourly expecting death. Men kept watch at a distance on their enemies and would not trust even their friends when they approached. Yet even while their suspicions were aroused and they were on their guard, they fell; so swift were the conspirators and so crafty in eluding detection.

Besides these there arose another body of villains, with purer hands but more impious intentions, who no less than the assassins ruined the peace of the city. Deceivers and impostors, under the pretence of divine inspiration fostering revolutionary changes, they persuaded the multitude to act like madmen, and led them out into the desert under the belief that God would there give them tokens of deliverance. Against them Felix, regarding this as but the preliminary to insurrection, sent a body of cavalry and heavy-armed infantry, and put a large number to the sword.

No sooner were these disorders reduced than the inflammation, as in a sick man's body, broke out again in another quarter. The impostors and brigands, banding together, incited numbers to revolt, exhorting them to assert their independence, and threatening to kill any who submitted to Roman domination and forcibly to suppress those who voluntarily accepted servitude. Distributing themselves in companies throughout the country, they looted the houses of the wealthy, murdered their owners, and set the villages on fire. The effects of their frenzy were thus felt throughout all Judaea, and every day saw this war being fanned into fiercer flame.

JOSEPHUS, *JEWISH ANTIQUITIES*
Book XX, chapter 8
Robbers in Judaea — Murder of Jonathan by the Sicarii

In Judaea matters were constantly going from bad to worse. For the country was again infested with bands of brigands and impostors who deceived the mob. Not a day passed, however, but that Felix captured and put to death many of these impostors and brigands. He also, by a ruse, took alive Eleazar the son of Dinaeus, who had organized the company of brigands; for by offering a pledge that he would suffer him no harm, Felix induced him to appear before him. Felix then imprisoned him and dispatched him to Rome. Felix also bore a grudge against Jonathan the high priest because of his frequent admonition to improve the administration of the affairs of Judaea. For Jonathan feared that he himself might incur the censure of the multitude in that he had requested Caesar to dispatch Felix as procurator of Judaea. Felix accordingly devised a pretext that would remove from his presence one who was a constant nuisance to him; for incessant rebukes are annoying to those who choose to do wrong. It was such reasons that moved Felix to bribe Jonathan's most trusted friend, a native of Jerusalem named Doras, with a promise to pay a great sum, to bring in brigands to attack Jonathan and kill him. Doras agreed and contrived to get him murdered by the brigands in the following way. Certain of these brigands went up to the city as if they intended to worship God. With daggers concealed under their clothes, they mingled with the people about Jonathan and assassinated him. As the murder remained unpunished, from that time forth the brigands with perfect impunity used to go to the city during the festivals and, with their weapons similarly concealed, mingle with the crowds. In this way they slew some because they were private enemies, and others because they were paid to do so by someone else. They committed these murders not only in other parts of the city but even in some cases in the temple; for there too they made bold to slaughter their victims, for they did not regard even this as a desecration. This is the reason why, in my opinion, even God Himself, for loathing of their impiety, turned away from our city and, because He deemed the temple to be no longer a clean dwelling place for Him, brought the Romans upon us and purification by fire upon the city, while He inflicted slavery upon us together with our wives and children; for He wished to chasten us by these calamities.

The Egyptian Prophet (see Acts 21:37, 38)
Date: around AD 58

With such pollution did the deeds of the brigands infect the city. Moreover, impostors and deceivers called upon the mob to follow them into the desert. For they said that they would show them unmistakable marvels and signs that would be wrought in harmony with God's design. Many were, in fact, persuaded and paid the penalty of their folly; for they were brought before Felix and he punished them. At this time there came to Jerusalem from Egypt a man who declared that he was a prophet and advised the masses of the common people to go out with him to the mountain called the Mount of Olives, which lies opposite the city at a distance of five furlongs. For he asserted that he wished to demonstrate from there that at his command Jerusalem's walls would fall down, through which he promised to provide them an entrance into the city. When Felix heard of this he ordered his soldiers to take up their arms. Setting out from Jerusalem with a large force of cavalry and infantry, he fell upon the Egyptian and his followers, slaying four hundred of them and taking two hundred prisoners. The Egyptian himself escaped from the battle and disappeared. And now the brigands once more incited the populace to war with Rome, telling them not to obey them. They also fired and pillaged the villages of those who refused to comply.

JOSEPHUS, JEWISH ANTIQUITIES
Book XX, chapter 8
The Sicarii
Date: Festus was procurator from AD 60-62 (see Acts 24:27)

When Festus arrived in Judaea, it happened that Judaea was being devastated by the brigands, for the villages one and all were being set on fire and plundered. They would frequently appear with arms in the villages of their foes and would plunder and set them on fire. Festus also sent a force of cavalry and infantry against the dupes of a certain impostor who had promised them salvation and rest from troubles, if they chose to follow him into the wilderness. The force which Festus dispatched destroyed both the deceiver himself and those who had followed him.

JOSEPHUS, *JEWISH WAR*
Book II, chapter 17
Menahem, son of Judas the Galilean
Date: around AD 67

At this period a certain Menahem, son of Judas surnamed the Galilaean
— that redoubtable doctor who in old days, under Quirinius, had upbraided
the Jews for recognizing the Romans as masters when they already had God
— took his intimate friends off with him to Masada, where he broke into king
Herod's armoury and provided arms both for his fellow-townsmen and for
other brigands; then, with these men for his bodyguard, he returned like a
veritable king to Jerusalem, became the leader of the revolution, and directed
the siege of the palace.

But the reduction of the strongholds and the murder of the high-priest
Ananias inflated and brutalized Menahem to such an extent that he believed
himself without a rival in the conduct of affairs and became an insufferable
tyrant. The partisans of Eleazar now rose against him; they remarked to each
other that, after revolting from the Romans for love of liberty, they ought
not to sacrifice this liberty to a Jewish hangman and to put up with a master
who, even were he to abstain from violence, was anyhow far below themselves;
and that if they must have a leader, anyone would be better than Menahem.
So they laid their plans to attack him in the Temple, whither he had gone
up in state to pay his devotions, arrayed in royal robes and attended by his
suite of armed fanatics. When Eleazar and his companions rushed upon him,
and the rest of the people to gratify their rage took up stones and began
pelting the arrogant doctor, imagining that his downfall would crush the whole
revolt, Menahem and his followers offered a momentary resistance; then, seeing themselves assailed by the whole multitude, they fled whithersoever they
could; all who were caught were massacred, and a hunt was made for any in
hiding. A few succeeded in escaping by stealth to Masada, among others
Eleazar, son of Jairus and a relative of Menahem, and subsequently despot
of Masada. Menahem himself, who had taken refuge in the place called
Ophlas and there ignominiously concealed himself, was caught, dragged into
the open, and after being subjected to all kinds of torture, put to death.
His lieutenants, along with Absalom, his most eminent supporter in his
tyranny, met with a similar fate.

JOSEPHUS, *JEWISH WAR*
Book II, chapter 17
Abolition of debts — the Zealots' demands
Date: AD 67

The royalists, now outmatched in numbers and audacity, were forced to evacuate the upper city. The victors burst in and set fire to the house of Ananias the high-priest and to the palaces of Agrippa and Bernice; they next carried their combustibles to the public archives, eager to destroy the money-lenders' bonds and to prevent the recovery of debts, in order to win over a host of grateful debtors and to cause a rising of the poor against the rich, sure of impunity.

Appendix III
Texts Related to Chapter 10

JOSEPHUS, *JEWISH ANTIQUITIES*
Book XVII, chapter 10
Futility of an armed resistance — Achiab's surrender
Date: 3 BC (Jesus is 4 years old)

Varus then sent part of his army through the country to search for those who were responsible for the revolt, and when they were discovered he punished those who were most guilty but some he released. The number of those who were crucified on this charge was two thousand. After that he dismissed Aretas' army, seeing that it was no longer useful for any purpose, for they had often been disorderly and had disobeyed Varus' orders and requests out of desire for the gains that their misbehaviour brought them. He himself, on learning that ten thousand Jews had risen in arms, hastened to capture them. They did not, however, face him in battle but following the advice of Achiab surrendered to him. Varus then pardoned the great majority of those guilty of revolting but sent to Caesar any who had been their leaders. Caesar let most of them go and punished only those relatives of Herod who had joined them in fighting, because they had shown contempt for justice in fighting against their own kin.

JOSEPHUS, *JEWISH WAR*
Book II, chapter 9
Nonviolent resistance under Pilate
Date: the time of Jesus

Pilate, being sent by Tiberius, as procurator to Judaea, introduced into Jerusalem by night and under cover the effigies of Caesar which are called standards. This proceeding, when day broke, aroused immense excitement among the Jews; those on the spot were in consternation, considering their laws to have been trampled under foot, as those laws permit no image to be erected in the city; while the indignation of the townspeople stirred the country-folk, who flocked together in crowds. Hastening after Pilate to Caesarea, the Jews implored him to remove the standards from Jerusalem and to uphold the laws of their ancestors. When Pilate refused, they fell prostrate around his house and for five whole days and nights remained motionless in that position.

On the ensuing day Pilate took his seat on his tribunal in the great stadium and summoning the multitude, with the apparent intention of answering them, gave the arranged signal to his armed soldiers to surround the Jews. Finding themselves in a ring of troops, three deep, the Jews were struck dumb at this unexpected sight. Pilate, after threatening to cut them down, if they refused to admit Caesar's images, signalled to the soldiers to draw their swords. Thereupon the Jews, as by concerted action, flung themselves in a body on the ground, extended their necks, and exclaimed that were ready rather to die than to transgress the law. Overcome with astonishment at such intense religious zeal, Pilate gave orders for the immediate removal of the standards from Jerusalem.

On a later occasion he provoked a fresh uproar by expending upon the construction of an aqueduct the sacred treasure known as "Corbonas"; the water was brought from a distance of 400 furlongs. Indignant at this proceeding, the populace formed a ring round the tribunal of Pilate, then on a visit to Jerusalem, and besieged him with angry clamour. He, foreseeing the tumult, had interspersed among the crowd a troop of his soldiers, armed but disguised in civilian dress, with orders not to use their swords, but to beat any rioters with cudgels. He now from his tribunal gave the agreed signal. Large numbers of the Jews perished, some from the blows which they received, others trodden to death by their companions in the ensuing flight. Cowed by the fate of the victims, the multitude was reduced to silence.

JOSEPHUS, *JEWISH ANTIQUITIES*
Book XVIII, chapter 3

But the Jews showed no faint-heartedness; and so, caught unarmed, as they were, by men delivering a prepared attack, many of them actually were slain on the spot, while some withdrew disabled by blows. Thus ended the uprising.

JOSEPHUS, *JEWISH ANTIQUITIES*
Book XVIII, chapter 2
John the Baptist

But to some of the Jews the destruction of Herod's army seemed to be divine vengeance, and certainly a just vengeance, for his treatment of John, surnamed the Baptist. For Herod had put him to death, though he was a good man and had exhorted the Jews to lead righteous lives, to practise justice towards their fellows and piety towards God, and so doing to join in baptism. In his view this was a necessary preliminary if baptism was to be acceptable to God. They must not employ it to gain pardon for whatever sins they committed, but as a consecration of the body implying that the soul was already thoroughly cleansed by right behaviour. When others too joined the crowds about him, because they were aroused to the highest degree by his sermons, Herod became alarmed. Eloquence that had so great an effect on mankind might lead to some form of sedition, for it looked as if they would be guided by John in everything that they did. Herod decided therefore that it would be much better to strike first and be rid of him before his work led to an uprising, than to wait for an upheaval, get involved in a difficult situation and see his mistake. Though John, because of Herod's suspicions, was brought in chains to Machaerus, the stronghold that we have previously mentioned, and there put to death, yet the verdict of the Jews was that the destruction visited upon Herod's army was a vindication of John, since God saw fit to inflict such a blow on Herod.

Two Documents Referring to Jesus

JOSEPHUS, *JEWISH ANTIQUITIES*
Book XVIII, chapter 3
Jesus

About this time there lived Jesus, a wise man, if indeed one ought to call him a man. For he was one who wrought surprising feats and was a teacher of such people as accept the truth gladly. He won over many Jews and many of the Greeks. He was the Messiah. When Pilate, upon hearing him accused by men of the highest standing amongst us, had condemned him to be crucified, those who had in the first place come to love him did not give up their affection for him. On the third day he appeared to them restored to life, for the prophets of God had prophesied these and countless other marvellous things about him. And the tribe of the Christians, so called after him, has still to this day not disappeared.
An interesting document: the same passage in the slavonic version of Josephus' *Jewish Wars* (from the Appendix of the *Jewish Wars* in Thackery's translation).

JOSEPHUS, *JEWISH ANTIQUITIES*
Book XVIII, chapter 4
Pilate returns to Rome after being accused

When the uprising had been quelled, the council of the Samaritans went to Vitellius, a man of consular rank who was governor of Syria, and charged Pilate with the slaughter of the victims. For, they said, it was not as rebels against the Romans but as refugees from the persecution of Pilate that they had met in Tirathana. Vitellius thereupon dispatched Marcellus, one of his friends, to take charge of the administration of Judaea, and ordered Pilate to return to Rome to give the emperor his account of the matters with which he was charged by the Samaritans. And so Pilate, after having spent ten years in Judaea, hurried to Rome in obedience to the orders of Vitellius, since he could not refuse. But before he reached Rome Tiberius had already passed away.

JOSEPHUS, *JEWISH ANTIQUITIES*
Book XVIII, chapter 8, paragraph 2-6
Nonviolent resistance of the Jews under Caligula (Gaius)
Date: AD 41

Indignant at being so slighted by the Jews alone, Gaius dispatched Petronius as his legate to Syria to succeed Vitellius in this office. His orders were to lead a large force into Judaea and, if the Jews consented to receive him, to set up an image of Gaius in the temple of God. If, however, they were obstinate, he was to subdue them by force of arms and so set it up.

. . . Meanwhile, many tens of thousands of Jews came to Petronius at Ptolemais with petitions not to use force to make them transgress and violate their ancestral code. "If," they said, "you propose at all costs to bring in and set up the image, slay us first before you carry out these resolutions. For it is not possible for us to survive and to behold actions that are forbidden us by the decision both of our lawgiver and of our forefathers who cast their votes enacting these measures as moral laws."

. . . "Equal to this determination of yours, O Petronius," replied the Jews, "not to transgress the orders of Gaius, is our determination not to transgress the declaration of the law. We have put our trust in the goodness of God and in the labours of our forefathers and have thus hitherto remained innocent of transgression. Nor could we ever bring ourselves to go so far in wickedness as by our own act to transgress, for any fear of death, the law bidding us abstain, where He thought it conducive to our good to do so. In order to preserve our ancestral code, we shall patiently endure what may be in store for us, with the assurance that for those who are determined to take the risk there is hope even of prevailing: for God will stand by us if we welcome danger for His glory. Fortune, moreover, is wont to veer now toward one side, now toward the other in human affairs. To obey you, on the other hand, would bring on us the grave reproach of cowardice, because that would be the explanation of our transgressing the law, and at the same time we should incur God's severe wrath — and He even in your eyes must be accounted a higher power than Gaius."

. . . "Will you then go to war with Caesar," said Petronius, "regardless of his resources and of your own weakness?" "On no account would we fight," they said, "but we will die sooner than violate our laws." And falling on their faces and baring their throats, they declared that they were ready to be slain. They continued to make these supplications for forty days. Furthermore, they neglected their fields, and that, too, though it was time to sow the seed. For they showed a stubborn determination and readiness to die rather than to see the image erected.

. . . Petronius decided to recognize the cogency of the plea of the petitioners. . . . He requested those in authority to attend to agricultural matters and to conciliate the people with optimistic propaganda. He thus did his best to encourage the masses. God, on His part, showed Petronius that He was with him and would lend His aid in all matters. For as soon as Petronius had finished delivering this speech before the Jews, God straightway sent a heavy shower that was contrary to the general anticipation. . . . The result was that, when much rain fell at that moment exceptionally and unexpectedly, the Jews were hopeful that Petronius would by no means fail in his petition on their behalf. Petronius, on his part, was struck with great amazement when he saw unmistakable evidence that God's providence was over the Jews and that He had shown His presence so abundantly that not even those who actually proposed to take the opposite view had any heart left to dispute the fact. He included this occurrence along with the other things of which he wrote to Gaius. It was all designed to induce him and entreat him in every way not to drive so many tens of thousands of men to desperation. For if he should slay them — and they would certainly not give up their accustomed manner of worship without war — he would be deprived of their revenue and would be put under the ban of a curse for all time to come. He said, moreover, that the Divinity who was in charge of them had shown His power to be unimpaired and was quite unambiguous in displaying this power.

Gaius Caligula's Answer

"Since you have held the gifts that the Jews have bestowed upon you in higher regard than my orders and have presumed to minister in everything to their pleasure in violation of my orders, I bid you act as your own judge and consider what course it is your duty to take, since you have brought my displeasure upon yourself. For I assure you that you shall be cited as an example by all men now and all that will come hereafter to point the moral that an emperor's commands are never to be flouted."

Such was the letter that he wrote to Petronius. But Petronius did not receive it while Gaius was alive since the voyage of those who brought the message was so delayed that before it arrived Petronius had received a letter with news of the death of Gaius. Indeed, God could never have been unmindful of the risks that Petronius had taken in showing favour to the Jews and honouring God. No, the removal of Gaius in displeasure at his rashness in promoting his own claim to worship was God's payment of the debt to Petronius. . . . Thus Petronius first received the letter which reported clearly the death of Gaius, and, not long afterwards, the one which ordered him to take his life with his own hand. He rejoiced at the coincidence that Gaius' disaster came when it did, and marvelled at the providence of God, who swiftly and punctually had paid him his reward for showing honour to the temple and coming to the rescue of the Jews.

Index of Scripture Citations

General Index

208

The Author

Andre Pascal Trocme was born in 1901 in Saint Quentin, France. He was married to an Italian girl named Magda, who was a faithful and supporting wife in his interests of peace and nonviolence until his death in June 1971.

Trocme came face-to-face with the violence and revolution of Hitler and his regime. He had experience first in the military and later in the various peace movements. His work in helping Jewish refugees flee from Hitler will never be forgotten.

Trocme was one of the rare Christian pacifists of the past fifty years who refused to choose between impassioned action and intellectual clarity. He repeatedly practiced and proclaimed virile Christian obedience in turbulent times while confronting actively situations of human conflict.

The Introduction of this book contains extensive biographical information about his work, conflicts, beliefs, and never-tiring efforts to promote peace and nonviolence.

Additional biographical information may be found in "Radical for Peace, The Story of Andre Trocme" by Constance Muste in *Fellowship*, September 1951, and in *Christians in the Arena* by Allan A. Hunter, Fellowship Publications, Nyack, N.Y., 1958.